D0860455

CRACK, COCAINE, METHAMPHETAMINE AND ICE

CRACK, COCAINE, METH- AMPHETAMINE AND ICE

Leslie E. Moser, Ph.D.

Multi-Media Productions, Inc.

Copyright © 1990 by Multi-Media Productions, Inc.

10 9 8 7 6 5 4 3 2 1

Multi-Media Productions, Inc.
P.O. Box 7428
Waco, Texas 76714

Library of Congress Catalog Card Number: 90-92781

ISBN 1-878-938-00-2

Cover design by Dennis Hill

To my grandson, Steven Moser.

<u>We</u> did it together.

CRACK, COCAINE, METHAMPHETAMINE AND ICE

INTRODUCTION

Introduction to Crack, Cocaine, Methamphetamine and Ice

I carefully and sadly examined the impoverishment of the human spirit in my book, <u>The Struggle For Human Dignity</u>. I found strong evidence that man has become an unwitting but willing pawn in a social structure that is robbing him of his freedom of will and his capacity for self-determination and self-control.

Grinding poverty, with its attendant squalor in housing, hunger, broken families and rampant crime contributes much to the broader social problems which accompany the drug-abuse phenomenon. On the other hand, Japan has the world's largest methamphetamine problem and few of the social problems described above. It is clear that the impoverishment of the human spirit occurs both amid squalor and amid affluence. We must have many spearheads aiming at different aspects of the failure to sustain human dignity in order to do battle with drugs.

Knowledge is Power

In this new book <u>Crack, Cocaine, Methamphetamine and Ice</u> I will examine in depth the two drug entities which I believe are the most dangerous we face, especially in their smokable forms. Methamphetamine and cocaine must be fought from as clear a knowledge base as we may possibly achieve. We must know how they impact upon the human body, mind and spirit. We must know how to deal with those persons who are in the grip of addictions, and we must know how law enforcements are being mounted against the creation and spread of these vicious chemicals.

We cannot return to self-control unless and until we release the victims and destroy the sources of victimization while seeking ways to rehabilitate man's belief in himself. Knowledge is the power we must marshal against these forces of enslavement.

Methamphetamines and Cocaine — So Different

These two drugs are being consistently abused and are causing unfathomable miseries. They have damaged the nation severely by depleting its human resources.

True, many drug abusers are polydrug users and drugs are legion. Yet, there is ample justification for isolating these two drugs for specific study, and this is what I have decided to do in this book. I have a strong feeling that many will benefit from my trying to clarify the issues relating to these two drugs, especially in their smokable forms of crack and ice.

Methamphetamine and cocaine are very different. Cocaine is a derivative of the coca plant growing both in wild and domesticated forms. Methamphetamine is a synthetic drug. The use of cocaine dates back many centuries, perhaps to the earliest contact between living man and living plant. Methamphetamine is a twentieth-century drug with amphetamine having been concocted in Asia in the latter part of the nineteenth century. The two drug forms are poles apart chemically.

Methamphetamines and Cocaine — So Similar

With such a vast difference in nature and origins, it is uncanny that the drugs have such similar impacts upon those who use them. That is basically why I am studying them together.

Cocaine was always there for South and Central American natives. In its most refined form of cocaine hydrochloride, as well as in cruder forms of powdered dry leaves, it was long known as the drug of the wealthy, of today's jet-setting chic and of the upper classes of eighteenth-century Europe.

Methamphetamine has, by contrast, always been more affordable — available to the common man, to college students and even to the inner city poor, many of whom are sustaining their habits by selling the substance in order to be able to use it. So, methamphetamine has become known as poor man's cocaine because the impacts of the two drugs are very similar and because methamphetamine is available and affordable.

As illegal and addictive substances, both drugs are water-soluble, and thus amenable to liquefaction and intravenous use. Snorting is common with both drugs, and now, both substances have been made available in smokable forms.

The smokable form of cocaine delivers exactly the same chemical to the brain as does other forms of administration. Yet, the freed-from-its-base vaporous cocaine has nuances of impact, addictive powers and dangers to the human body vastly enhanced when compared to other forms of administration.

Smokable methamphetamine known as ice or as crystal meth, has the same chemical properties as the most refined and powerful laboratory form of the drug, d isomer methamphetamine. However, methamphetamine which commonly has both d isomer and l isomer chemical make-up even in refined forms, becomes almost pure d isomer methamphetamine in vaporization, and the impacts of the vapor on the central nervous system have unusually dramatic and intensely harmful effects. In his appearance before the Select Committee on Narcotics Abuse and Control, Doctor Jerome Jaffe, M.D., Senior Science Advisor of the National Institute on Drug Abuse, made the following statement:

The toxic syndrome seen with amphetamines and methamphetamine seems clinically indistinguishable from that produced by cocaine. Cocaine addicts describe the euphoric effects of cocaine in terms that are almost identical to those used by amphetamine addicts for amphetamine. NIDA studies show that in the laboratory, subjects familiar with cocaine cannot distinguish between the subjective effects of intravenous cocaine and amphetamine. In addiction, animals exhibit similar patterns of self-administration of cocaine and amphetamine.

While it has been generally assumed that the subjective effects of cocaine are more intense and its abuse potential more significant than that of the amphetamines, the similarities in terms of subjective effects as well as pharmacological and toxic effects are more striking than are the differences.(5, p. 137)

The Flexing of Supply and Demand

Although individuals who can afford either drug have preferences, the two drugs in many respects have quite similar impacts on the central nervous system. That has profound meaning in terms of supply and demand. When cocaine was very expensive because of limited supply, methamphetamine was cheap because supply could easily flex with demand. This situation prevailed strongly during the 60's and 70's. When the supply of cocaine escalated in the late 70's and 80's because of illicit South American connections, the price of cocaine plummeted dramatically and the use of poor man's cocaine began to recede in favor of cocaine itself. When crack cocaine invaded the American marketplace after 1983, methamphetamine preference and use declined even further. Some self-described drug experts expect the price of cocaine to rise dramatically because of supply interdiction, and therewith they expect the availability, preference and use of methamphetamine to rise again because it will remain cheap and available.

The Real Truth

We are faced with two sobering, unexpected and almost unbelievable realities. These are: 1) The supply of cocaine remains plentiful and prices are changing very little. 2) Methamphetamine has shown a phenomenal rise in manufacture and in use although cocaine is still cheap and available. Many so-called experts have been saying that crack could not be seriously challenged as the number one drug form in America because ice would always be more expensive than crack. Some are conceding that even if crack remains cheap and available, ice may also become cheap and available. Thus, ice may become the drug scourge of the 90's.

At present and for some time to come, mainland users will not be securing large quantities of ice per se. A mixture of crack and methamphetamine HCL with a street name of croak is fast invading our schoolyards and other places of use.

By mixing a portion of methamphetamine HCL into the baking baking soda and cocaine HCL, a myriad of products may be formed, and we may be sure a number of street names will be applied thereto. These products may be even more dangerous

12

than the d isomer methamphetamine called ice. As the street people say, "Croak puts legs on the crack fix." The question of purity of these amalgamations will always be a threat.

What has happened? Cocaine in all its forms is largely unabated in supply. Crack is generally recognized as America's number one drug problem at present. But, contrary to almost every expectation, methamphetamine use and supply is at an unprecedented level in the 90's. Methamphetamine use, especially IV use, is taking an upward spiral. In some parts of the nation, methamphetamine use is up by 500 percent in the 90's as compared with the mid 80's. And that is not because the use of ice has strongly accelerated! Many users have a strong preference for methamphetamine via IV administration even though crack remains cheap and available. If ice becomes cheaper and more available, many will still prefer the IV mode of administration.

What is happening? The dramatic amphetamine comeback did not occur because of diminished cocaine use. Methamphetamine has developed a new and vibrant following for reasons not fully understood, although its availability and cheap price in its hydrochloride form are factors.

Some basic harsh realities struck home when a report prepared by Mark A. R. Kleiman of the Harvard University School of Government, working under the U.S. Senate Judiciary Committee, was released. This study found that earlier reports by the National Institute on Drug Abuse on cocaine addictions were very inaccurate. This most recent scientific study, which augments the earlier NIDA estimate with new and more accurate statistics, declares cocaine addiction to be two and one-half times as large as had been reported by NIDA.(3)

With this study on mushrooming cocaine addiction, we may be seeing only a little larger tip of the iceberg of drug abuse in America. We may expect updated statistics reflecting large increases in drug use with other drug forms, especially methamphetamine. Although tremendous efforts are being made under the war-on-drugs rhetoric, we are losing the war at a startling pace.

The obvious truth is that more cocaine and methamphetamines are being used in more ways than ever before. The nation is not ceasing its love affair with cocaine and is reentering a lost love affair with methamphetamine at the same time. Does this mean that those who have used drugs are using more drugs in quantity? Does it mean that there is a mushrooming wave of new users? Does it mean that the old addicts are becoming polydrug users? Undoubtedly the answer is "all of the above"!

The Future for Crack and Ice

The fact is that cocaine HCL is in abundant supply in spite of interdiction. There is also a mushrooming supply and a resurgence of the use of methamphetamines. Both drugs are gaining adherents for the more devastating smokable forms. The battle involving cocaine, methamphetamine, crack and ice as destroyers of the lives of the human body and spirit has entered a new phase. According to Jon G. Jackson, M.D. at the University of Hawaii, Manoa:

In psychiatry, a growing number of emergency room visits results from the use of crystal (ice). Most frequently, the presenting feature is an acute psychosis in chronic users, with auditory hallucinations and extreme paranoia. Often these patients demonstrate destructive behavior, and they have been brought to the emergency room by the police. Unlike the acute paranoid disorders seen in users of cocaine, these psychotic symptoms do not resolve during the next few hours, and they may persist for days, weeks, or even longer.(4, p. 907)

Recent Visits to Hawaii and the West Coast

In an effort to validate early statements concerning the psychological and physiological effects of ice, as emphasized in Dr. Jackson's statement above, this author was allowed to interview several inmates at the Waiawa Correctional Institution on Oahu. These inmates, imprisoned for trafficking in ice and for violent acts under paranoia caused by ice had been heavy ice abusers. Their testimonies given under camera confirmed earlier statements concerning ice effects. This author is convinced that ice effects are as horrendous as has been reported in the media.

A recent visit with Police Department Officials on Oahu finds them gratified with efforts to control ice distribution but highly alarmed at the sharp rise in the numbers of ice babies being born. The numbers of ice babies have more than doubled in two years, and studies are under way to accurately evaluate the damaging effects of ice upon the newborn. The consensus among those studying ice babies is that ice is more damaging to the fetus than is crack or other drugs and that the damage to the neurological systems of these babies is likely to be sustained for longer periods than is true for other drugs.

A number of on-site interviews held in Honolulu and San Francisco three days before this book was sent to press have convinced this author that:

1. The psychological and physiological effects of ice use are as serious as reported consistently in the media.

2. The most threatening and alarming aspect of the ice age in Hawaii is the rising incidence of ice babies, born of mothers who are using ice as a means of controlling body weight.

3. Interdictive and educational measures in Hawaii are working to control ice use in Hawaii at present.

4. The heralded ice epidemic in mainland states has to date been held in check through control of chemicals and education, although methamphetamine manufacture and use in mainland states is escalating alarmingly.

5. Drug traffickers everywhere are seeking markets for smokable forms of methamphetamine and mixtures of cocaine and methamphetamine, but they have not at this time been able to exploit the marketplace with either high intensity or high consistency.

6. Smokable forms of methamphetamine mixed with crack cocaine loom as the highest threat for mainland U.S.A.

Late in the year 1989 psychiatrist Dr. Herbert Kleber, who heads the Federal Drug Demand Reduction Office as a deputy director to the drug czar, met with health care professionals and government officials in Hawaii. Dr. Kleber expressed his belief that there will be a return to the numbing euphoria of the opiates rather than new stimulant epidemics of any kind in mainland states.

This author, in his most recent swing through California and Hawaii, conferred with Police Department Officials in Honolulu and workers at the Free Clinics in the Haight Ashbury District and found that ice use measured by arrestable offenses in Honolulu and by hospitalizations in San Francisco have leveled off. The future is unclear. This author fears that smokable forms of various mixtures of cocaine and methamphetamine will be exploited by drug traffickers.

Gloomy Predictions

What is likely to be the drug scourge of the 90's? Federal anti-drug forces, emanating from the Washington-based war on drugs, say, "To help win the war against drugs, the proposed federal anti-drug plan targets our nation's worst enemy: crack."(6, p. 8) Such a statement made in 1989 clearly labels crack as a continuing drug scourge of the 90's.

The NIDA (National Institute on Drug Abuse) noting the unbelievable resurgence of methamphetamine, said in 1988, "Domestically produced methamphetamine looms as a potential national drug crisis for the 1990's."(7, p. 1)

United States Attorney Daniel Bent in an address to the House Select Committee on Narcotics Abuse and Control, meeting to discuss the dangers posed by ice, said, "In effect, now that the barrier of administration by injection has been removed, we have a drug which chemically may be more popular than crack."(1, p. 64)

So obviously, experts have different opinions and thoughts. The harrowing reality that demands attention is that they are all probably correct. True, three drug forms cannot all be number one in threat and in toll taking. The fact that all forms of cocaine and methamphetamine are on the upswing at the same time spells gloom and perhaps doom.

The Vulnerable Subgroups for Ice

The vapors from ice are virtually odorless. Ice delivers an intense rush, a high that can be sustained over a period of a long working day. A horrendous crash comes after a few days of use. Most of us agree ice targets at least three population subgroups as being particularly vulnerable.

Targeted as victims are those who feel they might benefit from taking a drug which has privacy. Features of no odor and the lack of a need for periodic fixes during a working day appeal to these people. Factory workers and construction workers who must remain alert for repetitive tasks for long periods come to mind. Students who must sustain long periods of uninterrupted study come to mind. Young yuppie entrepreneurs, who must pack, run, fly and present their ideas to buyers and repeat the same sequence under heavy stress, come to mind.

Bad News, Good News

Visits to Hawaii have confirmed that these are the highly vulnerable groups, although there is a preponderance of garbageheads who are ready to try anything. A visit to the free clinics in the Haight Ashbury District of San Francisco confirms that the drug-saturated types commonly found in this area gleefully await the chance to try any new stimulant.

However, my latest visit to Hawaii and especially my contact with mental health functionaries in that state provide a hopeful note. "Ice makes these people crazy," John Joseph Blalock, Ph.D, Head of Mental Health Team for Courts and Corrections, State Health Department, State of Hawaii, told me. "They appear at first to be experiencing psychotic breaks, seem to be exhibiting classic signs of paranoid schizophrenia."

"And what about the college students, the entrepreneurs and the factory workers?" I asked. "Is it as bad for them as predicted?"

"No, Dr. Moser," he replied. "Lower socioeconomic groups of workers at tedious tasks are the principal users of ice. The more educated groups are showing that they are either too smart or too scared to use it." Hawaii, in reaction to the crack epidemic in mainland states, created an immense public awareness campaign. The dangers of crack were displayed via every media outlet including billboards on highways.

Police officials credit the media blitz with saving the island state from a crack epidemic like mainland states are experiencing. Daniel Bent, U.S. Attorney for the District of Hawaii, offered in his address to the Select Committee on Narcotics Abuse and Control the hope that the State of Hawaii might return the favor to mainland states by encouraging widespread media blitzes which are being made in Hawaii about ice.

Yes, education is demonstrably effective. Whether the tactic is one of creating usable knowledge for logical decisions or is one of fear, there is evidence that knowledge is power, and that it is effective.

Bottom-line Conclusions

Our society is clearly at a crossroad in the war on drugs. With the collapse of communism at hand, our struggle for survival makes possible and imperative, even demands an extremely high and sharply high-lighted priority for the war on drugs. This new focus must draw heavily upon a national sense of urgency and an absolute and total convictions that this war is clearly one which presages our survival as a nation and as human beings with dignity and worth.

The commitment and dedication required of each of us must involve our motivations as well as our high-tech skills put to use in the interdiction of imported drugs and the control of domestic drug sources. Recent signs of success in Colombia are heartening. However, the key to winning this war is, without question, our knowledge base about drugs — how drugs get into our bodies, what they do to our bodies and, summarily, how we can wipe out the demand factor — the nation's appetite for drugs. Unless we are able to control the demand, the problem cannot be solved.

Knowledge is the power that will fuel our motivations, our resolves and our capabilities of shutting down the demand factor. The supply factor, while important, can never be brought under control entirely. What human beings want, they most often get; for the most part, human ingenuity for attaining and obtaining what is desired is both blessing and curse. Our greatest hope must be to develop tools for influencing what people want or desire as a part of their lives. If this is counted as a big-brother feature — so it must be. At least it must be to a degree and for a time, until we can manage to bring a run-away love affair with mind-controlling drugs to heel. While we must not be guilty of robbing people of their personal freedoms, we cannot escape the conviction that some of us must intervene in order to bring order into a world gone mad because human freedoms have led paradoxically to a total loss of freedom. For many, drug addictions have become their private hells — their totalitarian despots. This will be the toughest war we've ever fought.

This war can be won, but not easily. This book is one small effort in an overall assault on a vicious enemy arising as it does from our indomitable search within ourselves for pleasure, for stress relief, for novelty and for meaning. Our dependence on drugs to give us courage and help us cope is far more threatening than anything we have ever known before. Not that we haven't known before about this enemy within; but this enemy has changed, has grown on an order comparable to the change from the muzzle loading rifle to the atomic MX. The idea that it is a "them" problem is asinine; this is an "us" problem. As a nation, we stand to lose our most precious assets — the sharp, uncluttered minds and the healthy bodies of all our citizens, especially the young who seem so vulnerable to the ravages of drugs.

Unless we can halt the onrushing despotism of drugs and therapize the devastations wrought already upon the personalities of the victims where the damage is already done, unless we can free human bodies from chemical abuse, we will have no nation, no society, no caring about quantity or quality of life. In short we will have no future. Ingested chemicals are devastating our sense of human rights and values as well as our capacity for caring along with our capacity for having or even

19

caring about personal happiness and tranquility. We are facing a devastation which is, in its own way, worse than the atomic annihilation we have feared for a half century and more. The time for changing priorities is now, or the time is never!

The Format of This Book

This author shares the feelings expressed by U.S. Attorney Daniel Bent of the District of Hawaii: "I think what we need in Hawaii, frankly, and the rest of America, is not $9 billion or $27 billion or $50 billion, but we need 200 million — 200 million outraged American, Americans outraged about the existence of drug use in their communities and Americans that simply won't tolerate it anymore."(2, p. 16)

This book adopts this declaration as its reason for being. The audience for this book is those 200 million outraged Americans. The book is presented in four parts with eleven chapters. An effort to engage readers emotionally is made in this book by beginning each chapter with a short "happening" — a believable and engaging story of what has happened and is happening to people. These stories are both dramatic and believable. The happenings are selective slices from life, but they are engaging and realistic. Although fictional, I know the people these things have happened to. These true-to-life happenings present graphic information about crack cocaine and ice. The happenings come from thorough, extensive research and from the author's experiences which include thirty-five years of hands-on work as a licensed psychologist in the State of Texas and as Professor of Psychology at Baylor University.

Sections called "The Facts As We Best Know Them" comprise the informative and scholarly parts of each chapter. In these sections, a careful, research-based analysis of the facts as they pertain to the chapter topic are presented.

Certainly, no book can attack all the tentacles of the enemy at once. Hopefully, I will be able, in this book, to make available to every member of our society a most thorough knowledge about crack, cocaine, methamphetamine and ice.

L.E.M.

Bibliography

1   Bent, Daniel. "Reemergence of Methamphetamine: Select Committee on Narcotics Abuse and Control House of Representatives." Washington, D.C. October 24, 1989, p. 64

2   Bent, Daniel. "Reemergence of Methamphetamine: Select Committee on Narcotics Abuse and Control House of Representatives." Washington, D.C. October 24, 1989, p. 16.

3   Dart, Bob. Cox News Service. "Hard-core figures on hard-core users." May 1990.

4   Jackson, Jon G. " Hazards of Smokable Methamphetamine." New England Journal of Medicine. Vol. 321 No. 13. September 28, 1989, p. 907.

5   Jaffe, Jerome. "Reemergence of Methamphetamine: Select Committee on Narcotics Abuse and Control House of Representatives." Washington, D.C. October 24, 1989, p. 137.

6   "Federal anti-drug strategy: 'Attack crack'." "Mayo Clinic Health Letter." November 1989, p. 8.

7   National Institute on Drug Abuse. "Methamphetamine Abuse in the United States. Public Health Services, Alcohol, Drug Abuse and Mental Health Administration." September 1988, p. 1.

PART I — IMPACTS

Chapter 1

Grandchildren of the Drug Culture

Happening One — The Inevitable

The Facts As We Best Know Them

Parents Are Role Models
Sexual Effects of Crack Cocaine
Crack Cocaine and Methamphetamine Increase
    Sexual Desire
The Drug Becomes the Master
Drugs and Personality Change
Behavioral Changes in Personality
Crack, Ice, Paranoia and Depression
The Power of Addiction with Crack and with Ice

Happening One — The Inevitable

From her position in the choir loft, Susan was aware that her mother who was sitting with a friend in the second pew. She could not see her mother clearly because of her own tears. Her mother's eyes , Susan knew, were shifting from her face to her husband Dr. Lewis Froman seated in the Pastor's chair on stage. She knew her mother had just a touch of her usual prideful smile on her face.

"She thinks I'm crying because I feel so happy, so close to the Lord," Susan thought. "Oh, God! what am I going to do? I know what I must do, but can I do it?"

Susan mouthed the words to the chorus, "Sweet, holy spirit, sweet heavenly dove." She could make no sound. She controlled her sobs, trying to smile and hoping Daddy wouldn't notice that she wasn't singing. The order of worship was to have the choir sing "Sweet, Sweet Spirit" before her daddy would rise and move to the podium. She heard Jimmy's deep voice behind her. She marvelled that Jimmy could sing normally when she couldn't. This madness had to end. She'd be dead, and her mother and daddy would never know the truth. She'd never let them be disgraced. Suicide would devastate them, but it was the only answer. She knew it was; it had to be.

The choir seated themselves, and Susan heard her daddy intone, "Let us pray." She heard only the drone of his voice after that. Her thoughts went back. Daddy came into the choir room a few minutes before they entered the loft. After his words of inspiration and his prayer with the choir, he had time to whisper something to her. "How's my angel? You're prettier than ever." Then, he pinched her at the waist, as only a daddy is allowed to do. "You're losing your baby fat, sugar; you're really becoming a woman!" Then he smiled, showing his obvious pride in her, and moved on to pat shoulders, to shake hands and to say words of encouragement to many.

"Baby fat?" Susan thought. He doesn't know I haven't eaten in a week. The memories, the smells, the tastes never left her. But she'd never have to do that again. She wouldn't; she couldn't. She couldn't tell anyone; she could only suffer alone, cry when no one was looking, fight the pain deep inside her and try to swallow the lump in her throat. "Oh, if I could just die," she thought. "I want to be dead. I'll have to do it myself. Oh, sweet Jesus, you'll understand; you'll know that my love for you hasn't changed. You'll take me to be with you. I know that some say suicide is the unpardonable sin, but my trust is in your understanding. Just be with me, give me enough courage and then take me home." She whispered, "Oh God, I so much want to live to bring glory to your name. I want to have Jimmy as my husband. I want my babies and my life. But it can't be."

She hated Jimmy now. "How could he be so uncaring, so calloused? He acts like he doesn't have a care in the world. He must know I'm dying of shame and hurt. He seems immune to it all. He won't even talk to me anymore. All he wanted was to use me to satisfy his need for the drug. How he has used me, shamed me, abused me, destroyed me! And he has no feeling about doing it!" she thought.

Thinking back to their earlier times together, she couldn't believe it. Jimmy was from a fine family. They had fallen in love when they were fourteen. That was two years ago. They had talked about their future together endlessly. He was going to become a lawyer like his father. They'd have a wonderful life. When they had started having sex about a year ago, there was nothing but joy. The great and glorious future they had planned put stars in her eyes. It simply wasn't true that having sex meant a boy didn't care for you as a future mate.

Her mother had agreed with her when Susan confided in her. Her mother had helped her get the pills from their doctor. Susan had been amazed at her mother's understanding. Mother didn't tell her daddy about it, Susan was sure. Susan and her mother had always had that kind of understanding. Susan knew her mother's secrets, and her mother knew she was aware of them because they shared their secrets. Her mother had said, "You're a grown woman, Susan, and you understand these things, I'm sure." She was referring to "these things" as the fact that Mother and Daddy had had sex before they were married, too. And other "things" Susan remembered. It seemed like a thousand years ago that she and Robert, her younger brother, were often sent off on Friday evenings to spend the night at Grandmother's.

Of course, Susan hadn't known about the special Friday night parties then, or at least she hadn't known what happened at those parties. Friday was Daddy's day off, coming just before his hard weekends as pastor —preaching twice on Sunday after preparing all week for the sermons, visiting the sick and all the things a pastor must do. Sure, they deserved "time to themselves" as Grandmother so wisely put it.

The odd thing Susan remembered about those early years was the funny smell about the house when she and Robert came home on Saturday afternoons. Looking back, now she knew that it had been marijuana smoke. She had been a little shocked about that at first; but, in time, she'd come to understand that Daddy had been to Viet Nam and that the "sixty" generation was, according to her school books, the "drug culture." Still, it had shocked her some, but she got used to it. And the sex parties — well, everyone knew about the "birds and the bees"; but, even so, when she was younger, it had seemed a little weird that Daddy and Mother were into that when they were constantly expounding the pious life to others. Now she knew that the kind of life people expected a minister to live was really impossible. They all were constantly exposed to the heavy sexuality of TV and movies. Sure, husbands and wives do these things; it is only natural — both the sex and the pot.

Susan should have expected that Mother would understand when she told her that she and Jimmy were having sex. Actually, she'd been a little ashamed to tell her and was pleased and surprised when her mother took it so lightly.

"Let's get you some protection, honey. I'll talk to Dr. Joe about a prescription right away. Just wait until we get the pills, and it will be okay. Jimmy is a fine boy, and the two of you will be able to have babies and be very happy when both of you finish the University." It had been so much smoother than Susan had expected it to be. She had been sure that her mother knew, too, that she and Jimmy were into pot. She had never been sure what Daddy knew, but she knew he was no fool. What girl talked to her daddy about things like that? But after all, somebody was paying for the pills.

It all "came down" about three weeks ago. Jimmy was excited when they went out on their date that Tuesday night. He drove out to the secluded place they often went and whispered, "I've got something new, baby."

"What is it, Jimmy?" she asked thinking maybe he had a bottle. A lot of kids were drinking, but she and Jimmy had only used marijuana. But Jimmy handed her a joint as usual. It felt a little funny, kind of hard instead of soft like the joints usually felt. Jimmy lit her joint for her and handed it to her.

From the very first drag, Susan knew that this wasn't just pot. The first drag didn't do much, but after the third or fourth, she was gulping and pulling that smoke into her lungs like crazy. The high hit her, and it was past describing or explaining. She was lifted up, felt herself floating, and her sense of happiness was like an explosion; Jimmy smoked his joint, too, and they grabbed each other in unspeakable joy. The high was absolutely sublime for what seemed like minutes. They were spaced out in each others' arms in indescribable bliss. They could feel each others' heartbeats. She felt like they were one and that the heavens had opened up, causing unspeakable contentment.

And then the sex began. Never before had it been like that! It lasted and lasted. She had never imagined sex could be so great. Oh, if married life could be like this, it would simply be a joy forever. Unbelievable!

Finally she was able to say, about midnight, she guessed, "Jimmy, what was that we smoked?" And he said simply, "It's crack, honey, crack cocaine. Well, not altogether crack; it's crack mixed with pot, what the guys call a 'primo.' Did you like it?"

"Like it? It was beyond belief!" she said.

She couldn't shake the feeling all the next day. Half the time she was expectantly elated, half the time, depressed and sad. And although she and Jimmy seldom went out on Wednesday nights, she just had to call him. "Jimmy, can't we do it again?"

But Jimmy was a little hesitant. "Was it that great for you, Susan? You know that stuff costs like crazy. It took most of my allowance just for those two joints last night. But I'll tell you what, I'll fix us a little pipe, and we can use just a little crack. I think I can get it."

"Jimmy, you've got to get some more. Please. Tell me you will. I've got some money."

Well, that was less than three weeks ago. And as she sat there in the choir loft, she yearned even through her anguish for that high again. The craving was unbearable.

But had it been just three weeks? Surely all this had not happened so swiftly. It was glorious at first, but it was a hellish nightmare now. She and Jimmy squandered every dime they could lay their hands on, but it just wasn't enough. And she knew Jimmy was almost as panicky, almost as hooked as she!

And then he started having plenty of crack and money, too. At first she didn't ask questions. She would have stolen her mother's jewels and hocked them just to have that feeling again. But Jimmy's bonanza couldn't and didn't last.

It was a shock of sorts for Susan to find out that Jimmy was pushing now. That was why he had crack and money. What a terrible thing — Jimmy had become a drug pusher! She couldn't allow that. But she did. For almost a week, Jimmy kept them supplied. And they had it every night; they couldn't get by even one night without it. Mother and Daddy seemed a little skeptical when she and Jimmy started going out every night. And as usual, they didn't really know what time she got it. But even then, at least up to a week ago, life couldn't have been better. It was simply great, too great to believe! Even so, a small part of her kept whispering, "This is not right. It can't go on. Susan, you're slipping in your school work. You're not paying attention to the right things. You're strung out and you're hung up. You're feeling no pain. This can't go on."

But it had to go on. There was no other way.

And then a week ago, it happened. "I just can't get enough money, Susan, honey. They want more for it now, and I'm selling all I can. Still, I can't keep them paid."

At first it didn't dawn on her. "Who's 'them,' Jimmy?"

"Why, the dealers, baby. They're ones who bring the stuff in and get it on the street. We've always depended on someone else to get the stuff in, even when we were only doing pot. Don't you understand?"

No, Susan didn't understand. She'd always depended on Jimmy. He'd always had the joints. How stupid she'd been to think that joints grew on trees or something.

"I've got a little burglary ring organized, honey. We're breaking and entering now. We're taking jewelry, TV's, VCR's and hocking them as fast as we can; but the pushers always want more. I just don't have enough money to keep us in the groove, and I don't know what to do. I'm afraid we are going to wind up in jail. The guys working with me are all our friends, and it's going to hit the fan one of these days. Susan, we're in real trouble."

Trouble? Real trouble? Susan hadn't had any trouble up to then. She hadn't known what trouble was, but, oh God, she knew now.

"I'll let you talk to one of the pushers," Jimmy told her one night in desperation. Did Jimmy know what he was getting her into when he said that? Surely not. But then, Jimmy was no fool.

So they met with one of the pushers. He was trash — Susan knew that right away. She'd been brought up properly — fine home, good clothes and impeccable manners. She'd stood at the top of her class and had heard fellows say about her from time to time, "Susan — that girl's got class!" And they'd shaken their heads admiringly, showing their jealousy of Jimmy.

But this dirty scum put his hands on her, "Honey, if you need the stuff, old Jesse will get you all you need, baby.

29

And then he gave her a pipe. Although she was nearly sick to the stomach just to smell him, she had no choice but to take it. She sucked the cocaine into her lungs, and everything became rosy again, scum or no scum. So he put his filthy hands all over her, and she didn't feel anything was wrong. She even enjoyed it! She looked around for Jimmy that night, but Jimmy was gone. The scum let her out of his car around midnight about a block from her home. She stumbled in using her key, slipped upstairs to her bedroom and looked at herself in the mirror. She vomited right on her dressing table.

It got worse, much worse, unbelievably worse. First, there was one of them, then a few nights ago, there were two. Then, last night there were three. And, "Please, God," she whispered, "don't let it be so." But it was so. Last night, Jimmy was there too. The things those thugs did to her and the things they made her do right in front of Jimmy couldn't be told, could hardly be allowed into her mind. And Jimmy just watched, stoned out, just as she was, of course.

And then the unbearable happened — the ghastly act that broke through even her cocaine stupor. One of them said, "Jimbo, you'd better get yourself a piece of this." And then there were four of them. Jimmy was just like they were!

Sure, he was sitting behind her now and was able to sing "Sweet, Sweet Spirit." How could he do it? How could she allow him to become a house burglar? How could he become a scum like the rest of them when he was on the stuff? How could he act like a big man on campus as he did all day Friday while she wanted all day to crawl under her desk?

No, crack was too big for Jimmy — too big for her. "God, help me; please, God, help me," she whispered to herself, pulling herself up, stumbling over the knees of the choir member between her and the aisle. She heard Daddy begin the invitation, "Come unto me all ye that labor and are heavy-laden, and I will give you rest."

Susan didn't make it to the rest room before she retched. "Please God, please God, please, please," she pleaded. "Will Mother understand that it is better for me to be dead than to have the truth known?"

****

Her mother didn't understand — she never understood anything at all.

The Facts As We Best Know Them

A great deal is being written about the effects parents' behaviors have on the surging crack and ice epidemics. In one "toughlove" support group, one woman in her fifties volunteered, "We cannot expect our children not to use crack when my husband and I are both alcoholics!" This was a tearful admission and was not accompanied by any declaration that she and her husband might ever try to give up alcohol. In fact, inherent in her verbal and emotional display was an unspoken declaration, "My husband and I cannot give up alcohol, so we must stand by and watch our children use crack and ice."

Parents Are Role Models

As pitiful as it may seem, this woman mentioned above had unusually sharp insights. With most parents, denial enters in and makes it possible for them to avoid any sense of blame for what their children do.

Some Deny, Some Are Unaware

Many persons who engage in denial will even deny their denial. It is usually the job of someone such as a counselor to point out the function and presence of denial. The fact is that many parents truly are unaware of the messages they are sending to their children. Other parents are somewhat aware of the effects of their own behavior on their children, but they seem to think they can keep their children in the dark concerning what they, the parents, do in their bedrooms or in their social milieus.

In "The Inevitable," Susan's parents, these conservative, high-profile religious persons, were themselves children of the 1960's drug culture. The pastor had been in Viet Nam where heavy hashish and methamphetamine use was the norm. It could be argued that such drug use was necessary for survival in Viet Nam. It was likely that both of these parents were marijuana users during their college years because that was the age of rebellion against establishment values.

Rationalization

Parents, who themselves are children of the drug culture, are rarely good role models for children in the 1990's who are becoming victims of crack and ice. Such parents, deep within themselves, are dealing not with denial but with rationalization. They are saying via their actions, "Marijuana didn't hurt us; we still use and enjoy it." But since they probably understand that marijuana use is often the entrée to harder drugs, they often try to use their drugs in private and not let their children know that they use them. The problem here, of course, is that these parents are almost sure to fail in their clandestine use of drugs. Children, by and large, are much too smart to be fooled.

Whether or not anything can be accomplished by remonstrating with parents concerning the effects of their continuing loyalty to principles they embraced in the 1960's is arguable. It seems that many such parents could be persuaded to change their behavior if they could be made aware of the impact their behavior is having on their children.

Parents Say By Their Actions That Drugs are Okay.

When parents use alcohol, marijuana or tobacco, there is a high probability that there is a subtle message to youngsters that "drugs are okay." In the mind of a child, the distinction between legal and illegal drugs usually doesn't function at all. Parents should remember that young children do not realize alcohol is a legal drug for adults, and marijuana is an illegal drug under many circumstances.

The acknowledged progression from "light" to "heavy" drugs often follows this scenario: 1) tobacco (cigarettes) 2) marijuana (smoked) and 3) crack or ice (smoked). A youngster who has never had a puff on a cigarette has more of a struggle in taking a puff from a crack or ice pipe.

The closest association of all is the association between pot smoking and crack or ice smoking. Indeed, this is almost a natural progression. Murray (6) reports through an article in The Journal of Drugs Issues entitled "The Cannabis — Cocaine Connection" that there is a social-recreational connection between these two substances. Anecdotal records from the field

33

support this strongly. It is at least unusual, although certainly not unheard of, for a youngster to smoke crack or ice as the first drug he uses.

All of the things said above can be substantiated by self-report studies. But rather than take time via literature citations from more important material ahead, a consensus agreement is logical — the high probability is that marijuana use often precedes crack or ice use.

Parents Can Become More Knowing and More Responsible

Two things must be said here: 1) Parents who use what youngsters believe to be dangerous drugs are setting bad examples. Saying to children, "Do as I say, not as I do," demonstrates weakness to the child. Many parents seem to be blind to the fact that lifestyles usually do pass from parents to children whether that is what the parents want or not. 2) Parents; who, through design or through neglect, fail to teach positively against drugs; are unthinking, unknowledgeable, neglectful or some combination of these.

On the other hand, lecturing parents is no more effective than lecturing children, unless we can provide some compelling reasons for parents who are children of the drug culture to change their ways. Some of us attempt to do so with strong dedication.

Parents of the drug culture probably argued with their parents thusly, "Pot is no more dangerous than cigarettes." That was a good point, and all the facts pursuant to such a claim are still not in evidence. What parents of this drug generation are telling their youngsters via their actions is, "Sure we use marijuana as a recreational drug. We hope you won't do it; but then if you do, it will be no worse for you than it is for us."

They are wrong! The marijuana they and their children are getting now is ten to twenty-five times as powerful as the pot the parents smoked in the 1960's. The gradual increase in potency of marijuana may not create massive problems for the parents because they have adapted to the change; but for the children, the impact is immediate and likely harmful.

In the 1960's cocaine was beyond the reach of all except the wealthy. Most important of all, **crack is here now, and it is easily available!** The easy availability of ice is a progressive reality.

To sum up, parents of the drug generation of the 1960's are proving to be a chief enemy to the welfare of their own children, and most of them haven't faced this reality. If we are to win against drugs, parents must shoulder not only blame but must take concerted action saying, "Enough is enough. No more drug use in this family!"

Sexual Effects of Crack Cocaine

There is a consistent message pervading the culture, especially among the upwardly mobile, that cocaine and more specifically crack cocaine is an aphrodisiac. The scientific literature reflects (not without contradiction) a two-tiered pattern of relationships between cocaine use and sexual behavior. In other words, yes and no.

Historical and Anthropological References

When the Spanish conquistadors arrived in Peru, they were amazed to find unbelievable etchings of sexual depravity (as interpreted by their clerics) on the pottery of the Incas and on anthropological artifacts thought to be related to the Moche people who lived in Peru even before the Incas. These etchings were reminiscent of pagan rites of fertility worshipers in ancient Judah and Israel. The chewing of coca leaves was forbidden by Spanish priests for the Spanish. But priestly demands largely went unheeded. Siegel (9) gives a lucid review of the sexual-cocaine connection.

Cocaine, the Lascivious Woman

Today, with the widespread, somewhat crude processing of coca leaves in the Andean jungles, the crossbred natives anxiously await the opportunity to acquire coca paste, the crude mixture of leaves, solvent and other chemicals deriving from the manufacture of cocaine hydrochloride. This paste is a cheap, easily obtained, smokable form of cocaine, although the cocaine

35

content is not as strong as with refined cocaine hydrochloride. On the other hand, coca paste is a dangerous form of the drug since it still has harmful chemical content which will later be filtered out. The young and the old men who work in these clandestine factories rest in the shade at siesta time and roll the dried paste into "joints." The young men, after the first few puffs, exchange sly glances and stroke the short joints with loving hands as if they were the budding breasts of little girls.

Juan looks with a knowing smile at Pedro and whispers, "La ninita (little girl)." Pedro smiles back nodding, "La muher bonita (pretty woman)." But the old man, smoking his joint in silence and trying to draw from it a new strength for the hard labor of the afternoon, sadly shakes his head and mutters, "El diablo (the devil)."

The Andeans always refer to coca leaf as "woman," "girl," or a number of cruder sexual connotations. The young men learn early about the sexual turn-on that the coca plant offers and have a lascivious regard for it. But the old have learned of the fickleness of the woman, the leaf.

Crack Cocaine and Methamphetamine Increase Sexual Desire

The literature, replete with controlled studies and statistical analyses, shows that cocaine as well as methamphetamine have aphrodisiacal properties during early use which may continue for months or years with casual use.

Sexual desire increases for many from a combination of drugs, sometimes methamphetamine with cocaine, sometimes marijuana with cocaine and even with a combination of alcohol and cocaine. Alcohol per se reduces inhibitions of all kinds because it is chemically a depressant. Obviously, with a combination of lowered inhibitions and elevated sensitivity, sexual desire increases.

The Causes of Arousal

The explanation of the power of cocaine and methamphetamine to stimulate sexually has many facets from chemical and neurological bases. Both of these drugs have an elevating capability over most bodily functions. Heart rate, blood pressure and respiration counts are are elevated. Psychologists are well prepared to defend the "general arousal syndrome." With general arousal, all emotions are sensitized, including sexual desire.

More importantly, the neurological effects are centered in the pleasure centers of the brain (the limbic system). More than a pure sensitizing of pleasure centers is involved however. Dopamine is one among four synaptic neurotransmitters; and dopamine itself, as a chemical, affects the entire body along a pleasure-pain dimension. With early drug use, there is an immediate uptake of dopamine into higher brain centers.

Cocaine and methamphetamine have effects on dopamine reuptake (dopamine recharge and release) with synaptic neurotransmitters and cause a general elevation bodily functioning. With further stimulation derived from other drugs and with inhibitory responses to downers such as alcohol and opiates, the increase of sexual desire is virtually guaranteed in the early stages of cocaine and methamphetamine use. This increase in sexual desire may continue over time if the drug use is optimally controlled. It is worth noting that among first users of cocaine, especially crack, dopamine molecules are moved at accelerated pace along the limbic pathway with accompanying libidinal arousal occurring, even when the persons using the drug do not expect this to happen.

Indeed, there are many anecdotal reports, especially from women, that knowledgeable men have manipulated them by introducing them to crack or methamphetamine. Under the control of a sudden, almost frenzied orgiastic outburst of sexual turn-on, women regularly report (especially to rape crisis personnel) that they have been manipulated into sexual acts which thirty minutes earlier would have been unconscionable to them.

Such reports are seldom heard from males, but logically a reverse gender manipulation is scarcely beyond imagination. Logically, rape crisis counselors and hot-line volunteers are urged to receive such reports cautiously. The rise in reported "date rape" seems to be related. Many times, females reporting "date rape" have actually been maliciously abused. At other times, they enter into smoking crack with full knowledge of

37

what could happen, fully believing they can handle the surge in sexual arousal when, as a matter of fact, they cannot.

The Role of Expectation

Still, another factor in sexual arousal is expectation. If a person expects a drug to turn him on sexually, then it likely will because the brain (where expectations reside) is clearly the most important sexual organ of all. If we add still another brain-associated factor, habituation, no one should be surprised at the aphrodisiacal capabilities of crack and ice.

It must be emphasized that these stimulations are more intense with early use of cocaine or methamphetamine in any form but is more pronounced with crack freebase and ice because of the "immediacy" effect. The affected person has less time, with actions precipitated by crack or ice, to marshal together opposing forces of conscience, training or scruples. He/she acts before cognitive processes of thinking and reasoning can be brought into play. Methamphetamine effects on sexual arousal with IV use is described in a summary of research findings used by the National Institute on Drug Abuse (7) as follows: "When injected intravenously, methamphetamine produces a rush which many users are unable to describe in words. Some suggest similarities to an intense orgasm."

This same NIDA report (7) on methamphetamine use quotes a study done in July, 1988 by Gawin and Ellinwood: "One third of females and males interviewed stated that sexual activity was enhanced with amphetamine use." These statistics for sexual arousal by methamphetamine are less dramatic than those usually cited for cocaine. Crack cocaine provides the most dramatic sexual turn-on of all forms of cocaine, and the sexual turn-on with ice is said to be more dramatic than that for IV use of methamphetamine.

Obviously, the stimulating sexual effects of cocaine or methamphetamine can last, perhaps for years, with persons who use the drug or combinations of cocaine and other drugs casually and not very often — say only once a week. With these persons, toxicity has not been reached. Whether or not it is inevitable that the hurtful level may ever be reached is arguable.

The Drug Becomes the Master

However, for abusers, there comes the onset of reversal. Drug tolerance becomes a factor. It may gradually require more and more of the drug(s) to achieve the desired level of excitement.

Cocaine Use and Methamphetamine Use Reduce Libidinal Energy

After being hyper-activated over a long period, the synaptic neurotransmitter dopamine goes into a depletion phase. Like any other aspect of bodily (or brain) function, calling upon the dopamine transmitter too often and not allowing maximal time for refraction and reuptake to occur causes a diminishing of the dopamine manufacturing processes which occur in specific areas of the brain.

Dackis et al (1), working in Hampton Hospital at Rancocas, N.J., say, "While cocaine produces euphoria through its stimulating effect on dopamine neurons, several lines of evidence suggest that dopamine depletion occurs after chronic cocaine abuse." This summary statement is repeated in essence over and over in continuing cocaine research. In short, the "use it or lose it" adage can be rewritten to "use it too much and lose it."

A Change in Priorities

Another dynamic of sexual dysfunction is that a change in priorities comes about as a person becomes more and more dependent on the drug hits. Sex is a powerful natural desire, especially among the virile young. But drugs become more important to many than sex. One young person described the pleasure of the crack rush as orgasm times one hundred. From this, one can easily see that anticipating and craving the hit occupies such a prominent place in the crack abuser's mind that sex per se may become relatively unimportant. The NIDA bulletin, Methamphetamine Abuse in the United States states, "Many who experience the intense euphoria as a result of IV use become regular mainliners, prizing speed over other drugs and sometimes over food or sex."(7)

This phenomenon of sex drive reversal is at the heart of many human problems. It is especially hurtful to the member of a sexual partnership, who continues with sex as highest priority while the hit is secondary, when the reverse priority is occurring in the other partner. Troubles of sexual dysfunction in marriage are legion without the drug factor. With a swing in priorities from sex to drugs in either partner to an intimate relationship, sexual dysfunction of the affected partner becomes a very threatening contingency for an intimate relating process. Marital discord with its vicious tentacles reaching into the domains of children is, of course, a major issue in American life.

Drugs and Personality Change

Most every parent knows what to look for when he/she begins to suspect that it is just possible that his/her child is using drugs. At one time, parents principally focused on possible marijuana use. Then the focus was turned to cocaine and methamphetamine, and now to crack and ice. The broad spectrum of drug use yields highly generalized behavior patterns among the young, especially if the young are using several drugs. Straight Inc. has suggested that parents watch for the following symptoms:

1. School tardiness, truancy or declining grades

2. Loss of motivation, energy, self-discipline, loss of interest in activities

3. Forgetfulness — short or long-term

4. Short attention span, trouble concentrating

5. Aggressive anger, hostility or irritability

6. Sullen, uncaring attitudes and behavior

7. Disappearance of money or valuables

40

8.   Changes in friends, elusive about new friends

9.   Unhealthy appearance and bloodshot eyes

10.   Changes in personal dress or grooming

11.   Trouble with the law in or out of school

12.   Use of visine, room deodorizers, incense

13.   Rock group or drug-related graphics and slogans

14.   Pipes, small boxes or containers, baggies, rolling papers or other unusual items

15.   Peculiar odors or butts; seeds or leaves in ashtrays, clothing or pockets(11)

All these warning signs could be subsumed under the heading, "Sudden change in personality." These are overtly obvious and fit a wide array of available drugs.

Siegel (10) has compiled a list of personality factors specific to freebase and crack smoking. His list encompasses characteristics more typical of young adults than of children. Siegel carefully tested thirty-two crack cocaine subjects and offers the following personality characteristics together with the number of persons demonstrating each behavior. He lists these characteristics in two categories, psychological and physical. Further, Siegel found, in the "physical symptoms complex," conditions far more severe for freebase smokers than those measured in cocaine abusers using nonsmoking routes of cocaine administration.

Psychological Evidence of Personality Change

Siegel reports the following data on psychological symptoms in thirty-two freebase cocaine abusers:

Symptom	No. Subjects
Paranoia	20
Visual hallucination	16
Craving	15
Asocial behavior	13
Problems concentrating	12
Irritability	10
Base dreams	10
Hyperexcitability	9
Violence	9
Auditory hallucinations	8
Lethargy	8
Depression	8
Business problems	8
Marital problems	7
Memory problems	6
Driving impairment	6
Tactile hallucinations	4
Sexual indifference	4
Improved sexual performance	4
Polydrug use	4
Family problems	4
Situational impotency	3
Robbery-burglary	2
Attempted suicide	2
Nightmares	2
Attempted homicide	1

Physiological Signs of Drug Impact

Siegel reports the following data showing physiological symptoms in thirty-two freebase cocaine users:

Symptoms	No. Subjects
Blurred vision	11
Coughing (black expectorate)	11
Muscle pain (back and shoulder)	11
Dry skin	9
Tremors	9
Weight loss	8
Chest pains	7
Episodic unconsciousness	5

Symptoms	No. Subjects
Difficult urination	5
Respiratory problems	3
Edema	3
Convulsions	1
Insomnia	1

Behavioral Changes in Personality

Most of the symptoms presented in the above tables can be overtly observed in the abusers. However, there are many other symptoms that cannot be so easily observed but are acted out. The personality changes for crack smoking have not been shown to be different in kind from those caused by cocaine introduced by other methods. However, crack not only brings about these changes, but the changes are often more noticeable because the changes occur more suddenly and more dramatically.

Ice and Violence

Ice brings considerably more violent behavior than does crack.(13) Historically, amphetamines have brought more violent reactions than have the many forms of cocaine. And then, too, with ice, just as with crack, there is the same immediacy and potency effect that comes from smoking this drug form. It is too early for research to have been done in laboratory settings on the effects of ice, so we shall have to depend upon reports from the field for semi-scientific evidence about the effects of ice.

The anecdotal reports we have show that ice yields a much longer high than crack with less of a rush effect within the first few seconds. It is being reported that ice is causing both sociopathic behavior and psychopathic behavior. Strangely, this drug increases sociability, sharpening the senses for social niceties — at least it does until toxicity occurs.

People who use ice in moderation can maintain a controlled high for many hours seeming only to be more outgoing. However, with intoxication, the lid blows off, and violent behavior erupts. These anecdotal reports coming largely from Hawaii pertain to casual or to moderate use. However, with ice toxicity brought on by overdosing, the reports are more frightening. Psychotic-like violence is being reported with ice toxicity, and elevated crime rates are a natural consequence. When it comes to media and anecdotal reports, we must understand that there may be polydrug effects upon behavior reported for both ice and crack.

Sociopathic Personality Change

In the story about Jimmy as given in "The Inevitable," there was evidence of an emerging sociopathic personality. Many anecdotal reports of sociopathic behavior have been brought to this author's attention and labeled as crack-induced. There is no substantial evidence that a change to sociopathic behavior is a drug-specific effect of cocaine in any form. However, in Jimmy's real-life case he was arrested for burglary and was labeled sociopathic by a court-appointed psychiatrist. It was suggested by the media that the sociopathic behavior was caused by crack. There is a possibility that Jimmy was using and had been using methamphetamine, and the research for methamphetamine does show strong sociopathic trends.

Estroff et al (2) in their article, "Adolescent Cocaine Abuse, Addictive Potential, Behavioral, and Psychiatric Effects," studied behavior patterns in 341 residents of seven Straight Inc. treatment programs who admitted cocaine use. These 341 residents were divided into categories of light users, intermediate users and heavy users. Heavy and intermediate users "used more sedative hypnotics to calm themselves and engaged in more criminal behavior, such as stealing from parents and stores and passing bad checks. They had more arrests for possession of drugs, stole more cars, sold more drugs and were more likely to trade sexual favors to obtain the drugs. Heavy and intermediate users were significantly more psychiatrically disturbed than light users."

The Estroff study further states: "This study suggests that cocaine is as addictive in adolescents as in adults; possibly more so." More importantly, in documenting sociopathic behavior as being possibly caused by cocaine abuse, this study reports, "It also causes psychosocial dysfunction ...." In a study by Griffin et al (4), it was demonstrated that males have more antisocial personality traits than do females.

In a study by Galanter (3), the mechanisms that underlie the apparent self-destructive behavior of addicted persons are presented. It is apparent that Jimmy experienced self-destructive as well as sociopathic qualities in the story, "The Inevitable."

Crack, Ice, Paranoia and Depression

While there is little scientific documentation for crack as a drug-specific antecedent for sociopathic behavior, there is well-researched information that crack cocaine causes paranoia. There is even stronger evidence for paranoid behavior in the use of ice. The NIDA report on methamphetamine abuse says, "Excessive doses can produce mental confusion, severe anxiety and aggressiveness."

In speaking about the first fifty cases seen at the Haight Ashbury Free Clinics, Director Dr. David E. Smith, said, "All of the ice users who entered treatment were paranoid." He continued, "With ice, they get real wired, and then they come down with something else. They drink or take Librium or Valium. They will use opiates to come down. There is a lot of polydrug use with ice."

It may be observed that of all personality classifications found in the study by Verebey and Gold (14), paranoia led all the rest. Twenty subjects out of thirty-two subjects were diagnosed as having paranoia. Eight were diagnosed as depressive. Working in a detoxification context, Wallace writing in The Journal of Substance Abuse Treatment reveals that the DSM III data for thirty-one adult crack users reveal high rates of depressive disorders. As a matter of fact, Wallace (15) suggests treatment residences specialized for crack addicts.

There is good reason why both depression and paranoia are associated with crack use.(5) According to Verebey and Gold (14), crack delivers the most sublime "high" to the user within eight to ten seconds of inhalation, and the high lasts only from five to ten minutes. This high is much shorter-lived than is true of the next cocaine form in line, IV cocaine use. The rush in IV use comes in 30 to 45 seconds and the high lasts 10 to 20 minutes. On the other hand, ice delivers a high that lasts up to eighteen hours.

It should be clear that both cocaine HCL and crack cause depression as the high leaves the victim feeling morose. Crack is the worst, but cocaine HCL is capable of producing demoralizing depression. Then, paranoia is sure to follow in either case, more acute for crack just as the depression is more acute.

These debates as to which of the two forms of cocaine is most destructive is at best a sterile one. And it is true that in lesser degrees, the other forms of use and abuse carry corresponding levels of depression and paranoia.

The Power of Addiction with Crack and with Ice

It is a much more meaningful dialogue to discuss the addictive qualities of cocaine IV use and crack.(8) Few deny that freebase smoking, of which crack is a part, is the most addictive use of the drug cocaine, and many researchers assert that freebase cocaine smoking makes freebase cocaine the most addictive drug in the long list of drugs, legal or illegal.

Ice use is similar, yet different, in its addictive qualities. Methamphetamine IV use brings about a quick rush and, depending on dosages, relatively quick crash and depression phases. Addiction through IV use of methamphetamine does not have the seduction that crack delivers.(12)

Ice cannot match crack for seductiveness. The ice high lasts longer than with any drug form commonly known with some observers and users reporting highs for as much as twenty four hours. Although ice is a dangerous drug form for many reasons, and ice is quite addictive; this smokable form of methamphetamine cannot match crack in its addictive properties.

Verebey and Gold (14, p. 517) described the actions of crack or IV use of cocaine as follows:

Intravenous cocaine HCL enters the bloodstream quickly, but the distance from the injection site to the brain is further than that from the lung to the brain. After freebase cocaine

46

smoking, brain concentrations are reached faster, resulting in greater behavioral effects than those experienced after IV cocaine HCL use, the duration of the reinforcing positive effects of cocaine is the shortest after freebase smoking versus other routes of administration lasting only five to ten minutes.

However, the dynamics of addiction are important because everyone must be convinced and impressed with the dangers of addiction. When the rush, especially that of crack or ice, comes on suddenly and with great intensity, that is the beginning of addiction — pleasure is the beginning. When the rush ends suddenly, having been for a few seconds sublimely pleasurable, the depression and paranoia is more severe as a result. With more severe depression and paranoia, the urge to return to the former unbelievable euphoria and elation rises in stark contrast to the depression and paranoia. Can anyone wonder that a user must use again and do so quickly? **Indeed they must!** Addictions come from quick shifts from heady euphoria to degrading depression-paranoia and then back again, because of the effort of the individual to regain the euphoria. Few people can resist the reaching-out from great pain toward intense pleasure. Few people can resist dependency on crack once this cycle has been repeated. One repetition is sufficient for many people. Two or three repetitions may be required for most.

Bibliography

1 Dackis, Charles A. MD and Gold, Mark S. MD. "Psychopharmacology of Cocaine." Psychiatric Annals. (189) September 1988, pp. 528-31.

2 Estroff, T.W. and Schwartz, R.H. and Hoffman, N.E. "Adolescent Cocaine Abuse, Addictive Potential, Behavioral and Psychiatric Effects." Clinical Pediatrics. Vol. 28(12). December 1989, pp. 550-555.

3 Galanter, Marc. "Self-destructive Behavior in the Substance Abuser." Psychiatric Clinics of North America. Vol. 8(2). June 1985, pp. 251-261.

4 Griffin, Margaret L. et al. "A Comparison of Male and Female Cocaine Abusers." Archives of General Psychiatry. Vol. 46(2) February 1989, pp. 122-126.

5 LeBlanc, P.E. et al. "Effects of Intrauterine Exposure to Alkaloidal Cocaine." American Journal of Disabled Children. Vol. 141(9). September 1987, pp. 937, 938.

6 Murray. "The Cannabis — Cocaine Connection." Journal of Drugs Issues. Vol. 14(4). Fall 1984, pp. 665-675.

7 National Institute on Drug Abuse. "Methamphetamine Abuse in the United States. Public Health Service, Alcohol, Drug Abuse and Mental Health Administration." September 1988.

8 Perez-Reyez, M. "Free-base Cocaine Smoking." Clinical Pharmacological Therapy. Vol. 32. 1982, pp. 459-465.

9 Siegel, Ronald V. "Cocaine and Sexual Dysfunction: The Curse of Mama Coca." Journal of Psychoactive Drugs. Vol. 14(1-2). January-June 1982, pp. 71-4.

10 Siegel, R.K. "Cocaine Smoking." Journal of Psychoactive Drugs. (14) 1982, pp.272-341.

11 Straight, Inc. "The Adolescent Drug Treatment Program That Works." St. Petersburg, Florida. 1989.

12 Thompson, Larry. "Ice, New Smokable Form of Speed." Washington Post Health. November 21, 1989, pp. 11,12.

13   U.S. Department of Justice. "A Special Report on 'Ice' (d-methamphetamine hydrochloride)." October 1989.

14   Verebey, Karl and Gold, Mark S. "From Coca Leaves to Crack: The Effects of Dose and Route of Administration in Abuse Liability." Psychiatric Annals. Vol. 189. September 1988, pp. 513-520.

15   Wallace, Barbara. "Cocaine Dependence Treatment on an Inpatient Detoxification Unit." Journal of Substance Abuse Treatment. Vol. 4(2). 1987, pp. 85-92.

Chapter 2

The Innocents — The Youngest Victims of Drugs

Happening Two — Good Luck, Randy

The Facts As We Best Know Them

The Impact of Crack Upon the Fetus
Crack Cocaine and AIDS

Happening Two — Good Luck, Randy

Christy Malone was thirty-eight, receptionist and Girl Friday to Dr. Nolan Brazil, the most prominent OBGYN (obstetrician-gynecologist) in Deerfield. She was living with Dr. Jeb Hunter, a much younger OBGYN than Dr. Brazil. Actually, Jeb was in his first year of practice at the Family Practice Center.

Jeb was thirty. That made him eight years younger than Christy. But age made no difference. Christy and Jeb had been drawn magnetically to each other while Jeb was doing internship training under Dr. Brazil. He had helped Dr. Brazil with several deliveries at Deerfield Presbyterian Hospital, the teaching hospital for the State University Medical School.

Jeb had asked her to marry him right away, but Christy doubted he had been really serious about it. "Impulsive young kid," Christy had chided him. "Wait until you've lived with me long enough to see what a bitch I can be!"

"You're a lovely bitch," had been Jeb's comeback. He was definitely more sexual than amorous. But weren't all men? Christy thought so but really had no regret about it.

****

But after living with Jeb for nearly a year, she began to get a different itch. She was no stranger to the biological clock thing and knew time was running out for her. She had thought long and seriously about it, and she knew that her love for babies had been at the heart of her decision to grab the chance to work as Dr. Brazil's receptionist. How she loved the tiny creatures, and she really envied every mother who brought her baby in.

Jeb didn't know how badly Christy wanted a baby; and at times, she felt bad about leaving the pills off the last five months. Was this her way of entrapping Jeb? "Of course not," she had reassured herself over and over, "Jeb wants me to marry him. Maybe Jeb is the one with the problem, maybe he ought to take a fertility test." She had never asked Jeb whether or not he even wanted children. But if she became pregnant and Jeb didn't go along with the baby idea, Christy was prepared to be a single mother for as long as necessary.

But nothing was happening! She was staying just as unpregnant as anyone could be! After six months of sex without pills and without any signs of pregnancy, she went for a full evaluation to Dr. Nita Miller, her personal friend and gynecologist.

Christy told Nita about her bout with gonorrhea when she was eighteen; and Nita reported, after thorough fluoroscope plus radiology, that both tubes were completely blocked. "There's no way to know that the gonorrhea did it," Nita tried to console Christy. Nita discouraged surgery, declaring the condition couldn't be corrected. Christy, taking the prognosis very hard, cried herself to sleep that night, while Jeb was delivering at County Hospital.

Thinking back on the day, Christy remembered that after the terrible diagnosis, she had told Nita about her marijuana use, and Nita had assured her that there was no connection. "Pot won't keep you from getting pregnant, Christy, and pot isn't going to open those tubes, either. Why don't you adopt?"

Christy had been on the verge of confiding to Nita about how Jeb and she had started doing marijuana and crack together, but had caught herself in time. "No use telling her that," she thought. "Crack won't open or close the tubes either." After all, she and Jeb were only casual and recreational users. "Jeb got me started on crack," Christy confided to herself, realizing it was a stupid thought.

Finally and inevitably, adoption came to be Christy's fondest hope. She thought seriously of telling Jeb about her visit to Dr. Miller and about the results but decided not to tell him anything, because she did not want to tell him about leaving off the pills.

Christy's biggest surprise of her life two weeks ago. She and Jeb had done the crack and sex bit and were relaxing in bed when she had asked, nibbling Jeb's earlobe, "Still interested in making an honest woman out of a sexy little bitch?"

Christy had expected him to grab her and say, "Yes, yes, baby, let's set the date." It was a real surprise when he hadn't really reacted at all. Very cautiously, he'd simply said, "I'll think about it," and got up to put on water for coffee, leaving her feeling like a cast-away whore. That had been the first time she'd ever felt a tinge of conscience about their sleeping together all these months.

Then, with coffee cups cradled in their hands at the kitchen table, Jeb had come back to it. "What about kids, Christy? You want kids?" Before she could explode with a very firm answer, he'd continued, "I really want kids — lots of them!"

So Christy had had to tell Jeb about her blocked tubes. She played it cool, as if she'd known about it a long time. "We could adopt, you know, honey," had been her well-prepared declaration.

"Yes, but it wouldn't be the same. How about artificial insemination?" he'd asked. "I've got plenty of the right stuff!"

"Chauvinist!" Christy had responded. But, then, why not? Several successful inseminations had been done at Presbyterian during the last few months.

Christy had made an appointment for evaluation the very next day. "Now, you're not going to back out on me?" She had asked Jeb and received his expected rebuttal, "No way, baby!"

It hadn't gone well at all. Dr. Ned Jayroe at the fertility clinic had told her after a thorough examination, "I don't think you are a good candidate, Christy. I'm not sure you could carry a baby to term, because you not only have the bad tubes, which are a risk factor, but your uterus has been affected, too. Actually, there may be no connection. Your uterus is considerably smaller than the norm. We don't have high success rates in the first place with either inseminations or embryo implants, and we don't like to go into it without having the pluses in our favor."

Well, that was that! It was back to adoption with Jeb being a good sport about it. "He's a darling," Christy thought, "I think I'm really falling in love with him."

****

It was about three o'clock on a Wednesday morning that Christy's dream child was been born. Actually, he was an impatient little thing, taking a "swan dive," as Dr. Brazil had explained it, before he could get his garb on.

The mother was a teen who, months ago, had chosen adoption over abortion. Christy felt for her when she left the hospital, not even seeing her baby. "Very sad," Christy thought, "and from a well-known family, too." But at least the girl had been well prepared for her ordeal; she was very real in her grief — not at all the hardened bitter kind she and Dr. Brazil saw in the office so much these days.

Christy fell head over heels in love with "Randy." The baby boy was born with a full head of curly, dark hair. "A perfect doll! He's mine," she exclaimed to herself when she first saw him.

Jeb was nearly as excited as she. They started the adoption process immediately. Christy and Jeb were surprised when the social worker insisted on in-depth interviews with them. "You will need to get the wedding bells ringing," she told them without humor. Jeb had started calling the baby Randy, too, and Christy had started calling Jeb Daddy. Jeb was bursting with pride about it all.

Somehow, Dr. Brazil was left out of all this. He had known about the artificial insemination screening being negative and about their desire to marry and adopt. When Christy went into the office that fateful morning, Dr. Brazil quipped, "Aren't we happy today! What's up Christy?"

"You don't know about Randy?" she asked in an unbelieving tone and then realized that Dr. Brazil had made only one trip to the delivery room, and had gotten bloody all over before he could get his full garb on. He had never even heard the name, Randy.

55

"We've been to the nursery a dozen times to see him," she declared, and then she calmed down long enough to tell all to her dearest friend. She thought he'd be so excited over the love affairs between Jeb, Christy and Randy. Christy caught a sharp breath when Dr. Brazil frowned instead of smiling.

"Come into the office and sit down," he said simply. And then in fatherly tones he said things that put Christy into deep gloom. "Christy, I can't stand by and see you do this. You weren't there when that baby came. He's a drug baby, Christy. I suspect he's a crack baby; I knew about the mother using drugs. He was gray, not pink or purplish as most babies are. The color was enough for me. But then, the nurses handling the cleaning made me aware even more specifically that he was a drug baby because of the way they handled him. The blood and urine screenings are bound to show cocaine. The aftercare is not ours Christy. The residents will take care of him until he's adopted. I absolutely can't stand by and let you and Jeb adopt that baby, Christy!"

"But Dr. Brazil, can't we get Randy detoxified? Won't he be all right, as good as new?" Christy realized these were not the right words, but she was completely shaken.

"Christy, think girl!" Dr. Brazil's fatherly demeanor came on stronger than ever. "There is high risk of damage in the limbic region, and dopamine balance is likely to be affected. He may not show it for four or five years, but that kid is high risk for A.D.D. He's sure to have a lot of learning disability." Christy suddenly got dizzy and thought that she would hit the floor. She knew well what Attention Deficit Disorder was like; her five-year-old nephew was into that now. It was pure hell for her sister —for everyone connected in any way to that kid.

Seeing Christy become very upset, Doctor Brazil said, "Easy Christy, we'll find another baby."

"But you don't understand, damn it. I'm thirty-eight years old. In another year or two, the social workers are not going to let me have a baby at all." Christy stumbled out of the room wiping her eyes, not wanting Dr. Brazil to see her so distressed.

Christy waited anxiously for Jeb to get home that evening. She met him at the door. "My baby...," she exclaimed tearfully, "Oh, my God, Jeb, Randy, my baby, I can't have him! He's a drug baby, Jeb. I can't stand it. I've just got to have my baby! I'm dying over it, Jeb."

"Not your baby. He's not just yours. He's ours!" Jeb declared fighting his own tears.

Then she fell into his arms. This was genuine love. They were married the following weekend.

****

Christy missed her period the second month after marriage. Nita Miller, shaking her head in disbelief, confirmed her pregnancy two weeks later. "You're pregnant, Christy. You can't be — can't possibly be — but you are. Congratulations! But we've got to set up a bunch of ground rules, Christy. You're pregnant — that's good — but from conception to birthing can be a long, dangerous road for you, honey. Evidently, your uterus is willing but is it able? I don't know...."

There was jubilation in the apartment that night. Christy was aglow with joy; Jeb was strutting like a peacock. "Told you I had the right stuff," he bragged. "Those little critters of mine lash their little tails and go for broke."

Christy, puzzled at first, realized he was talking about his sperm. "How silly," she thought, "but who wasn't acting silly around that apartment?"

"We've got to go into a huddle," Jeb said seriously.

"A what?"

"A huddle with Dr. Brazil. You're probably going to have to quit work and stay off your feet, my darling."

"Oh, my God!" she said, "I hadn't thought of that."

57

Jeb grabbed Christy by the shoulder, turned her around and looked her straight in the eyes, "Something else you hadn't thought about, I'll bet."

"What are you talking about, Jeb?" she asked earnestly.

"The drugs!" he exclaimed sharply and firmly. "That little guy in there is mine, kiddo, and if he ever gets a hit of crack, it will be after he goes off to college. Damn it, Christy, I mean it! No more crack! No more hash!"

Christy was shaking her head "yes," but she couldn't resist getting in a lick on this chauvinist pig. "Who do you suppose started me on crack, Jeb?"

"No difference," he said. "You quit and I'm game. I quit it, too. Deal?" And Jeb stuck out his hand soberly.

"Deal. But I'll give you a hundred to one you won't quit, Jeb. I can quit because I haven't been using it all that long. And besides, I've got to quit. Your little critters with their lashing tails breaking through my blocked tubes don't carry crack piggy back, but my blood does. It won't be the same motivation for you as for me," she said. "You may quit because you want to and to be a good sport; but for me, it is the eleventh commandment, 'Thou shalt not do crack when pregnant.'"

****

The pregnancy dragged on and on. Christy went to the office most days, but it was pencil pushing all the way. Dr. Brazil put his foot down. "Your job will be here when you deliver, Christy; until then, you'll be on sick-leave pay schedule." She argued that it wasn't fair to him, but in the end Daddy always won — and she realized that Dr. Brazil had become Daddy while Jeb had become her jailer. Jeb watched her like she was a prized piece of special ming. This made her as tense as hell and very angry. She never knew pregnancy would be like this.

Christy knew, too, that Jeb was using, although never at home. She lasted two weeks without a crack hit; and then, she

58

had only a little one. But the little one demanded a big one! It was then that she realized she couldn't quit cold turkey. "Jeb will never find out," she assured herself, "and I won't use enough to hurt the baby."

She fought it real hard for the first month, but crack was winning and she knew it. She used up all the rocks that she'd hidden around the house. It required a mighty effort at first to get a new supply. She had been across the river with Jeb several times to pick up a supply in a housing development over there. She knew Jeb just drove slowly through the run-down housing development until someone stepped out from an alley or from behind a tree and asked, "Looking for somebody in particular, Mister?" From there to the exchange of money for crack had always taken no more than a minute or two.

She borrowed Jeb's car on pretense that hers needed to be put in the shop for its annual inspection. Jeb obligingly followed her in his car, surrendering it to her in the hospital parking lot. She knew that the pushers would recognize that car and would come to it quickly. She was right. She fumbled around for the words, trying to remember how Jeb said it. "No sweat, baby," the pusher said. "How much do you want, little lady?" She kept her purchases small, making a trip about every two weeks.

After that first trip, she took her own car and had no trouble buying. She bought only one hundred dollars worth at a time, assuring herself, "You aren't using very much, really, not enough to hurt the baby." But she realized deep down that as the pregnancy wore on, she had to have her hits more often. However, she still kept the hits small. "Thank goodness drugs affected everyone differently," she thought. She knew some pregnant women used a lot and had perfectly normal babies — at least, she thought she remembered someone saying that.

Dr. Miller had insisted on amniocentesis at eight weeks. Christy was totally aware that abortion might follow immediately if the cell study should show Down's Syndrome. She knew there would not be a drug screen on any of this material. "No need," she thought. Naturally, the baby might show some cocaine traces if they should do a screen, even from the amniotic fluid. But Christy knew the amount of crack she was using

59

wouldn't harm the baby. After all, many mothers who were users delivered perfectly normal babies. Oh, maybe they showed a little irritability at first, but they soon got over that.

Christy was very nervous when Nita called her in for the report on the amnio. Nita's eyes told her what she wanted to know as she embraced Christy at the office door, saying, "Everything's perfect, Christy. Absolutely no problems — beautiful!"

Dr. Miller had become a mother hen about this baby. Part of it was brought about by the bad judgment she'd made early on, Christy figured. But then, Christy and Nita were friends! Even so, Christy felt like Nita was overdoing it on all that ultrasound monitoring. But Christy realized that Nita was still deeply concerned that she couldn't carry the baby to full term. Somehow, Christy wasn't really worried about that.

Oh, how boring life could be without her work! She didn't go to the office very much anymore. She sat for hours just staring at the wall.

It was during the fourth month that she had a bad scare. She always looked forward to Jeb coming home. Trouble was, he was so irregular. That day, he came at least two hours before she expected. She knew she would have to be careful to cover because she'd had a hit less than an hour ago. Thank goodness crack didn't smell up the place, at least not like pot did. So she met Jeb at the door and grabbed him around the neck. She was really glad to see him, and the words gushed out. "Oh, Jeb, darling, I'm so glad to see you. So glad! Oh, my God, how I've missed you!"

Jeb held her at arms length, looked at her eyes and said, "You okay, honey?" She knew that Jeb suspected something.

"You haven't been doing crack, have you?" Jeb asked right out of the blue.

"I'm just so glad to see you, Jeb. Of course not, silly. I wouldn't do that," she said.

"Well, be sure you don't," he said commandingly.

Christy had a hard time with that remark. "Who is he to be so bossy?" she raged inside. But she regained control quickly. She was smart enough to realize that his suspicions were aroused, because coming off the flush, she had been a little out of control, a little too hyper, too jittery.

Being a doctor's receptionist, she knew about dilaudid, the synthetic opium. She heard that they were called dilos or big D's on the street. So after that scare with Jeb coming in so early, she asked the pusher if he had dilos. And, of course he had plenty of pills.

By the fifth month, Christy was getting her hits; and then to keep the rush in control, she took the dilo. But it was a tricky game. She couldn't afford to be caught crashing down when Jeb came in anymore than she could be caught with a rush on. It got harder and harder. It was up with the hit and down with the dilo. She got to where she liked that routine. It seemed to make the hits even better.

Oh, how boring it was. She wasn't even having morning sickness anymore, no pain, no dizzy spells. She had nothing but boredom, hits and dilos. And then came just about the worst. After the 250th day, with about thirty more to go, Jeb suddenly announced, "No more sex."

"You know better than that, honey. If we're careful we can do it, right up to the night before. You're a trained OBGYN, Jeb. Surely, you weren't trained in the dark ages."

"I don't care," he said. "We can wait a month. You can hold your breath for a month," he quipped.

"It's not funny, Jeb."

"So, who's laughing? Nothing is going to happen to my kid — nothing," he said with finality.

Within a week from that day, Christy entered deep depression. She wanted the closeness of making love; but Jeb wouldn't relent. "Where are you getting it, Jeb? You're not a priest. You're getting it somewhere."

61

"Don't be silly," he said; and in a rage, he walked out slamming the door.

It got worse and worse — boredom, boredom, boredom. Nobody came; nobody called. Jeb, who usually called her at least once during the day, didn't call anymore. He came in late every night, it seemed, and he wouldn't talk to her — didn't seem nearly as excited about the baby as before. "He can't be that scared, that uneasy like a new father on first delivery — not with as many babies as he's delivered," she thought.

****

"One more week," Christy whispered to herself on Monday morning after Jeb had gone out for the day. She knew that some firstborns were late. And, at her age, who could tell when a baby might be late? She remembered one of Dr. Brazil's patients who had gone to the hospital with false labor in late August and hadn't delivered until mid-October. An eleven month old fetus! Even Dr. Brazil had pronounced it that.

God! She couldn't stand it, not even another week! So, she had a great idea. She and Jeb were sleeping in different rooms now, and she knew that a really big hit following several smaller hits could induce labor. She had to get out of this just as quickly as possible. So, she had several hits during the day and didn't follow them with dilo.

They had dinner that night, and after the news, each faked a fond goodnight. It seemed to her that they had been doing this for ages. She went to her room, telling Jeb she believed she'd close the door between them because his snoring bothered her. "Okay, by me," he said. She thought he said this almost sullenly.

Could she be getting paranoid? She didn't think so. "People just don't realize what sex means in a marriage," she counseled herself as she lay down awkwardly. She sprayed the room with deodorant and put the biggest rock she had into the pipe. She inhaled deeply. She'd have this baby by morning even if she had to use two or three hits during the night.

Christy woke up screaming with pain. Jeb was at her side quickly. "Labor? Christy! Labor?" he asked. Fighting back the pain, she realized that Jeb was acting like a first-time father after all. For a moment, it kind of amused her; and then the pain hit again — hard.

"Christy, where's the pain," Jeb demanded.

"Up here," she placed her hand upward toward her navel.

Jeb put his hand on her distended abdomen, felt the rigidity there. "Goddam it! Christy. I knew you'd been hitting the crack," he screamed at her. "Oh, my God!" he said, "it's an abruption — Goddam abruption." Jeb headed for the telephone.

****

Christy was barely conscious of the wild ride to the hospital. She wasn't conscious at all after they put the sodium pentothal in her veins. As she went in and out of consciousness after the C-section, she knew she wasn't rational. But realized at a subconscious level that she was saying, "Where's my baby, my baby," and then mixing it in with a few curse words of her own, "I don't really give a damn — to hell with all of them!"

And then Dr. Brazil, who had been there during surgery, was shouting, "Wake up, Christy! Wake up, Christy!" When she was half awake, he said, "You've got a cute little boy, Christy. He looks a lot like Randy."

"It is Randy," she said. She knew it would always be Randy. Soon, Randy was in her arms, but it wasn't like she had expected. He never stopped crying, not even for an instant. She couldn't cuddle him. He refused her breast. He acted like he was being tormented.

The nurse from the newborn unit took the blanket from around Randy. "It's a soft blanket, but he's very sensitive to it. Let's just let him lie between your breasts. He'll be more comfortable," she said softly.

Christy heard his crying as if he were far away. She could not feel his weight upon her chest although she could see him there. She moaned and the tears came profusely. "He's a crack baby, isn't he, nurse?" The nurse turned away without answering, returning only to take Randy back to the nursery.

Jeb came in. "He picks the most awful times," Christy thought.

"He was as gray as a ghost," Jeb said. There was no love in his voice, only gut-level belligerence, "You've done extremely well, Christy. You've given us a crack baby."

"How do you know it's a crack baby?" Christy asked defiantly.

"The damn drug screen on the urine sample doesn't lie," he shot back at her.

"On whose authority did you do a drug screen?" she screamed at him.

"On my authority; I'm his daddy." Jeb answered gritting his teeth.

"You bastard! You had no right to do that. It's my baby and my body." Her anger and body movements made the stitches pull, and she fell back in pain holding her stomach.

"I'll sue you, and I'll sue the Hospital," she shouted angrily.

"Go to hell!" Jeb turned on his heel and left her moaning.

****

Three months later, Christy was back at work. Jeb had obtained a no-fault divorce and was taking her to court for custody of Randy. Christy had fought a mighty battle, had been in detox a week and was taking both group and individual counseling. She used crack only in the evenings now.

64

The Facts As We Best Know Them

The Impact of Crack Upon the Fetus

Drug and AIDS babies are being born in considerable numbers in delivery rooms across America. It is reported by dependable sources that 11 percent of babies born in 1989 showed overt signs of infection or addiction transmitted from mother to child during the gestation period.(12, p. 6)

Through talking with a number of hospital administrators, this author has found that so far as these hospitals are concerned, drug screening of the mother's blood or urine is seldom done for a routine pregnancy.

Laws have been enacted in some states to make it possible for health-care workers to do drug screening even without the patient's consent in some cases. The laws (usually at the state level) allow health-care workers to do this only if they perceive a clear and present danger to themselves whether in prenatal care or in the delivery process. When a prospective mother is highly suspected of having HIV, the test is almost always done; however, when the patient is a citizen of high community standing, the hospital often waives this legal prerogative. Actually, such a mother often will refuse both drug and HIV screenings, and her wishes often prevail over the best judgment of hospital personnel.

When the fetus is delivered and shows clear signs of drug intoxication, the hospital has little difficulty in getting parental consent for drug screening pursuant to helping the child survive withdrawal symptoms. Obviously, this applies only to the mother who wishes to keep her baby; with abandoned children, hospitals can do screening tests without consent.

A test for HIV is often a different matter inasmuch as the danger to the staff is unclear when only overt signs of drug addiction are present. The hospital is hard pressed to know what test to administer regardless of legal prerogatives since the drug baby, while demonstrating symptoms common to drug addiction but not HIV infection, is sometimes regarded as a high-risk for HIV as well. HIV infections are often masked under drug addiction symptoms, but the hospitals are hampered

65

because they must be able to cite clear danger to health-care workers in order to override a mother's objection to HIV testing.

Crowding the Hospitals with Crack Babies

Thousands upon thousands of newborns who are abandoned by the mother at birth are taxing the infant-care capacities of hospitals across America (and around the world) to the point of catastrophe for infant-care facilities. Babies whose mothers use crack cocaine are exposed to the drug through the placenta and are referred to as crack babies. The designation "crack baby" is common, yet vague and often misleading 1) since the mothers are often polydrug users and 2) since many babies whose mothers used drugs other than crack are labeled "crack baby" as a popular connotation. It is likely that babies being born in Hawaii are being called "ice babies" under similar circumstances.

After being delivered, crack babies must be stabilized and nursed through withdrawal. The average hospital stay for such babies is forty-two days as contrasted to three days for a healthy infant. Obviously, HIV babies often must be held for even longer hospitalization.

When the babies are abandoned at birth or soon thereafter, they are left to board in hospitals until they can be placed in the care of relatives, adoptive parents or a foster home. Boarder babies' long stay overcrowds pediatric units in many hospitals. This crowding has been so extreme that at one point last year, doctors couldn't find an empty neonatal, intensive-care bassinet in any hospital between Philadelphia and Richmond.

Crack, a Financial Burden on Health Care

It is obvious that there are drug babies who have many and sundry drug effects coursing through their veins at birth. And usually, an HIV positive baby is both a drug baby and an AIDS baby. It is well-demonstrated that most mothers who use drugs at all ingest several drugs, chief among which is alcohol.

According to the Mayo Clinic, "Given the magnitude of the costs required to treat crack babies and AIDS babies, you may wonder how hospitals can continue to deliver this type of care without better reimbursement or different treatment approaches, short of rationing care. The fact is some can't."(12, p. 7)

Research suggests that the cost of treating one infant born to a crack-addicted mother may be as high as $250,000.00. This drain on health resources which, of course, includes tremendous upsurges in emergency-room costs inevitably means 1) health costs across the board must soar to allow hospitals to overcome these costs, 2) health care in myriads of other critical areas must be short-changed or 3) many hospitals must fail.

There is a dearth of good news for anyone. Rural areas and small cities have long counted themselves lucky to have low crime rates, clean air and a low incidence of drug-related problems. If drug use and addictions are used as criteria, there are few if any rural areas left in America. Rural hospitals for these same reasons as well as for other fiscal pressures are closing at an alarming rate.

The Placenta as a Barrier

The infant characterized as having "fetal alcohol syndrome" has been with us forever (or at least for the millennia that alcohol has been available and used). However, only in the last twenty years has attention been given to babies who are identified with this "syndrome." Before the "syndrome" was conceptualized and identified, those babies were dealt with as simply premature, small in size and having symptoms not directly related to the alcohol use by the mother.

Indeed, medical technology has been late in researching and admitting that drugs and viruses can abrogate the placental barrier. For thousands of years, it was generally held that the placenta was a very effective barrier to penetration of most of the bacterial entities the mother may have had.

Indeed, the placenta is an effective screen for many bacteria which being larger do not invade as readily as do viruses. Until the last twenty-five years or so, it was generally held that the barrier was an effective shield against nicotine, alcohol intrusion and, of course, most of the drug entities which can now be found in infants with relatively simple urine drug screening processes. These elements are neither viruses nor bacteria. The placenta is not as effective a filter as many persons think it is.

For various reasons medical science was a very long time in finding that the placental barrier is not as effective as was once believed and hoped. It is virtually certain that well-meaning mothers were shielded from these truths because their physicians, knowing that the barrier was pregnable thought it best for the mother's "psychological" health to permit her to continue to smoke, to drink or to use drugs during the gestation period. One mother of a drug baby reported that her physician told her, "Trying to give up your habit of smoking or alcohol will make you tense, and thus harm the fetus more than the substance will."

But now, it is known with certainty that even though the blood supply of the fetus and the mother are not commingled, many drugs (including nicotine and alcohol) do get through to the fetus. The substances may not enter the fetus in the same chemical form they had upon ingestion into the mother's system, yet the drugs as experienced by the fetus often exert a hurtful effect.

Drug babies and HIV positive babies have a lot of symptoms in common, especially if the HIV baby is also a polydrug baby. Some obstetricians and gynecologists can tell on sight, or think they can tell, which drug or drugs a newborn baby has in his veins. But this is hands-on inexactitude at best; drug screening tests, being what they are today, reveal ultimate realities even though these tests are costly.

Kaye, et al (10) reporting on birth outcomes of drug abusing mothers, offer the following: Infants of all drug abuses weighed an average of 423 grams less than control babies, and the gestational age of these babies averaged four to ten days less than the controls. The report concludes that babies of polydrug users (principally cocaine plus opiates) fared worse than infants whose mothers used a single drug in terms of birth weight, gestational age and length of hospital stay. An important finding of this study was that infants of crack users fared worse than did infants whose mothers abused cocaine in other forms. These crack babies were lighter in weight and had more adverse neurological signs than other babies exposed to alternate forms of cocaine intake.

Cherukuri et al (6) compared 55 crack-using mothers (during pregnancy), with a cohort of 55 non-drug-using women who delivered babies during a common time period. The groups were matched for age, parity, socioeconomic status, alcohol use and presence or absence of prenatal care. "A significantly larger number of women using crack delivered early (50.9 percent versus 16.4 percent). Crack exposed infants were 3.6 times as likely to have intrauterine growth retardation and 2.8 times more likely to have a head circumference less than the tenth percentile for gestational age. Premature rupture of the membranes was 1.8 times more common in the crack group."

Research on the effects of methamphetamines on prenatal growth has been scant using human subjects. Martin (11) did a study using 25 female Sprague-Dawley rats divided into two groups and a control group. Twice daily, beginning on the first day of pregnancy, he subcutaneously administered 3.0 mg/hg of methamphetamine HCL to one group, 5.0 mg/kg to another and a saline solution to a control group.

The rats given either dosage of methamphetamine delivered earlier. Weight gain during gestation decreased as a function of dose level and litter size also decreased. Four out of seven of the female rats receiving the higher dosage failed to deliver viable offspring.

This study has significance when examined in connection with the "ice baby" phenomenon in Hawaii. Daniel Bent, U.S. Attorney for the District of Hawaii, told the House Select Committee on Narcotics Abuse and Control, "A nurse who specializes in neonatal care has advised that ice babies appear to be even more profoundly affected and difficult to get to respond to care and nurturing than cocaine babies."(1, p. 65)

Chasnoff et al (3) report that cocaine-using mothers have a significantly higher rate of premature abortions than the control and comparison group. In this study, the Brazelton Neonatal Behavioral Assessment Scale revealed "that infants exposed to cocaine had significant depression of interactive behavior and from organizational response to environmental stimuli." There was no sub-group of crack abusers per se in this study. Many similar studies using cocaine HCL demonstrate almost identical results.(4,5)

Crack and Abruption

In the study by Chasnoff et al cited above (3), 4 out of 23 cocaine-using women studied in the Institute's perinatal-addiction program, experienced abruptio placentae. These abruptions occurred at various points late into the pregnancies and in each case, occurred immediately after intravenous self-injection of cocaine.

Abruption is a condition usually experienced during the third trimester in which the placenta separates from the fetus before delivery. This condition causes acute bleeding without any blood emission through the birth canal. There is usually intense pain higher up in the thoracic cavity than is the case with labor pains. The blood quickly distends the uterus and the abdominal rigidity along with the pain clearly indicates to nurse, gynecologist or obstetrician what is taking place. Ultrasound monitoring is sometimes done for confirmation. The condition is life threatening for both baby and mother, and a Caesarian section must be performed quickly to save both lives. There have been no studies of which this author is aware that might differentiate the incidence of abruption as a function of freebase smoking versus other forms of cocaine usage.

The Impact of Cocaine on Brain Development

It was reported earlier that cocaine affects the limbic system as well as other centers of the brain, releasing dopamine to these brain centers in early use and causing dopamine deficiency eventually. Actually, L'dopa and other dopamine derivatives are used widely to treat drug addicts with dopamine deficiency in much the same way as L'dopa is used in the treatment of Parkinson's Disease.

However, there are other brain-damage effects deriving from cocaine use quite distinct from dopamine deficiency and problems deriving from faculty neurotransmitter output. Howard (9), working at the University of California School of Medicine Rehabilitation Center in Los Angeles reports in

Developmental Medicine and Child Neurology, "The in utero turmoil of cocaine-using, pregnant women puts the development of their newborns at risk." Howard goes on to say that impairment is likely to be specific to the parts of the brain system which determine mood states and the experience of pleasure.

The Amazing Absence of Guilt

When parents of adolescent who are under treatment meet in "toughlove" support groups, the emotion most shared among members of the groups is guilt. At this stage, parents are likely to feel that they are to blame for what has happened to their children. Often the support group members try to reassure each other that they are not the responsible ones. "It it a function of a culture gone mad," they assure each other. Still, the guilt most often persists.

A most amazing phenomenon prevalent among many mothers of newborn drug babies is the absence of guilt at the stage when the infants are suffering severely from withdrawal symptoms. Most mothers go through the gestation period knowing full well the risk they take in having babies with built-in addictions. They are using drugs sufficient to harm the baby but deny to themselves that they are doing so. This denial cannot be allowed to fail, because, if it did, these mothers would represent a high-risk group for depression and even suicide.

Discussions with scores of gynecologist-obstetricians, with delivery room nurses and with nurses charged with caring for seriously disadvantaged neonates reveal that few mothers overtly express guilt even when they know their baby's condition is a result of their own drug use. "They will simply ask you for prescriptions drugs as a substitute for the illegal drug they have been using," one OBGYN told this author. "Most often you can't give them prescription drugs sufficient to the task, so they just get right back on the illegal drug, get pregnant again and repeat the cycle." Obviously, there are many exceptions.

A Blow to Adoption

For many years adoptive parents have anxiously waited for babies to be put up for adoption. Black markets in adoptable babies have flourished. Waiting lists are long at present for available babies, and pregnant mothers are being urged, especially by right-to-life groups, to consider adoption over abortion. Many are doing so.

Obviously, the information about possible, even probable, deficiencies in adoptive babies has become widespread. Many adoptive parents have been wise enough to inquire into the genetic backgrounds of babies they are considering. Physical virility of the babies has always been a factor, too. But now, wise adoptive parents would do well to inquire into the drug habits of the mother. Unfortunately, these facts are most often obscured and do not usually become a part of a social worker's information file.

Perhaps, it is good that information about drug use by mothers is withheld. The facts are, of course, that with the upsurge in drug and AIDS babies, the odds are getting worse that a couple may hope to obtain an unblemished child for adoption. With eleven percent of babies born having come from drug-using or drug-abusing mothers and with the knowledge about the short and long term effects of neurologic and other damage accruing to these babies, we may expect a revolution in the "good idea" principle now so prevalent as it relates to adoptions.

Crack and A.D.D. (Attention Deficit Disorder)

Crack babies (and other drug babies as well) have an inability to lock into the world around them — they seem oblivious to the environment. True, they may seem to overcome this as parents demand their attention in early months and years.

However, when the child enters kindergarten or pre-school, the teacher often reports a lack of capacity for maintaining attention to learning tasks. Crack babies are at high risk for A.D.D.!

At the stage of having their attention called to this deficit, some mothers belatedly enter into a guilt phase. The denial which served them so well earlier has often lost its power, and there is a period of suffering extant in many if not most mothers as they see that their child cannot "keep up" with the others.

Tears will be shed then, and psychologists are often tempted to say, "At last they feel what they should have felt years ago." And psychologists, being human, may allow a fleeting thought, "It serves them right!"

But second thoughts always follow. Denial is a protector, a defense mechanism. It serves a good purpose much of the time. When, at last, the mother feels guilty, she becomes angry at herself and is torn with frustrations, anxieties and depressions; the caretakers of the fragile human spirit must think, "There except for the grace of God go I." Because psychologists know drugs are no respecters of persons — not even of psychologists.

Crack Cocaine and AIDS

At present, the most identifiable causes of the mushrooming spread of the HIV virus are the reuse of infected IV needles and homosexual-bisexual contact with persons already infected.

The most obvious factor in the spread of the HIV virus as it relates to drug use of any kind is that in the frenzy and panic which results from the anguish demanding the drug hit, all caution is thrown to the wind and that users in need of a hit will use any instrument available to get the drug into their veins. Smoking cocaine is infinitely safer than are dirty needles relative to HIV spread. This has not been viewed with elation!

Don C. Des Jarlais of the New York State Division of Substance Abuse Services offered the following in a letter published in JAMA (Journal of the American Medical Association): "One form of AIDS risk reduction the IV cocaine users might adopt would be to switch from injecting cocaine hydrochloride to smoking 'crack' or freebase (cocaine with the hydrochloride removed). Smoking crack gives a high that is comparable in intensity to the one obtained from injecting cocaine without a risk of transmitting AIDS."(8, pp. 1945,1946)

Under criticism for these remarks, Don Des Jarlais responded in another letter to JAMA, "At no point were we 'approving' the smoking of crack as a form of AIDS risk reduction."(7, p. 1556) It is clear that Don Des Jarlais was not alone in noting the possible trend toward crack as an AIDS reduction measure, and all who may have made statements of such trends do strongly oppose this substitution principle.

As a matter of fact, smoking crack by persons already using IV injections has not been shown to reduce IV injection or other forms of cocaine use. Rather, the pattern that is emerging is that people trying to move away from using cocaine hydrochloride by any route simply become addicted to the quick exhilarating rush of crack and then use the earlier mode(s) to sustain the high caused by crack and/or to avoid the painful crash which follows crack use.

This author was in San Francisco during the Sixth International Conference on AIDS beginning June 19, 1990. At this conference, it was reported by Don C. Des Jarlais of the Mount Sinai School of Medicine in New York City that the use of crack cocaine is a risk factor in the transmission of HIV. It was also reported that AIDS cases in women have grown from six percent in 1982 to ten percent in 1989.

The crack epidemic is obviously a potent source of upsurge in the spread of HIV. The elevation of libidinal urge is at the center of crack's influence because as a consequence of elevated sex drive, there will inevitably be a multiplicity of sexual partners. Safe sex, as it has become known, usually implies a reduction in the number of sexual partners and a more careful screening of sexual partners. In addition, protective devices (especially condoms) have become a part of safe sex.

Consider the effects of a heightened libidinal drive on safe sex! The elevated hunger for sex sets aside what otherwise would be protective elements which derive from fear, guilt, preferences and scruples. A person under an intense sexual urge will throw caution and scruples to the wind. Under the urgency of sexual drive the selectivity of safe partners as well as the good judgment to use condoms is diminished if not obliterated. Further, out of group smoking come group orgies.

The HIV Virus is Already Within the Heterosexual Bloodstream

In our present state of HIV spread, it is clearly conceded that not only do males have more HIV than females, but that the source of most of the spread is from infected males. Sexual congress between an infected male and an uninfected female has large potency in spreading the virus from male to female, especially with what some would call perverted sex such as anal sex. As late as the mid-80's, however, we were told that uninfected males could have sex with infected female partners with a considerable measure of impunity.

However, this reality (if it ever was a reality) has been severely challenged, and there is reason to believe the invasion of HIV into the heterosexual bloodstream is, at present, far advanced, especially in certain areas of the country. Many believe that the virus will eventually become thoroughly intruded into the heterosexual bloodstream. In the interests of safety, some researchers are insisting that the virus should be considered to be fully within the heterosexual bloodstream whether or not it actually is.

Whatever may be said at this time in our fight against HIV, it is a reality that female prostitutes are spreading the virus to male customers. The exact mechanics of this spread are relatively unimportant. On the other hand, too much emphasis may be placed on the spreading of HIV through hyper-sexual activity of crack-using prostitutes per se. Generally, prostitutes perform sexual activity as a way of making a living. For them it is the proverbial world's oldest profession. Still, even for female prostitutes, who typically do not feel horny while they are doing tricks, crack smoking has a double impact on HIV spread. The prostitutes do more tricks because they may be sexually aroused by crack, and they do more tricks in order to obtain enough money to support their crack addictions.

Female crack addicts, as opposed to prostitutes, may do tricks in order to satisfy desire on the one hand and to get money to support their habits on the other hand when there is no professional self-identity of "prostitute." As evidence that we are losing the battle with HIV and that the heterosexual bloodstream has been seriously compromised, Bowser reports in the Journal of the National Medical Association on his careful

75

ethnographic surveys in the Bayview Hunter's Point section of San Francisco. "Female crack addicts who support their habits with sexual activity may transmit HIV far more effectively than women addicted to heroin or other forms of cocaine. If crack increases sexual desire and impairs judgment, teenaged addicts may spread HIV to other populations."(2)

Crack, HIV and Group Sex

When infected females have sex with a number of male partners, what once was a homosexual bloodstream contamination gets more and more into the heterosexual bloodstream. Obviously, when groups of male-females use drugs, there is most often a broad spectrum of drugs present, some orally ingested, some snorted, some self-administered by needles and some smoked.

When crack is a part of the group drug scene, there is likely to be elevated libidinal drive in individuals, followed by visible sexual acts promiscuously performed between and among the sexes. Such scenes are typically erotic and especially so if downers have removed inhibitions and if uppers have brought about general arousal. If, in a group of eight, there is one infected person, the probability of spreading HIV is greatly multiplied. Luckily, with logical caution having been created from very credible knowledge about the horrors of AIDS, there has been a general downplay of group sex.

At the present time, most researchers agree that there is more HIV infection in the homosexual than heterosexual bloodstream. Some feel secure that HIV will be slow getting into the heterosexual bloodstream. Evidence from primitive societies where HIV has been in evidence for much longer periods than in the Americas demonstrates that once HIV gets well established in the heterosexual bloodstream, disaster follows. HIV is fast gaining a foothold in the heterosexual bloodstream in America, and the mounting numbers of HIV babies is stark evidence of this. Under the pressures created by the drug crack, usually used with other drugs, there is more and more evidence that caution in partner selection and in avoiding contaminated needles has been thrown to the wind. Group orgies in particular bring on the "garbagehead" phenomenon. Anything and everything goes! And that includes caution!

Crack and Male Prostitution

Crack use has been just as elevated among male prostitutes as among female prostitutes, perhaps even more so. These sex-sellers often have been recruited by madams and pimps through drug enticement. Many prostitutes have found prostitution to be the only way to survive after having endured shattered homes and exposure to street demands in uncountable ways. It is only reasonable that the incidence of HIV among male prostitutes has risen dramatically.

Male prostitutes are a particular and specific menace in the spread of HIV. Many if not most male prostitutes are bisexual. A much larger proportion of male prostitutes are carriers of HIV. Thus, male prostitution in either homosexual or heterosexual contact is a particular menace so far as HIV spread is concerned.

Many if not most females who engage male prostitutes are aware of the extra dangers they take. Because of this knowledge, safe sex with a male prostitute demands condom use and mitigates against anal sex. However, under the heightened arousal of crack and other drugs, the elements of safe sex are often forgotten, and HIV becomes more and more widespread.

Bibliography

1   Bent, Daniel. "Statement Before the House Select Committee on Narcotics Abuse and Control." Department of Justice Bulletin. October 24, 1989, pp. 1-11.

2   Bowser, Benjamin P. "Crack and AIDS: An Ethnographic Impression." Journal of the National Medical Association. Vol. 81(5). May 1989, pp. 538-540.

3   Chasnoff, Ira J. et al. "Cocaine Use In Pregnancy: Perinatal Morbidity and Mortality." Neurotoxicology and Teratology. Vol. 9(4). July-August 1987, pp. 291-3.

4   Chasnoff, Ira J. et al. "Effects of Cocaine on Pregnancy Outcome." National Institute on Drug Abuse Research Monograph Series. Monograph 67. 1986, pp. 335-341.

5   Chasnoff, Ira J. et al. "Cocaine Use in Pregnancy." New England Journal of Medicine. Vol. 313(11). September 1985, pp. 666-669.

6   Cherukuri, R. et al. "A Cohort Study of Alkaloidal Cocaine (Crack) in Pregnancy." Obstetrics Gynecology. Vol. 72(2). August 1988, pp. 147-151.

7   Des Jarlais, Don C. "In Reply to Grove." Journal of the American Medical Association. Vol. 260 No. 11. September 16, 1988, p. 1556.

8   Des Jarlais, Don C. and Friedman S.K. "Intravenous Cocaine, Crack and HIV Infection." Journal of the American Medical Association. Vol. 259 No. 13. April 1, 1988, pp. 1945, 1946.

9   Howard, Judy. "Cocaine and Its Effects on the Newborn." Developmental Medicine and Child Neurology. Vol. 31(2). April 1989, pp. 255-257.

10   Kaye, K. et al. "Birth Outcomes for Infants of Drug Abusing Mothers." New York State Journal of Medicine. Vol. 89(5). May 1989, pp. 256-61.

11   Martin Joan C. "Effects on Offspring of Chronic Maternal Methamphetamine Exposure." Developmental Psychobiology. Vol. 8(5). September 1975, pp. 397-404.

12   "Medical Essay: Mayo Clinic Health Letter." Mayo Foundation for Medical Education and Research. Rochester, MN. November 1989.

PART II —
ENFORCEMENTS

Chapter 3

The Control of Methamphetamine and Ice

Happening Three — The Sting of the DEA

The Facts As We Best Know Them

Happening Three — The Sting of the DEA

"We're going in tomorrow evening at nine," Chet told me in the DEA office in the Federal Building. Chet is my buddy but also is the SAC (Special Agent in Charge). Chet is naturally my superior since I am the ASAC (Assistant Special Agent in Charge), but Chet and I don't relate on rank. We are friends, buddies really. Chet says I saved his life once in a raid on a crack house, but don't believe that stuff. The bullet was meant for me; Chet just happened to step behind me. My name is Billy Townsend.

Chet was taking over on this one because it was big. "We're going in after documents," Chet explained for the umpteenth time. Something big is brewing. We don't know who the kingpins are in this, and we've got to find out. We think organized crime is all set to take on the Koreans and the ice trade in the States. So far, the Korean mafia have had all the gravy. They've been able to keep the price up so high because crack is booming in the States because of its cheap price and easy availability. These Asians have been acting like the ice business is exclusively theirs. Why, they've even been operating a clandestine lab in Oregon and sending the whole stash to Hawaii through Seattle. They can get $50,000 a pound in Hawaii whereas crack goes for about one-tenth that in California."

"Isn't that good?" I asked. "If that will keep the ice age in Hawaii and Asia, why wouldn't we be pleased as punch to just go on cracking the houses, or better yet, maybe we ought to leave the crack dealers alone, even legalize the stuff."

"Bullshit!" Chet exploded. "I know you know better than that, Billy. Legalizing any of this stuff would be stupid. We'd be swimming in it, and it would get a thousand times worse than it is now." I knew that, and Chet knew I knew it. I'd only been kidding him. But Chet was really steamed, and he was chewing my ass just like nobody had saved his life, much less me.

"We're in a pretty hopeless situation," Chet continued. "With all the interdictions of the Columbian coke, the stuff still hasn't slowed up, and the price hasn't gone up either as the experts thought it would. What a hell of a double bind we're in! We've got to hope crack will stay cheap, and when we hope that, we're encouraging kids to use crack. Talk about the devil and the deep blue sea. We're shafted."

"Still," he explained as if I didn't already know, "the cost of making ice isn't all that much; only the ephedrine is expensive. Actually, there is a killing waiting for organized crime in ice even if they put it on the market at the same price as crack. We could wind up with a drug war like we have gasoline wars with dealers cutting prices to keep their customers even if they go broke. Once that happens, we are going to have real holy hell."

"We ain't seen nothing yet," I said as if I were looking forward to it.

"Damn it, Billy, don't make jokes about it. The world is about to explode, and here you are with the funny crap."

Like I said, Chet was really steamed, but he came off it when Joe Lindsey and Alfred Stoddard came in. We had an SAC, an ASAC and two entry squad leaders in the room now. These guys were muscle men, the storm-troop leaders. They'd take charge of the platoons made up of California Highway Patrol narcotics officers and sheriff/police personnel when we made the raid. One would have a bunch coming in the back while the other would come in the front.

"These hills around San Bernadino are full of meth factories," Chet told the three of us. "We've shut down a lot of them, but this one is big. I got word from Dave Stebbins, the undercover agent yesterday." I was getting a little pissed off at Chet because this was really my territory, and I was the one Dave had called. But I canned that feeling quick-like. I knew Chet was doing his job, and I'd been the one that called him in on it. It was too big for us to handle. I knew it was a big deal when Dave said over the phone, "The ephedrine is here." Just like that, two seconds and pop, he hung up. I don't know where he was calling from but he had to get the word to us, risky as it was. I sure hope he had a clear phone line into us but doubt it since he was so abrupt. "The ephedrine is in." Well, that was all he really needed to say.

The tip-off on the location, an old, abandoned ranch house with big barns way back in the hills, had come when Frank Meadows, owner of the Circle T Ranch about two miles downwind from this abandoned place, had called in to report the smell. Those Chinook winds blow down the mountains regularly this time of year, and the guys at the so-called abandoned spread further up must have known that sooner or later, the smell of the chemicals they were using to make meth was going to be noticed. Hell, they all know we're coming after them sooner or later. They know it, but they just keep cooking. The profits are so big that these yahoos don't seem to mind a little jail time now and then. Occupational hazard! These guys are expendable so far as the kingpins are concerned. And it was the kingpins we wanted. San Bernadino County has been the methamphetamine capital of the world for years, unless you count San Diego. We are constantly busting up their equipment and jailing the personnel. But the jails don't hold them, and the stuff we mess up is a drop in the bucket. It goes on and on while we try over and over to get a line on the big guys, the money changers. Maybe they are connected with the bikers; or maybe they are bankers, lawyers or businessmen in L.A. Who knows? That's what we've got to find out. Chet was lecturing again.

"Look guys, we need every shred of paper we can find— bills of lading, invoices, letters, phone bills — anything we can trace. The Assistant U.S. Attorney and a squad of detectives and attorneys will be less than a mile away when we go in. They sure as hell don't take any chances. The bastards wear coats and ties, no less. They'll be there as soon as the rough stuff is finished, if there is any. They'll take over.

"We'll take all the powder they've got as usual but it's the ephedrine we're most interested in. Not that we want the damned stuff. We've got to find out where it came from. We've got special guys to take all the plastic bags or anything else the ephedrine might have come in to the lab; and if there's a mark on anything that'll show where it came from, they'll find and trace it. We've got to hope they haven't mixed the ephedrine with the red phosphorus and the hydriodic acid yet. I guess it would be good for morale if we busted an ice lab all right, but we'd rather have the chemicals unmixed than a bunch of big crystals. Remember, documents are top priority, not chemicals.

"They've got an old landing strip up there, and Frank's boys have heard a plane late at night several times. There is some road traffic past Frank's place at night, too. But the clincher was the butane truck. It was seen going up there in the daytime. They've filled the butane tank twice in the last six weeks or so. The sheriff contacted the gas company. The Sheriff's Office checked with the electric company, too, and the electricity is on up there. That old ranch is not the abandoned place it used to be.

"Now we'll have everybody at the Circle T horse show barn just after dark. Frank says we can seal the place up and have a great staging area from his place, and we are welcome to anything he has. But it'll be squad cars, unmarked cars and riot equipment all the way; we won't need Frank's horses or hay balers. We'll go in like cavalry all right but not on horses."

"What you want us to do in the meantime?" Joe asked.

"Well, let's see. I have the warrant all properly executed. You'd better check with Peters at the California Highway Patrol to be sure the copter is cruising the area. They'll go out in daylight to get a read on the exact location. Say, Billy, why don't you get Peters to take you up, and you guys locate the area together. That's the only way to be sure that Peters locates a good landing area as near the barns as possible. He'd better use his binoculars to be sure there are no fences or power lines or anything. He really needs to make a trial landing, but that's out. You know the place pretty well, Billy; so, you can help him pick out the landing area. You and Peters can work out the signal on the red beam for him to come in. Hope we won't need him. He needs to stay at about 10,000 so they won't hear him and needs to be up there by 8:45."

"You want me to check on the sheriff's office and the other back-ups such as the Highway Patrol narcotic agents and squad cars?" I asked meekly.

85

"No," Chet said, "I've already taken care of all that. No use taking any chances on leaks by having too many cooks in the kitchen." Chet paused to pull on his earlobe, a sure sign he was thinking.

Chet was acting like Eisenhower getting ready for Normandy. It was beginning to piss me off just a little. Sure he was the general, but why not give the troops a little room for judgments. I knew Peters would cuss if I made all those smart-ass suggestions to him. He'd done this kind of thing before. He was a pro, and Chet was the amateur. Oh, well.

"Too many cooks spoil the broth," Chet ruminated. So that was what all that deep thinking produced. He had been thinking deeply trying to come up with that bullshit line.

"Hey, wait a minute!" I sputtered. This was getting to be too much. He was telling me to keep my snotty nose out of it, and I was about to blow. The damn phone rang just before I made an ass out of myself. It was Frank Meadows at the Circle T.

"Yeah, Frank, I'll get the word to all of them to kill their lights when they turn into your place. You're right. No need to advertise. And you'll have blankets over the windows in the horse barn. Good boy!" Chet turned to us giving me the jaundiced eye. "Now, there's real cooperation for you."

****

The moonlit night was perfect. We could have killed our lights when we turned off the highway two miles from Frank's place, and there would have been plenty of light to see by. There must have been a dozen unmarked cars in the parking lot when we got there. We had two squad cars. It was 8:30 when all of us got settled on Frank's seats in the little grandstand. We bunched up close together and talked in whispers. It was crazy; we were two miles away from the old ranch house.

Then Chet took over. Even he talked kind of soft, like maybe he was afraid the horses might be spies. "Okay guys, this is it." Chet was really enjoying himself, a real ham. "We don't expect any trouble."

"Like hell," I thought. Maybe I was a little jealous and a little stupid, too. Everyone of us in law enforcement know we are living with danger. That's what keeps us going, really. But we have to have some built in thing that makes it bearable. I know Chet's "big commander" act is what keeps him going. Maybe mine is being snotty. I guess maybe the reason I resent Chet when he gets bossy is because his gimmick is maybe working better than mine.

"Everybody got your markers on?" Chet asked. The markers tonight were red bandanas. We looked like cowboys about to go on a round-up. Not too far off at that.

"Now, I don't want to seem stupid," Chet was saying. (I was thinking that he'd been doing a poor job on that so far. There I go again!) "Maybe we'll get no resistance, but believe me, I want you to keep those hand guns and those 9 mm Colt machine guns ready. Safeties on, but ready. Don't be trigger happy, but take out anybody that shows a weapon. The sheriff's squad will have tear gas if we need it, and we'll have three Uzis with us. The Sheriff's Department also has three shotguns loaded with rifle slugs. One other thing.

"Dave Townsend is in there, and if they get wise to him at the last minute, it could be bad for him. He's a local boy who has connections in these hills who take messages in and out. We've gotten word from him on two things: First, he will try his best to have the front door unlocked. Maybe he can, maybe he can't. Second, he will be wearing his shirt tail out. Watch for him. He's about thirty, blond hair, one-eighty and clean shaven. He's Caucasian and wears jeans, and I do mean blue. He'll lay back and lay low. Take him in like you do the others. We may be able to use him again.

"Now remember, meth labs have explosive capabilities. The ones who are going inside will wear full gear including Scott Packs and level-three bullet proof vests.

"Joe Lindsey will take the two squad cars up a little lane that goes to the old hay field, and seven men will come out of the woods behind the barn and cover the back. Frank is sure the cooking has been in the main house since the bottled gas only serves the house; he doubts there is anything in the barns but musty hay, but Joe and his men will keep their eyes on the barns anyway.

"This is Alfred Stoddard right here." By this time Joe and Alfred were standing. "Alfred has his group ready to go at the front. I'll be with them because I'll need to show the warrant. Since we have a warrant, we'll march right in as if we owned the place. I'll holler, 'This is the law.' If Dave doesn't leave the door open, don't knock; just kick it in. That violates the warrant, but we'll take our chances.

"Billy will be in charge of bringing the copter in if needed, and he'll meet the Assistant U.S. Attorney, detectives and legal eagles when they pull up fifteen minutes after we've hit the front door. Now, this is important! Nobody gets away! If they run, then tackle them. No shooting unless they show a weapon."

A few questions and answers, and we were on our way. We knew that Peters was overhead with the Highway Patrol copter and that the Assistant U.S. Attorney and his men were somewhere close.

****

We went in with lights only on the two squad cars. It is very unlikely they didn't see or hear us coming. We knew it wouldn't be a surprise because we didn't want it to be. They showed lights in nearly every room.

We all got out of the squad cars and the unmarked cars, which had circled the front yard like in cowboys and Indians. We got down while awaiting Chet's signal.

I was mad as hell that I wasn't going in. Chet wasn't doing me any favor making an errand boy out of me. But I guess he thought he was. He'll never really forget that bullet he thinks I took for him. Bullshit! I was just doing my job, and the copter had me in the hospital in twenty minutes. No big deal.

Suddenly, it happened. A small barn, more like a garage, I guess, was over to the left only a few yards from the front porch. The big door on the barn suddenly burst open, and there was a mighty roar. I think that was the biggest tractor I've ever seen. Chet and the five men with him were half way to the front door. The tractor had lights as bright as what you see on a locomotive. It was coming straight at Chet and the guys. You'd think the guys could get out of the way, but it happened so fast that the guys were falling over one another.

The guy next to me was a sheriff's deputy, I knew, and he had a shotgun. But he was petrified. I wasn't. I grabbed the shotgun and let off a blast right into the grillwork of the tractor. One light went out. Then several other shotguns and Uzis joined in, and the sound of the bullets shredding that tractor, and the noise of the shotguns, Uzis and the 9 mm machine guns all together was like the end of the world had come. The "Big Bang" theory in reverse.

But the damn tractor had up a lot of speed. Evidently, the engine was still revving full throttle. The tires were going flat, and the steering gear of the thing had been smashed. I guess the gas tanks didn't go because they were at the rear. Joe and his guys didn't open fire because it would have been a cross-fire on all of us. Just as well, the tanks didn't go anyway. They might have set off the ranch house like a bomb. Chet and his guys were scattering like chickens, but one of the big tires swung sharp right when the right tire was blown to bits by a powerful, hollow-tip slug. The big left wheel caught Alfred Stoddard. Alfred screamed as the big wheel went across his pelvis. The guy in the cab was slumped over; no way could he be alive.

I went into action calling Peters down with the red beam on the designated squad car. Chet went right on with the other men to the front door and violated his own orders. The big guy kicked the door down when it probably wasn't even locked. Can't say as I blame him.

****

I met the Assistant U.S. Attorney and his men at the turn-off into the place. They had come up just at the right time.

They all wanted to know about the shooting. They had seen the copter come down and take off. I didn't really have any information for them except for the tractor caper and Stoddard getting hurt.

It was a good hour before I got Chet aside to find out what had gone on while I was out chasing helicopters and U.S. Attorneys. "Well, it was a good bust," he said. "There was no resistance inside. There was a lot of crystal meth and a lot of equipment, but the main thing was the ephedrine. It was there and it was intact.

"We don't know about Alfred yet. The kid on the tractor was out in the barn when the action came down," Chet went on. "He panicked and turned that thing loose on us. All the guys inside were told to offer no resistance, and they didn't. Well, Dave Townsend did take a swing at the guy who handcuffed him and they swatted him one across the jowls." Chet and I halfway hugged each other. We didn't quite know what the manly thing was to do, so it was kind of awkward. We'd been successful. Sure. But we were both thinking about Alfred Stoddard.

****

Alfred Stoddard and the young man who drove the tractor were both dead on arrival at the hospital. You just have to shrug it off. It's easy enough when it is somebody in the next county it happened to. But we all know a lot of us are going to die before this war is over. The ephedrine led to a bunch of big businessmen in Los Angeles. They had made arrangements with some guys in Hawaii to transport the ice out there. They had an Asian chemist out at the old ranch who was going to help them with the chemicals. I hope they have enough room in jail for them.

The Facts As We Best Know Them

For those of us who lived through the 60's and 70's, seeing the devastation wrought by speed, crank, crystal meth or christy, and those of us who thrilled at the seemingly remarkable success of the "speed kills" media ads in the 70's; it has been a relief to believe that methamphetamine was a receding drug form. Many have believed methamphetamine use was receding because cocaine, especially crack cocaine, was flourishing.

Methamphetamine Rises Again

With cocaine being so cheap in both powdered and rock forms, it seemed only logical that "poor man's cocaine" would be abandoned in favor of the "real thing." That seems not to have happened. Thus, our relief that methamphetamine use was abating has been short-lived.

The NIDA Surveillance System

The National Institute on Drug Abuse (4) maintains several information networks designed to monitor drug use and abuse patterns. One of these is the Drug Abuse Warning Network (DAWN), and another is the Community Epidemiology Work Group (CEWG). The CEWG is a panel of researchers from twenty metropolitan areas who prepare semi-annual reports on drug abuse epidemiology in their local areas.

In September, 1988, NIDA released a pamphlet entitled "Methamphetamine Abuse in the United States."(4) Data from two reports given in this bulletin, the DAWN alert report mentioned above, CEWG reports from December, 1985 through December, 1987 and supplementary material provided by CEWG members during the summer of 1988, are included in the pamphlet.

The DAWN Report

NIDA's Drug Abuse Warning Network (DAWN) keeps surveillance on metropolitan areas which are reported to have high levels of methamphetamine and cocaine. DAWN monitors Emergency Room "mentions" and Medical Examiner "mentions" *vis à vis* Emergency Room incidents involving specific drugs

91

and reports on deaths deriving from abuse of a wide spectrum of drugs. NIDA's monitoring and reporting are not intended to be scientific in the strictest sense but are reasonably accurate indicators of trends in drug use and abuse.

The cities selected in the NIDA Drug Abuse Warning Network report on methamphetamine use for input in the report of 1988 were: Philadelphia, San Diego, Dallas, Phoenix, San Francisco and Los Angeles. These cities were selected because they were the six cities reporting the highest levels of methamphetamine abuse. The following statistics are drawn from "DAWN Drug Alert, 12 Quarter Summary: adjusted data January 1985 to December 1987, run date: May 17, 1988."

Methamphetamine ER "mentions" from all DAWN cities rose from 726 in 1985 to 1523 in 1987, representing an increase of 110 percent. The largest increase occurred between 1986 and 1987 when 533 additional ER "mentions" were reported; Phoenix experienced an 825 percent increase during the three-year period reviewed; San Diego ER "mentions" increased 501 percent and Dallas reported a 271 percent increase. By contrast, Philadelphia was the only city to reflect a decrease in ER "mentions" during this three-year period.

The above illustrations are selected from among the most dramatic upstagings. Some cities, including Philadelphia, reported little change, and Miami reported very low levels of activity presumably because cocaine traffickers have committed themselves to keeping methamphetamine competition under control to the benefit of cocaine use and trafficking.

It is clear that drug abuse is regionalized. These data concerning amphetamine use in the cities cited above need to be examined carefully. What are the implications for the future?

The CEWG Report

The CEWG report uses data from among the twenty researchers making up CEWG and includes state reports as well as major city reports. The research sites chosen for this report on methamphetamine were: Philadelphia, Minneapolis, Dallas, Texas, Oklahoma, Denver, Phoenix, San Diego, Los Angeles, San Francisco and Miami. This selection was a cross-sectional one and did not choose only those research sites reporting highest abuse rates. As a matter of fact, these sites range from the highest (probably San Diego) to the lowest (undoubtedly Miami).

The thrust of this NIDA report was that although methamphetamine abuse had declined sharply during the late 70's and continued to do so in some locales until the first half of 1985, the sharp rise in methamphetamine use following mid-1985 for most areas was phenomenal. The message clearly is that methamphetamine, a drug thought to be waning in popularity and use is on the rise again.

In fact, these data were so sobering as to cause NIDA to make the following statement: "Just as cocaine was introduced and successfully test-marketed in the 1970's before its expansion in the later half of that decade and the 1980's, domestically-produced methamphetamine looms as a potential national drug crisis for the 1990's."(4, p. 1) From the CEWG research reports, the following highlights emerge:

San Diego: In December of 1985, there was a 72 percent increase in methamphetamine treatment admissions for the first half of the year as compared to the same period in 1984... By early 1986, a glut of the drug was reported due to a proliferation of independent laboratory chemists who obtained the formulas for producing methamphetamine while in prison... By the end of 1987 methamphetamine clients accounted for 47 percent of the city's treatment caseload. Treatment admissions had increased 87 percent in a single year and more than 400 percent over 4 years. Emergency room mentions more than doubled for the second year in a row, going from 208 in 1986 to 451 in 1987... In the first quarter of 1989 San Diego ranked first in the nation for arrestees testing positive for the drug.

Los Angeles: Between 1983 and 1985, CEWG reports indicated that treatment admissions, ER mentions and related deaths for methamphetamine all declined. In contrast, law enforcement seizures increased almost 1000 percent between 1984 and 1985. In 1986 E R mentions nearly doubled over 1985, and deaths increased from 3 to 23.

Denver: Emergency room mentions of amphetamines increased from 13 in 1984 to 35 in 1986... Denver police had recovered 29 times as much of the drug as they had the previous year... In 1988, emergency room mentions for methamphetamine have continued to rise.

Dallas and Texas: Treatment admissions records indicate methamphetamine abuse peaked in early 1975... This indicator declined sharply to 6 percent by the end of 1976. At the end of 1978 treatment admissions began a steady rise for 3 years climbing back to the 24 percent level by 1981. Methamphetamine abuse data then slowed for 5 years. Then in 1986, several drug abuse indicators marked a sharp increase of methamphetamine activity. Emergency room episodes more than doubled over the previous year. Treatment admissions rose again and law enforcement seizures began a dramatic increase with 162 methamphetamine labs closed in Texas during 1987. The data from Dallas comprise a most graphic illustration of the decline of meth use in the mid 70's and the sharp rise after the mid 80's.(4)

A Dual Upsurge, Cocaine and Amphetamine

For some of us these data are very puzzling. The credibility of these reports can be questioned only on points of exactitude. The trends are well documented.

Facts About Methamphetamine Upsurge

The word had been that poor man's cocaine was being put aside in favor of the "real thing." If the price of cocaine had risen sharply and if its availability were seriously curtailed, then the resurgence of methamphetamine would be easily understood. The facts are that in spite of interdiction measures carried out in South and Central America, the cocaine pipeline is still operating without noticeable change. The crack epidemic is often labeled as a "summer of 1988" debacle which, without question, has not yet been slowed. In fact, crack cocaine continues to gain in notoriety. How can it be that simultaneously with the crack explosion there could be such a resurgence of methamphetamine use?

Many of us have thought that the amphetamine abusers, who for the most part were IV users, had switched to crack in part because of the HIV dangers. Also, for new users, especially, it is much less foreboding to smoke than to stick a needle in one's arm. Indeed, there is ample evidence that such a change from IV use to smoking of cocaine has taken place. The supposition that methamphetamine users had switched to crack cocaine has been based: 1) on the belief that cocaine is a more appealing drug than amphetamine and 2) on the belief that the fear of HIV was strong enough to bring about a switch from one drug form to another. Apparently, both of these suppositions have been wrong. It seems likely that IV users of methamphetamine did switch to crack in large numbers, but it seems likely, too, that such a switch has not been permanent.

At the same time we must remember that the drug-using population in the mid 70's is not the same population we have in the 90's. Everyone agrees that drug use comes in waves, but usually it is from an old drug to a new drug. The phenomena we are now experiencing is a new following for an old drug and a switch from a new drug form crack back to an old drug form amphetamines.

Conclusions About Upsurge in Cocaine and in Methamphetamine

One undeniable conclusion must be that more people are using drugs than ever before. It is doubtful that the mass of methamphetamine abusers, most of whom used the IV route, have simply added freebase cocaine to their polydrug habit repertoires. That undoubtedly is happening with many, and likely, some who left meth in favor of crack are drifting back to methamphetamine.

Most people believe that a switch from IV use to smoking the same or a different drug is based upon the physical pain of sticking a needle into a vein and the ugliness of needle puncture marks. But this is true only for new users. The facts are that a person who is addicted to cocaine or methamphetamine is addicted to the needle as well as to the drug. The needle has become a secondary reinforcement, and those who have used the needle for years miss the needle just as they miss the drug. The association between the sting of the needle becomes so strong that hardened addicts denied the drug will inject saline solution knowingly because the needle is at least one pay-off.

Thus, if a person is persuaded because of the AIDS threat to take up smoking crack or ice, he soon returns to the IV use partially because the needle is a reinforcer and partly because the IV dosages help him come down easier during the crash. This is especially true of ice use since the crash is so much harder with ice.

Smokable Methamphetamine

Methamphetamine in smokable form similar in appearance to crack cocaine is being seen as a distinct threat. When NIDA (4) suggested that methamphetamine might produce a potential national drug crisis in the 1990's, it is reasonable to suppose that ice, as smokable methamphetamine is called, was involved as part of the prediction.

The Movement from West to East?

Ice is in process of moving into the American drug scene. Ice first became a dangerous drug form in Hawaii about 1986. This rock form of methamphetamine was imported to Hawaii from the Philippines, Korea and other points in Asia and was for a time controlled by Filipino and Korean gangs. Rather than a consistent West-East movement, it is logical that ice concentrations in America may first occur in New York City because of the large Asian population groups there.

As a matter of fact, high-ranking officials of the Police Department in Honolulu revealed to this author that they felt sure that the ice arriving in Hawaii via airline flights from the mainland were not being transhipped from Korea or points in the East. They are convinced that this ice is being made on the mainland and sent via couriers to Hawaii because the price is so much higher in Hawaii than in mainland markets.

When drugs exist, one may be sure that they will be utilized in many ways and wind up in the bloodstream and then the brain. Just as crack has become a popular, cheap and available form of cocaine, it is inevitable that ice will cause methamphetamine to become an even greater problem.

Actually, the first surge of smokable methamphetamine in the 90's is occurring with a drug form widely known as croak. Croak, a mixture of crack and methamphetamine HCL, is cheaper than ice, delivers a longer high and most importantly is new. Drug forms by many names are proliferating from this basic combination of crack and methamphetamine. These mixtures are the beginning of the smokable amphetamine scourge of the 90's.

In the fall of 1989, the House Select Committee on Narcotics Abuse and Control chaired by Congressman Rangel (D., N.Y.) called together a number of experts to discuss problems inherent in smokable amphetamine. They had been apprised of the new resurgence of methamphetamine use in the mainland states and had heard of the "ice storm" being fully developed in Hawaii. A strong contingent of Hawaiians were invited including Daniel Bent, United States Attorney from the District of Hawaii.

"This is our chance to get ahead of the curve and not make the same mistake that we made in dealing with the rise of crack several years ago. I'm very concerned about heading off at the pass any illicit drug phenomenon that threatens to add to the existing drug problem," Congressman Rangel said. The purpose of the meeting, he said, was "to provide the impetus to devise some type of strategy or plan to control the spread of methamphetamine and ice."(5, p. 4)

Ice is described as odorless and has a high that can last through an eight-hour day. Workers who do boring, repetitious types of labor find, in the beginning, that an ice hit can sustain their alertness throughout a long, usually tiring day. However, tolerance to the drug builds quickly, and workers who continue to use it develop physical and mental problem of many kinds.

There has been much bad information growing out of the meeting of the Select Committee on Narcotics Abuse and Control. These testimonies have presented ice as a drug of Asian origin, which ostensibly presents considerable mystery to all except Asian or Hawaiian chemists. Clandestine methamphetamine lab operators have been seen as a possible source of made-in-America ice but have been a long time in solving the intricacies of ice production. This is probably not the real reason why ice has not proliferated in the mainland states.

Ice Is Not A New Drug Form

Testimonies have always been that ice is not a new drug. It has been available in Asia for many years and Asian mafia forces have only recently decided to capture markets in the United States much like the Asians have captured markets for electronics and automobiles. With this, lip service has been given to the idea that American genius in clandestine labs might well outsmart these "masters of the science" and start making ice in mainland America.

The facts are that ice is not a new drug — not in Asia, not in Hawaii and not in mainland America. Smokable amphetamine, more likely called glass rather than ice, has been around for a long time. The forms have been widely varied, and the forms have not become popular to American tastes.

The easiest way to make smokable methamphetamine is to start with meth HCL as a powder. Mix it with water to solution, and then add more powder until the solution is supersaturated. Allow cooling, and you have hardened methamphetamine ice, or glass or whatever you may want to call it. This form of ice has been available for many years. But again, the typical user prefers to shoot liquefied methamphetamine basically because this ice or glass tastes bad and smells bad.

Making Ice

The formula for odorless and tasteless ice follows several possible paths using a variety of precursors or main ingredients. The most popular formula is what has been designated as ephedrine hydrogenation, which requires a mixing of ephedrine, hydriodic acid and red phosphorus. This formulation requires more adventuresome cooks as opposed to chemists. There is danger of inhalation of noxious fumes from this concoction, and contrary to some bad information, cooking is required for expeditious processing. Further, there is more odor deriving from the cooking process than has often been reported. However, the product produced is an odorless, smokable form of d amphetamine.

American lab operators have been slow in converting to this smokable form of methamphetamine for two reasons: 1) The key ingredient, in most cases ephedrine, has been put on the closely-watched "hit" list by the DEA, and manufacturers of ephedrine are closely monitored. and a twenty-one day waiting time is required between ordering and delivering. 2) The ingredients, especially ephedrine, are quite expensive if and when available, thus causing a relatively expensive product. To date, methamphetamine HCL is very cheap, and ice is more expensive than the family of street drugs such as crank or speed. Ice is more expensive than is crack cocaine as well. Cheaper ice with the qualities of odorlessness, tastelessness and powers of producing long and euphoric highs is certain to follow.

Ice Effects

The ephedrine hydrogenation method produces d isomer methamphetamine which is ninety to ninety-eight percent pure. Chemists can achieve this in laboratories by meticulous work, but a clandestine operation in a kitchen can accomplish the task just as well given the ingredients and a cursory knowledge of handling them.

Dr. Jerome Jaffe, Senior Science Advisor to NIDA, citing the long duration of the ice high said, "Ice may pose even more of a social danger than crack."(3) Although ice is more expensive than crack, it is considered "a better buy" in that it delivers a high lasting many times longer than the crack high. Ice may present a special danger for those who desire a long-lasting high such as entrepreneurs, students and blue-collar workers.

The physical degeneration of a person who becomes addicted to ice is swift. Under the goading of the drug, the body literally burns itself out. The drug stimulates the central nervous system, causing users to experience little sense of a need to rest. Weight loss can be rapid, and severe stress is delivered to kidneys, heart and lungs.

When a user comes down from an ice high, he experiences a very depressing crash and may actually go into a coma. Typically, a person who has driven his body for days under a series of ice hits damages his body and stresses his neurological system to the point of entering a psychotic-like state. Psychiatrists describe this state as being very much like paranoid schizophrenia.

The Hawaiian Police Department's Statements

The Hawaiian Police Department declares their ice problem is their number one drug problem, twice as great as their crack problem. The U.S. Department of Justice counters by saying the statement is overblown, that Hawaii does not and has not had a terribly severe crack problem at any time. Careful consideration of the level of credibility of the Hawaiian Police Department is important. One position is that they are closer to their own problem than anyone else and that they must be taken seriously. The opposing view is that there is a tendency Hawaiians may have to follow a "media-blitz" format. This author has made a thorough and recent on-site evaluation of the situation in Hawaii and cannot escape the following conclusions: 1) The Hawaii authorities; be they police-oriented, treatment-oriented, hospital emergency specialists or even Department of Justice personnel; generally consider the media as an ally in their war on drugs. 2) Law enforcement personnel from top to bottom are experiencing what for them are dire circumstances involving ice as the precipitating cause. 3) Medical authorities declare that ice is creating havoc with pregnant women, babies and both short-term and long-term abusers in terms of physical breakdown and psychotic states. Consider the following information about ice taken from the Hawaiian Police Manuals:

Physical Effects

The drug tends to overtax the body and causes the body to literally burn itself up. Vitamin and mineral deficiencies are common due to inadequate nutrition, as the user keeps pushing beyond what the body can tolerate and may lead to a rapid and noticeable loss of weight. There is lowered resistance to disease, and prolonged use will cause damage to organs particularly the lungs, liver, and kidneys.

Psychological Effects

Continued use of methamphetamine can cause a heavy degree of psychological dependence on the drug which leads to a psychotic state, insomnia, anxiety, depression and fatigue. Toxic psychosis similar to paranoid schizophrenia can result from heavy short or long term use as well as delusional states. Prolonged use can also produce a heavy degree of psychological tolerance, and users find they have to use heavier dosages.

Dangers

Withdrawal from methamphetamine does not involve physical discomfort but can involve acute depression and fatigue. Depression can reach critical proportions since life seems boring and unpleasant. Progressive toxic effects of amphetamine abuse may include restlessness, tremor, talkativeness, irritability, insomnia, anxiety, delirium, panic states, paranoid ideation, palpitation, cardiac arrhythmias, hypertension, circulatory collapse, dry mouth nausea, vomiting, abdominal cramps, convulsions, coma and D E A T H. Other dangers include rapid deterioration of physical and psychological health since methamphetamine erases feelings of periods of time and creates the same sort of stress to the body that any long period of exertion creates; however, the user does not let his body recuperate, and permanent damage or death is the result. Recently, a survey was conducted with a select group of pregnant mothers. Twenty-five percent of the mothers tested showed their babies to have traces of Crystal meth in their systems. Queens Hospital is averaging approximately a half dozen methamphetamine overdoses a day compared to one a day last year.(2)

The Clientele of Ice and Crack

NIDA reports (4) that whites are the principal users of methamphetamine. In a random study of clients in treatment programs in five treatment centers in five different cities, the average first use of methamphetamine was 20.6 years with the average for males being 18.7 years and for females 23.6 years.

Crack use has quickly moved downward not only in the age of the users but in the socioeconomic levels of users. Children of eight use crack regularly and its popularity is greatest in low-income, minority populations. As ice becomes cheaper a similar spreading in age groups and economic levels may be expected.

It is not inevitable that ice will take the place of crack or become as popular as crack. Many users do not wish a long-lasting high; such a high does not serve their needs. However, the glass pipes used in ice smoking easily allow titration of the drug; that is, measured dosages may be taken simply by inhaling a little smoke at a time. The ice, unlike crack, is never exposed directly to the flame; and the flame may be withdrawn anytime, allowing the residue to remain in the pipe for future use. As Dr. Smith of the Haight Ashbury Free Clinics says, "Ice is not replacing crack. It is widening the groups of people who are smoking drugs."(6)

Daniel Bent, U.S. Attorney for the District of Hawaii, addressed the meeting saying, "My purpose in sharing information about the spread of ice in Hawaii is to prevent history from repeating itself... We may experience a higher level of violence because, in early reports, it appears to us that ice users are often more violent than crack users... Ice is likely to spread into a larger part of the population base than crack... In Hawaii ice has spread quickly among blue collar and service workers and has established itself in the workplace."(1, pp. 4,5)

Bibliography

1   Bent, Daniel. "Statement Before the House Select Committee on Narcotics Abuse and Control." Washington, D.C. October 24, 1989, pp. 4, 5.

2   Hawaii Police Department. "Ice Age in Hawaii." 1989. pp. 3-4.

3   Jaffe, Jerome. "Statement on Re-emergence of Methamphetamine." House Select Committee on Narcotics and Control. Washington, D.C. October 24, 1988.

4   National Institute on Drug Abuse. "Methamphetamine Abuse in the United States." September 1980.

5   Rangel, Charles B. "Opening Statement." House Select Committee on Narcotics Abuse and Control. Field Hearing on the Drug Crisis in Hawaii. January 13, 1990.

6   Thompson, Larry. "'Ice,' New Smokable Form of Speed." Washington Post Health. Washington, D.C. November 21, 1988, pp. 11,12.

Chapter 4

Local Law Enforcement and Drug Trafficking

Happening Four — Little Steps to Mr. Big

The Facts As We Best Know Them

Drug Enforcement at the Local Level
Federal Assistance
Multi-level Drug Dealers
Crack and Ice Houses
The Undercover Agents
Street Gangs
Informants Can Be Helpful but Sometimes
    Nuisances
The Drug Sweep in Low-priced Housing
    Complexes
Plea Bargaining in Drug Enforcement
New Laws Against Solicitation to Buy Illegal
    Drugs

Happening Four — Little Steps to Mr. Big

The well-dressed dude had driven his Camaro through the housing development twice already, and he was easing back through for the third time when the four of us sauntered out to the curb. Two of the these guys were pushers; the third was a street dealer who had just dropped off a five-hundred-dollar packet of rocks to each of the other guys and one to me. I am undercover for the Jade City drug enforcement unit. My name is Bubba Scott.

I'll tell you straight. I got into this job because I'm too fat and to lazy to work. I dropped out of high school after the coach booted me off the football team. He was a nice guy, never insulted me; but one of his assistants did. They put me at right guard, and I thought I had figured out how to use my weight to an advantage. I'd wait until the guys stacked up, and then I'd stabilize things by falling on top of the pile. I didn't get my uniform dirty like the other goof-offs did. The assistant coach yelled at me, "Hey, bottle butt, you're crushing our men to death."

I like being fat; it feels good. But don't get the wrong idea; there's a lot of muscle inside under there. I can hold my own in anybody's fight. I'll fight when I have to, but I'd rather stay out of ruckuses, really; it's just too damn much work.

Now, don't get the wrong idea. I'm the luckiest guy alive to have found this job. I never realized there was a place like this when I was in high school. I just can't believe my luck, really. I may joke about it; that keeps me loose, I guess. But I honestly think the Good Lord has led me into my niche where I can really do a job and be proud of what I do. Believe me, I know the danger, but there's no boredom here. I can get as scared as anybody; but in the long-run, I'll shake a little, but I'll get the job done.

I had been mixing with the other two pushers for about a week, shooting the bull with them a lot and shooting craps from time to time just to pass the time. I can make it with these kinds of guys. I always liked to hang out. But I am too smart to use all this pot, crack, or whatever. Two things I learned from my old lady: First, don't do drugs; and second, if I did, she'd beat the hell out of me and make me mow the lawn.

I bought a little rock every time I came over, pretending I didn't have much bread and always telling the guys I was saving it for a big date that night. They said that if I could raise five hundred, they would front for me with the street dealer. They said that I should take the rocks in dimes and quarters, meaning ten-dollar and twenty-five dollar rocks. They explained that the dealer charged six dollars for one and fifteen dollars for the other, and I could maybe double my money. They'd been doing that for a long time, they said. Real pals! I knew one or both of them would get an extra quarter for recruiting me.

Anyway, the lieutenant figured it was about time we busted the whole bunch and he wanted to use the new solicitation law at the same time. The department had copied Houston in getting the city commission to put this solicitation law on the books. Only a few cities are doing this — busting the people who solicit to buy along with the pushers who do the selling. This would be our first time to try for the solicitation bust.

Anyway, I had been carefully bugged that morning. The little bug was taped under my breastbone. I'd have to throw my shoulders back for it to even show. And you never saw such a small recorder. It fitted snug right under my big, old belt buckle. My belly kind of laps over my belt in the middle, so nobody could tell a thing.

The van was just then parking a little way down the street heading away from us. I'm sure the guys were eyeing it, but they thought it was just another buyer sifting through.

The guy in the Camaro was easing over to us on the right side of the street. I stepped out into the street and scooted around to his window just as he came to a stop. You could tell he was nervous. Who wouldn't be? He had to have money, or he couldn't buy rocks. He knew we knew that. For all he knew, we'd just as soon roll him as to sell to him. It happens.

"What can we do for you, Mister. Looking for somebody?" I asked kind of grinning because nobody was really fooling anybody.

"Thought maybe I might get a dime," he said.

It's an old trick. If I seemed to him like a police plant, he'd say a little louder, "I thought maybe you could give me the time." So I gave him the password, "How about a quarter, buddy?" I said smiling. I've got a winning smile; the girls at school always told me that.

"Well, I guess that's all right," the guy said.

The lieutenant had briefed me on the day I signed up and had taken my drug screen. Would you believe that my football coach fronted for me in getting this job? The coach and the lieutenant were buddies, and somehow the coach knew I was clean. Guess he knew a lot of things about me.

Anyway, the lieutenant had shown me how to punch the button turning the recorder on, and I had punched it when I stepped off the curb. I knew the guy was coming in loud and clear, but the lieutenant had said, "Be sure the target says what he wants in a way that he can't make up some bullshit and say he's been misunderstood."

So, I got the guy to spell it out. "You sure you want a quarter instead of maybe two dimes?" I asked.

"Damn it, fella, I want two quarters and two dimes," he blurted out.

"Now maybe you'd just as soon have some crank," I said. I knew what to expect.

"Hell no, I want rocks, crack. Understand? And raise it to three, no four quarters." He was really going now, and I was kind of afraid my buddies were getting the idea that maybe we ought to roll this bastard. I could see the wheels turning in the pushers' heads. If the street dealer hadn't been with us, I think I would have been in trouble. The dealer figured to get a lot more in the long run out of this dude than he was carrying right now, and he'd have to answer to the dealer above him if this turned into a roll.

So, I said innocent-like, "You want to smoke it, huh?"

"I'll tell you one more time. I want four quarters of crack, and I know perfectly well how to use it." The dude was getting mad; and one of the pushers, thinking I was messing up the deal, came around with four quarters in his left palm and his right hand out to get the century. It was time to move. I took off my cap. That was the high sign the van man was waiting for.

The guys in the van must have had the motor idling. We all heard a terrific roar and the squealing of tires as the souped-up van swung into a U-turn and accelerated right at us. As it straightened out, the bright lights came on. It couldn't have been better. When the cops spotlighted us, the century note was in the pusher's hand, and the dude had the rocks in his palm. I saw the flick of his wrist as he scattered the rocks on the street. At the same instance, I saw a bright flash. The police photographer was leaning out the window and caught that exact action on camera. We were caught by the headlights and the spot.

It happened so fast that the guys seemed unable to move. In less than ten seconds, two cops were standing there with handguns on us, and another one had a police shotgun. Nobody ran.

"Get your hands up and don't reach for anything," a cop barked. It took about a minute for them to get the four of us spread, frisked and handcuffed. Boy, those guys were fast. The cop that spread me knew the score. He didn't shove me down hard because he knew where the recorder was.

"Out of your car, Mister," a sergeant barked at the dude.

"Look, officer, I ..." That was all he got out. They jerked him out, had him spread and handcuffed, and all of us were getting our Miranda rights read fast and furious. That included me.

109

I thought the dude would have a seizure. "Damn it, you can't do this!" he screamed. "I'm a law-abiding citizen trying to find a baby sitter." Oh, my God, what a shithead!

"Lock your car," a cop spat at him.

The long and short of it was that four guys — one street dealer, two pushers and an outraged citizen — were crammed into that van. A cruiser picked up three of the five guys who were in the van, and a car with no markings sidled up. The door on the passenger side was opened from the inside for me. I lost no time getting my fat ass in. Being my first time, I guess I didn't know the whole score because I expected to be thrown into the van with the others. I turned to Sergeant Bean, the case agent, whom I knew from the debriefing session. I was about to ask him for a key to the cuffs when I felt them slide off. You guessed it; they hadn't even been snapped.

I let out a roar, "We made a good bust, man. And we got the solicitation guy cold."

The sergeant grunted. Old stuff to him.

"We're following them to the jail, right?" I couldn't hold my voice down.

"Wrong, man," he said, "we've got another stop to make."

"You mean you're just going to leave those four pukes in the van? What about the dressed-up citizen? He's going to be awful mad."

"Tough," he said, "that's a part of his penalty. He'll get off with no jail time if he can get five hundred in bond money. He'll get a maximum fine of two thousand dollars, and he'll have an arrest record.

"He's going to be one mad and embarrassed son-of-a-bitch. He's probably high society in this town. We'll hear from his lawyer tomorrow, no doubt. But if you got it on tape like I told you to, we're home free, and this solicitation law may be the greatest thing since crackerjacks." I believed him.

"The new bug we've got coming in won't have a recorder on you, just a radio sender. The conversation will be heard and taped in the van," he said.

"Gee." That was all I could say.

"We've got another bust takes place in fifteen minutes over on East Main. Woman dealer works out of an apartment, and our informant says she got a shipment from Raleigh yesterday." The case worker acted kind of bored. "You just stay in this car which I'll park in an alley at the back of the apartment. You can't go in with us because you weren't debriefed on this one. I want you to watch the back door though. And have this camera ready to snap a picture of anyone who comes out the door. You been briefed on the camera?"

"Yep," I said proudly.

"It's ready. Just aim and push the button. Take off that bug and recorder and put them in the glove compartment," he instructed. I did it.

The sergeant looked at his watch, got out and slipped in the back door. He'd said the woman's apartment was on the second floor, and there were back stairs. I knew from the training sessions I had attended that a flex squad would be going in at the front at the same time as the sergeant had gone in at the rear. I kind of wished I could have been in on this one, although I hate like hell to climb stairs.

The flex squad would have the department rammer, a six inch piece of heavy pipe about six feet long with two handles welded onto each side so two men could bash down any door with it. They'd all have sock caps pulled down over their ears, and you wouldn't be able see their eyes at all. Scare the hell out of anybody! And they'd all have their 9 mm pistols out and ready. One man would have a shotgun, and one would carry a couple of stun grenades. I've never seen one of those things go off myself except on a training video they showed me. Believe me, the sound of it would knock your ears off, and the bright flash of it would near put you to sleep. These guys go prepared for anything. You never know what kinds of things you'll encounter. There's nearly always a stash of guns and ammo in these joints.

There would be about five of the flex squad and maybe three or four other officers right behind them. They'd knock on the door first, polite-like. The case agent would holler, "Open up, it's the law" and would be standing there with search warrant in hand. If the door was opened, the search warrant would be served. If the woman refused to open the door, then they'd knock it down. The search warrant would be placed on a table, and a couple of guys would control the woman without manhandling her. If they found substances, they'd arrest the woman, read her rights and put her in the nearby van, cramming her in with the other four assholes. I couldn't help wondering what the dude with the Camaro looked like by now. I'd bet anything there was no crease left in his pants by now. It was bound to be plenty steamy and smelly in that van. Somehow, I couldn't quite see shoving a woman into that.

But like my sergeant said when I asked him if we were taking the four others to jail, "No use wasting gas. No use making two trips."

I'd been sitting there propped against the hood of the car with the police camera in hand for maybe ten minutes when I heard a commotion. I knew somebody was scampering down the back stairs in a hurry. I stepped around a bush, so I could get a clean shot of the back door. I was just in time when it busted open.

I got off a great shot of the case agent. "Damn," he spat out, but he wasn't into chewing my ass because I had followed orders to the letter.

"Put that thing in the car, lock it up and come around the front," he barked, losing no time scooting around front himself.

When I got there, a cop I didn't know was getting a real cussing from a slip of a girl maybe twelve years old. She used words I'd never heard, and when the case agent got there, she turned a full volley on him. The sergeant beckoned me to come quick-like. I did.

"She was the only one in the apartment. She's yours. Don't let her get the best of you," he said.

Can you believe these two guys left me alone with that spitting wildcat? She went through the whole vocabulary again with me. The only thing different I could tell was that I caught "fat bastard" in there a couple of times. Thank God, I'd heard that words-can't-kill-you crap. I'd heard it, I had believed it, but now I was doubting it.

The thing that happened next was hard to believe. Several of the neighbors were beginning to gather round. The girl was screaming and cussing, and people from apartments up and down the street were forming a ring around us. Some of them looked tough and mean. I began to get the drift. These were customers and friends of this woman dealer, and they were not on our side. They pulled the ring in tighter and tighter, and the women started cussing me. I didn't have on a uniform,of course; and, I guess, they maybe honestly thought I was a crook. Well, I'd been posing as a crook thirty minutes ago, so what could you expect?

"You dirty child molester. You fat slob of a motherfucker," one old lady maybe in her eighties screamed at me. I'd never heard that kind of talk from an old lady before. And man! That really turned them all on.

"Call the law," some female screamed.

"We don't need no law," one big bruiser growled, and several like him started moving in.

You'd think the twelve-year-old would be happy by now. But no. I heard cloth ripping behind me, and I glanced around. Her dress was barely hanging; one little bud of a breast was pointing out at me like it was accusing me. Then, she started screaming, "The bastard's gang raped me!" And she started crying like her little heart would break. I kind of wanted to console her myself, but hell, I was about to become one big spot of grease right there on the front lawn. Talk about scared!

I just about pissed in my pants. I looked up hoping some of the guys upstairs would come down and show this gang that the good old law was in charge. But no such luck.

Hot breath from these brawlers was hitting my face, and the girl was screaming, "Rape! rape! he raped me!" I knew I was a goner.

My mama always taught me that prayer changes things, and I was getting serious into it when a shotgun went off, and two uniformed cops came down the stairs at the same time. Everybody knew these cops hadn't shot off that charge. It came from near the front curb. I couldn't see anything but all those big bruisers, women and kids scattering like a bunch of quail flushed out of the brush by a good bird dog. They scattered like leaves in a stiff north wind as the swat team came in with gun butts up, never actually hitting anybody. Six uniformed men, who were wearing stocking caps pulled low over their eyes were swinging shotguns, would flush the toughest motor cycle gang, I bet. I had to hold on to myself to keep from running, too. Probably would have if the sergeant and the other cop from upstairs hadn't been right at my shoulder. I got a glance at the little girl. Poor little thing was trembling, holding her torn dress in place and all.

****

We were all back in the main DEU office by eleven o'clock. The two case agents and the lieutenant cleared it all up for me. These two raids were planned one to follow the other. I had been debriefed only for the solicitation case. They had gotten a big surprise when the little girl opened the apartment door. The woman wasn't there. It seemed she hardly ever was there. This twelve-year-old girl collected the money from the street dealers and handed out the rocks which were pre-packaged in one-thousand-dollar packets, a mix of dimes and quarters. The dealers had about cleaned out the supply the woman had got the previous day. There was just enough left to nail her on possession as soon as they could find her.

They hadn't known just what to do with the girl. She was a minor and that's sticky business. Unexpected and confusing! So they had led her into the front yard and made me her guardian — me, who didn't know from zilch about this raid. This night had been hard on my sensitive nerves; I was about ready to get me a job busting rocks bad as I hate anything physical. Hey, I'm kidding. I love this job. I'd work at this for nothing. Tonight was a real pay-off for me.

But the lieutenant was glowing proud of his men. "Great job, Bubba," he told me, and that was just the shot-in-the-arm I needed. Man, they'll never get me out of this work, as scary as it is. It's my life. I've found my calling. They still haven't found the woman and have put the little girl in juvenile. What they did find was about thirty thousand bucks, mostly in hundreds. They confiscated that. But that wasn't what was making the lieutenant smile.

"We'll get the bastard now," he kept saying. Only trouble was I didn't know which bastard he was talking about. But I caught on.

"The papers are more important than the money," the lieutenant kept saying. There was a letter from the woman to Mr. Big whose name I'd better not call although the lieutenant wasn't shy about calling it right out. She hadn't mailed the letter yet; she was cussing him for not getting her share on time and a few extra things. There were other bits of paper the lieutenant seemed to think were important; I never understood why.

"We've been waiting a long time for this," the lieutenant was saying. "He's got maybe a dozen dealers like this woman, and he's running the Busy Bee and The Rosy Queen topless clubs as fronts for the big money. We've known for a long time he was into this up to his balls and was laundering the money through his clubs which he operates at a loss.

"We'll get him for conspiracy," the lieutenant gloated. This will be a Federal case — conspiracy to distribute a controlled substance. With what we've got, and maybe we'll plea bargain the woman, a Federal grand jury will indict him in a minute. The bastard will get fifty years!

****

Mr. Big is in the Federal Penitentiary at Petersburg, Virginia. They have more room in the Federal prisons, so he's going to be in the slammer for quite a while.

The Facts As We Best Know Them

Drug Enforcement at the Local Level

More men and women are putting their lives at risk; seizing caches of drugs; arresting pushers, dealers and manufacturers — in short, keeping drugs off the streets more within local enforcement contexts than within glamorous careers such as the DEA. They do not get the good press, nor do they conjure up images of grandeur and drama as do the Federal agents. Few movies or TV shows are made about local police activity unless they operate in major cities such as Los Angeles or Miami.

The Drug Enforcement Unit Concept

There are hundreds, if not thousands, of drug enforcement units (or organizations of slightly different names) in the smaller cities and counties. There are some county enforcement organizations, (Sheriff's Offices, in particular) which find wisdom in setting up part of the law enforcement personnel into specialized drug enforcement units.

The units, while being organizationally separate, are in most instances administered through centralized Police Departments, County Sheriff's Offices and the like. The smaller drug units have access to manpower and equipment from the bigger units of which they are a part.

Cooperation is the Watchword

Indeed, most of the city, county, state and Federal drug units intermingle their efforts. Any one of these multi-level units may initiate a sting, a sweep or an interdiction and ask help from the others. Typically, helicopters used for surveillance purposes are at the call of any unit while being properties of state departments of public safety or of the more wealthy counties and cities.

Law enforcement officers of any description may arrest those violating substance abuse laws. For instance, a sheriff in a sparsely-populated county in Wyoming has the authority and obligation to enforce substance abuse laws. However, where

117

drug enforcement is more a specialized function of designated units, such units can bring more power of expertise, training and specialization to bear on the problem. The work of units results in more arrests and more convictions because these units are composed of specialists.

Federal Assistance

The work of the DEA is an immensely complex operation that covers the globe. A main thrust is interdiction of drug supplies. But there is a network of DEA agents which in one form or another covers every city, county, and parish in the United States. The DEA agents help with personnel support, educational programs, undercover agents and with legal interpretations. They help drug units of any size anytime, anyplace. Actually, since the crack epidemic, the DEA has started becoming involved in actual street confrontations with miscreants. The DEA considers a twelve-year-old kid who has three ounces of rocks in a plastic bag to be a major threat to the lives and welfare of citizens.

Federal Charges Are More Indictable

DEA agents can often find good reason to bring Federal charges to bear upon violators. Federal laws of conspiracy and transportation of goods and persons across state lines would otherwise be overlooked by local units.

One DEU official demonstrated for this author how the DEA assists his unit in providing forms of various types of warrants, which are word-processed into the unit's computer so that a specific warrant form can be quickly obtained.

Securing Warrants

Warrants to search premises must be secured from judges. If the action necessitating the search warrant derives from the violation of a local law, either a district judge or a justice of the peace may issue a warrant or sign one, which has been properly prepared. If there has been a Federal violation which prompted the need for a warrant, a Federal judge must approve the warrant.

The Federally executed warrant can be sealed, while others cannot be sealed. This means that unsealed warrants may be examined freely by defense attorneys; a sealed warrant prevents such examination except through a lengthy process.

A Federal warrant is not always better than the others. It does serve as a prelude to a Federal indictment and should be sought: 1) if there is good reason to believe a Federal law is being broken and 2) if there is a perceived advantage in having a Federal indictment or a perceived better chance of getting a Federal grand jury to indict as opposed to a grand jury at another level.

Multi-level Drug Dealers

There have been hierarchies of illegal drug handlers for a long time. These were rampant during the 70's when crank and speed were heavy favorites in many locales.

Cheap Crack Creates New Levels

However, crack distribution seems to have spread these hierarchies into far more levels than any other drug form. Before crack, it would have been very unusual to find a cadre of pushers among elementary school students. There are several levels among school-ground pushers now. These levels move upward through perhaps half a dozen disparate levels of distribution before reaching the supplier level.

With methamphetamine, the age of maximum use is in the low to upper twenties. Few children of elementary school age use methamphetamine. Crack use reaches downward, because crack is cheap enough that an elementary student can buy it with his lunch money plus a dollar or two filched surreptitiously from family sources.

Wholesalers and Manufacturers

A typical high school has three levels of dealers although all are called pushers. The suppliers for these pushers are usually street dealers where another three-tiered group operates. The street dealers obtain supplies from still other levels, which are in direct touch with suppliers further up the chain, not always local. There is still a higher level where a kingpin operates a network of wholesalers who supply street dealers.

At the warehousing and supply (manufacturing) levels there are still other levels and often the topmost tiers have ties to organized crime. Obviously, this hierarchy can be violated as when a street dealer gets smart enough to manufacture his own supply. However, he does this at a risk of violence to himself.

Crack and Ice Houses

There is probably no other entity as well known to TV viewing America as the crack house or the ice house.

Retail Sales

The typical public view of these houses, which are usually run-down rental properties, is that they are hang-out places for smokers who buy at the houses and smoke on premises. This is an accurate description of what some frustrated citizens know as crack and ice houses because these are located in their neighborhoods. An expanded view is that in addition to on-premises use, crack and ice are sold to those who drive up in automobiles day and night. These automobiles buy crack or ice retail, taking the drug to other premises for use.

Crack and Ice in Wholesale Distribution

Drug enforcement agents have broadened their concepts of the crack and ice houses. Such houses are seen as warehouses serving as jobbers or wholesale outlets. True, such houses may have some clientele who hang out and smoke on premises, but these are more for cover of the wholesale trade than a cherished element of the business.

It is the wholesale crack or ice houses that drug agents are most anxious to raid because the arrests and convictions they get have a larger impact. Arresting and getting an indictment against one person for possession, another person for solicitation and another person for street dealing, is not as important as busting a kingpin who manages a cluster of crack or ice houses and launders the money through business fronts.

Actually, indictments come easier when the larger prey is netted. Then, too, with larger operators, there is more probability of getting a Federal indictment.

The Undercover Agents

Without undercover agents, there could scarcely be a credible drug enforcement program. These undercover agents are a central fixture on every level and in every context. The DEA uses undercover agents to find out about cocaine and methamphetamine processing plants. Their work takes them from the ghettos to the Andean jungles. Perhaps, these global operations have been over-glamorized by modern fiction and television.

Selecting, Recruiting and Training of Undercover Agents

At the local level, undercover agents are also indispensable. These agents are commissioned officers in full standing with the sponsoring enforcement entity. They are carefully selected and trained. They are carefully recruited.

As one enters an undercover job, he is usually subjected to drug screening and to polygraph tests. He must test clean, and he must stay clean. He is periodically drug screened inasmuch as it is difficult to deal with drug users and not become a user oneself. Such agents are strictly instructed by reputable trainers not to use drugs to impress those whom they are trying to entrap.

Certainly, if an undercover agent is challenged to overtly use a substance by hostile traffickers who have a gun to to the undercover's head, he would inject, smoke or swallow. But he would check in with his superiors as soon as possible, letting them know what had happened.

Dangers in Undercover Work

It is difficult to overemphasize the dangers inherent in undercover work. True, a majority of local pushers, dealers and solicitors (people who buy drugs) are unlikely to maintain long-term hatred or resentment toward undercovers. However, persons involved in major operations, such as processing labs for ice and crack and wholesaling operations, often feel strong anger commensurate with the threat undercovers pose to their persons or their operations.

With gang activity involved, the undercovers' work becomes intensely dangerous. It is not an understatement to say that typical gang members have attitudes which do not place high value on human life.

Many have expressed disbelief that anyone in his right mind would go undercover because the dangers are so intense. Fortunately, there are those who relish the excitement of such work. They are built that way.

However, persons who have this kind of derring-do in their make-ups, are often blemished with overdoses of macho self-image or even self-destructive neuroses. This makes the finding of committed undercovers who do not have these negative qualities a tremendous challenge and one where caution and careful evaluation must be a central element. Periodic re-evaluation of undercovers' personalities must be sustained. The unswerving loyalty of a Matthew Helm is not something easy to find.

Street Gangs

The selling and money handling of crack and ice have come under the influence of street gangs in the larger cities. These gangs originated probably out of other motivations; but once formed, a street gang catches on quickly to the opportunity to make big money with crack, ice, and other methamphetamines.

These gangs take on colorations of motorcycle gangs and of ethnic gangs. Oriental gangs may control ice in one city while another ethnic gang may control crack. There is a strange mix of camaraderie and competition among gangs in a large city or even in large costal corridors such as that from San Diego to Seattle. There is more often than not warfare or turf battles which, while always a part of the scene, have become intensified with high traffic in ice and crack.

There are price wars and efforts to control prices by keeping the price high for crack in one locale, say Seattle, while allowing lower prices in Los Angeles. On the other hand, the price of ice may be higher in Los Angeles than in Seattle. A part of this scenario revolves around supply factors.

Gang activities in drug trafficking, in battling for turf and in competing with organized crime are creating a violent world and exacerbating the tasks of drug enforcement units including the DEA.

Informants Can Be Helpful but Sometimes Nuisances

Drug enforcement units cannot function without information. Undercovers are trained informants, to be sure. Yet, some of the most useful information comes from untrained sources. Generally, all drug enforcement entities, including the DEA, encourage call-ins who can tell them about unusual smells, sounds and traffic. Many clandestine labs are found only because people furnish reliable information.

The Frustrations of Dealing With Informants

The fact that citizens are anxious to clean up their neighborhoods is both a blessing and a source of headaches for drug enforcement personnel. The trouble is that people expect too much too soon. They want action now. If an informant sees a group of young people hanging out and smoking, his mind turns immediately to either crack, ice or marijuana. Citizens do not often realize just how difficult an officer of the law finds it to make a bust under such circumstances. The officer must see or have good evidence that a law is being broken. If he pulls up to a group of hangers-out who are smoking, he will find some of them smoking cigarettes. He may smell marijuana ever so sharply, but no one will be openly smoking it. The joint was thrown behind a convenient bush seconds before the patrol car arrived.

Laws of search have been liberalized, but an officer must still find "probable cause" to be able to justify a search or shake-down. The young people will have a good time kidding the officer, and he must withstand this with good grace. The informant, who is likely watching to see what will happen, reports to neighbors that the officer did nothing at all and even is on friendly terms with the ne'er do wells.

123

The well-trained officer knows exactly what is happening up and down the street, at the police switchboards and in the group of hangers-out. The group causing the problems gets a bang out of it, the taxpayer pays for time and equipment and no one gets arrested. The joints are lighted up again as soon as the officer pulls away from the curb.

For the most part, the missing ingredient in well-meaning citizens is patience. They want what bothers them stopped and stopped right now. Happily, other informants do a lot of good in bringing scrutiny to bear on houses and premises where laws are being broken; they are accurate in their reporting and patient in their hopes of good results.

Informants Who Are Drug Abusers

Often a person hooked on meth, crack or another drug comes into the unit declaring that he is tired of his habit, has decided to quit and wants to inform on boyfriend, husband or lovers. Such informants seldom turn out well. Once an orderly investigation is mounted with their initial help, these people will decide not to quit using, not to be instrumental in getting a lover or friend in trouble. They may get paranoid and accuse the officers of misconduct.

The Drug Sweep in Low-priced Housing Complexes

It is generally conceded that a large part of inner city drug activity occurs in environs of housing complexes where poverty pockets exist. There are several reasons for this. The people in these districts are often unemployed with nothing constructive to do. This encourages the hanging-out of youth groups, and the easy money of drug dealing becomes a strong motivator. Street dealers are ready and eager to exploit the situation. Pushers can easily be recruited, usually from among the apartment dwellers. However, it is a puzzle to some how drug trafficking can flourish in an environment where there is little money with which to buy drugs.

Why These Housing Units Encourage Drug Traffic

Two answers to the above question come readily into view: First, the demand for drugs is created in the poverty pockets by pushers who get unemployed youth to use drugs. They purposely create habits even if they have to sell drugs very cheaply. This creates a money demand that finds expression in crime. These sections are highly infested with theft, burglary and the like. Still, there are limited sources for productive burglary in such neighborhoods. Crime ultimately spreads into more affluent neighborhoods where goods are stolen and then sold perpetuating a vicious cycle of crime and drug use.

Then, too, the more affluent citizens depend on these neighborhoods to fill their own drug-related needs. Citizens of affluent neighborhoods certainly use drugs, but they do not wish to have the scandalizing influence of drug trafficking in their own neighborhoods. Therefore, they contribute to the problem by driving through these shoddy quarters, putting their own safeties at risk, but in the long-run, feeding money into a perpetual-motion machine. To be sure, some quite affluent citizens do not themselves go to such neighborhoods to secure drugs but pay and send others who are not intimidated by the public scrutiny and embarrassment attached to buying drugs. Either way, the machinations of drug trafficking are perpetuated.

This situation offers drug enforcement units good opportunity for arresting and jailing pushers, dealers and, more recently, persons who solicit to buy. Often, they will run a "sweep" through several of these housing complexes in a single sustained operation.

Techniques of the Drug Sweep

There is a lot of careful planning for a drug sweep. First, there is the personnel —getting together enough men to pull it off. Small cities may call on nearby large cities to send swat teams, on county officers and on state troopers attached to narcotics units.

The case agent in charge will acquire blueprints of the buildings to be raided. Undercovers will be planted in these buildings several weeks before the big sweep. Often, these

125

undercovers will carry bugs (recording devices) and get a lot of conversation which they sneak back to headquarters. The case agent has to be satisfied that everything is in place, or the sweep won't be carried out.

An hour or two before time to go with the sweep, a debriefing takes place in a convenient, secluded place. Every man who is going to take part in the sweep has to be at the debriefing from its beginning. If someone gets there a little late, he just won't be allowed to participate in the sweep.

The case agents utilize maps and tell the personnel exactly how the sweep is going to move — which building will be hit first and so on. Specific rooms in the buildings will be targeted based on undercover information. Group supers will be assigned to lead certain groups. Every man and woman understands his/her role. There will be several rammers used to break down doors, a shotgun for each squad of eight or ten people and 9 mm handguns for everyone. One person in each squad will have stun grenades, which can be thrown into a room if necessary. These make a demoralizing loud noise and a brilliant light giving personnel time to beat their opponents to action. Resistance is expected although it often doesn't occur. On the other hand, the number of weapons found on these sweeps is usually amazing and justifies the intense focus on sufficient personnel and weapons.

Every person will have a two-way radio. The case agent cruises the area in an unmarked car during the sweep and is the principal one who sends on the radio equipment. Only a few key persons are authorized to send out messages. The case agent relays messages from squad to squad keeping the sweep going according to plan or changing the plan slightly when necessary.

Every person is dressed alike, for example, with black jackets over uniforms. The people almost always wear sock caps down over their ears, partly for identification one to the other so no one accidentally gets hurt and partly for the psychological effect on the miscreants. The sight of what looks like a bunch of goons with guns is usually enough to scare the dopers, and unfortunately the citizens, into paralysis.

The undercovers wear pre-arranged markers, so they can have some measure of protection. They usually don't enter into the action. Sometimes, they are taken into custody with the dopers to protect their identities.

The Work of the Case Agent

The case agent is in full charge. Every person may be in place, but no one moves until the case agent says its a "go." As the sweep races from one end of the string of apartments toward the other end, people, especially the guilty ones, will scurry from the building under attack to the next building which will be attacked in a finely-tuned sequence. Once the operation starts at one end, it is usually continued. A helicopter usually circles overhead calling in information about movements into the complexes, out of the complexes on foot or any other salient activities. The streets are usually sealed.

A large percentage of those arrested have been pre-identified by the undercovers. Some are arrested for resistance, and some for possession. Those in apartments where illegal substances or illegal firearms are found are taken in.

Confusion and Chaos Is the Rule

Children usually present many problems. Which one belongs to whom is always a question. Stun grenades are not used where children are known to be present. Well-meaning neighbors usually help with the frightened children.

There usually isn't a lot of shooting. A small war may break out in one particular building, but when the would-be resisters find out they are overwhelmed, they usually give up meekly. The firepower is held in check except when necessary to protect the officers, but casualties sometimes occur with officers, offenders and innocent bystanders.

Many times, a sweep will net fifty or more dealers and pushers who are crowded into vans for a ride to the jail. Sorting out the various charges often takes days. These sweeps are necessary in most cities as a means of closing down known hotbeds of drug activity and as demonstrations of law enforcement power. A threat to those who create such hotbeds must be sustained.

Plea Bargaining in Drug Enforcement

Plea bargaining is frowned upon by many citizens as mollycoddling of criminals. It can be that, but it is often an effective tool and lends itself well to drug enforcement.

Why Plea Bargaining Works

A street dealer who figures he may get thirty years in the penitentiary will usually furnish evidence on his supplier if he can be convinced that he can get a lighter sentence by informing. True, everyone knows these sentences seldom are served; but still, no one wants to go to the slammer. Even if a thirty-year sentence typically gets reduced to five, it is still a harsh penalty. Overcrowded jails, prisons, halfway houses and court dockets present still problems in cleaning up the drug mess; but these must be seen as facts of life. Strong efforts to correct these deficiencies are under way.

Perhaps, the most effective plea bargaining occurs with adolescents and young people who have not yet become hardened criminals. Drug enforcement personnel are largely in favor of rehabilitation although many have a logically dim view of rehabilitation.

Some Can Be Saved From a Life of Crime

The young person who has taken only a few wrong steps is more salvageable than a person who has been into this lifestyle for many years. These young people are among the most approachable for plea bargaining. Most of those with no previous arrests or convictions are well aware that they may get off on probation.

Probation often serves to turn young lives around although recidivism rates are much higher than they should be. A principal fault lies in the environments to which these young people must return. If an environment or lifestyle spawns a criminal the first time, it has a high probability of doing so again.

New Laws Against Solicitation to Buy Illegal Drugs

Houston, Texas was among the first to pass a law "prohibiting solicitation to purchase or acquire a prohibited substance." A few cities have copied this and it could be a wave of the future.

Supply and Demand

People in drug enforcement may be prone to gloat over . the number of "busts" they make. Who can blame them? But many are seeing that the buyers of drugs are the true source of sale and manufacture of drugs. Some social experiments in foreign counties, notably China, have shown the effectiveness of punishing the buyers.

We are told that buyers in China have been placed in jail under strict penalty to the extent that the dealers and pushers have no source left for profiteering. It is not likely to be as easy as it sounds, but the idea is finding acceptance slowly but surely in American cities.

Solicitors Are Seldom Indicted

True, the penalties under the solicitation laws in this country are not severe. But some law-abiding citizens who feel they have a perfect right to buy and use crack or ice. The point is arguable. Nevertheless, a person probably wouldn't buy drugs if he faced a series of embarrassing penalties. A person would not openly solicit a second time if, on his previous try, he were: 1) arrested, handcuffed and thrown into a police van with smelly characters, 2) wound up in a jail cell, even if for only an hour or two, 3) had to post a five-hundred-dollar bond to get out of jail and 4) had to pay as much as two thousand dollars in fines. Most people would be inclined to hire a lawyer thinking their rights have been violated. Then, when the attorney advises that the law is strictly against the person and that the consequences cannot be avoided, the message strikes home. *Don't solicit to buy illegal drugs.* This law will not be a panacea, but will deter many who do not want to pay these penalties.

Law enforcement first against suppliers and then against solicitors to buy controlled substance is like a candle with a wick at both ends. We light both ends of the candle. When the supply flame and the demand flame meet in a mass of molten wax, we will be closer to solving the drug problem.

PART III — SETTINGS

Chapter 5

Family Dysfunction — Seedbed of Drug Abuse

Happening Five — Scrambled But Not Well Done

The Facts As We Best Know Them

Bottom Line — The Wounded Human Spirit
Where We Went Wrong
The Dysfunctional Family
Success Identity or Failure Identity
Healthy and Unhealthy Reasons for Wanting a
Child
The Late Appearing Child, A Special Challenge
Feelings of Abject Dependency Must Be
Disallowed
Breaking Family Rules — Guilt Trips
Abusive Parents
Family Therapy

Happening Five — Scrambled But Not Well Done

I am really scared! This is the first time I've really run away. The other times weren't for real. I'd only hid out in vacant houses for a few days the other times. The juvenile authorities had called these runaways, but they really weren't. I've never intended to split forever until now. But this is it! It's either get away or kill myself.

How do you catch a ride anyway? I've heard about thumbing and about women hiking their skirts a little — all TV stuff, I guess. But these tight hip huggers won't hike. Besides, at thirteen, I'm a little overdeveloped upstairs; but I haven't got that much to show — really. All I know to do is stand here a little down the highway from the big truck stop. Maybe one of the truck drivers will pick me up before he gets up any speed. They're bound to see me, and I'll look sad and lonely. But I've got to keep my head up; I've got to make eye contact with them. Hard to do since they all wear dark glasses. Gosh, I wish I had someone to go with me. If I did, maybe I wouldn't be so scared.

I figured it right. The big eighteen wheeler is slowing up. I know the guy is glooming me; it seems like he's going to stop. He almost decides against it; I can tell by the way the big engine sounds — it gives a read-out of the guy's feelings. He probably knows I am underage, and that could spell trouble for him. But he's stopping, believe it or not. The door is swinging open on my side. All I have to do is climb in.

I never realized what it's like getting into one of these big things. It's like scaling the side of a mountain. When I finally make it up those steps and into the seat of the cab, my feet are six inches off the floor. I am totally out of breath. For the first time, I look around at the driver.

He has his dark glasses off, and he is a lot older than I expected. Oh, he's not real old. But he is grey at the temples, maybe fifty; I don't know — about like my granddad, Big Joe was, when he died. He really looks a lot like Big Joe did.

132

"Well, little lady," he says with a nice friendly smile, "where are we off to today?" Almost fatherly, well, maybe grandfatherly.

"Oh, I'm going up to Albuquerque. I got an aunt up there I visit pretty often. She's in bad health, and I need to look out for her, you know."

"Sure," he says. "How old are you, honey?" I pretend not to hear him. You can read a lot into a "honey." This guy isn't a masher, for sure, and I'm glad about that. I can feel a patronizing tone in the "honey." I'm kind of glad because I am really shaking. My first real runaway is starting out real good.

The guy is staring at me. No sweat. He's got a kind face. But he's not revving up to move out. I think he's going to change his mind and dump me back out. Now, he knows now I'm really a minor and is figuring he's in trouble.

But he's finally deciding to risk it. He's turning his eyes to the rear view mirror and he's gunning the big engine. This is kind of thrilling. That engine picking up is music to my ears. I'm getting out of this hell hole. The engine is saying, "Goodbye to hell. Goodbye to rotten mother, bitchy little sister and to friends who love you for your money." That motor is playing a refrain for me. It is a golden oldie, and it all comes rushing in: "That's the only thing I've plenty of, baby. I can't give you anything but love." Bullshit, the only thing my sleazy friends were interested in was my money; they didn't know the meaning of the word love. My mom and my grandmother Alma likewise; they are interested only in themselves.

"How old are you, honey?" There it is again. Wish to God I was twenty-five and was out of these stupid teenage years as well as out of this town. But I can't keep on ignoring the guy. He could still dump me.

"I'm eighteen," I lie, "eighteen last month." I'm trying to look this old geezer in the eye to convince him, not quite knowing which way to go with him. Do I give him a come-hither, eye-batting act, or do I play the business-lady role like we're both adults and we've got our own business to tend to? I can't decide, so I drop my eyes and pretend I'm hunting for a

133

cigarette in my purse. Another old song comes back to me. The words go: "I've got plenty of nothing, and nothing's plenty for me." "That's the only thing you've got, baby nothing," I whisper under my breath. All I have are the clothes on my back and my purse which has nothing in it but three twenties, a five and a little change, a lipstick and six or seven dime rocks hidden behind the lining. My copper stem is right there in plain view, and I'll have to tuck that into the lining, too.

"Sorry, lady," the man says. And there is something wrong with that "lady" thing. He's pretending to go along with the eighteen bit, but he knows better. Why change from honey to lady? "I don't smoke," he says, "and I wish you wouldn't in the cab. We've got a stop about thirty miles up and I've got to get gas. You can smoke in the ladies room there." There's a short pause. "Sorry," he says again, not meeting my eyes. I'm shaking again feeling it's no use. The guy isn't into believing, and I can't tell anybody the truth.

No way could I just pop and say, "I'm thirteen years old, my mother is a rich, alcoholic bitch, my granddad is dead and my grandmother is sleeping around like a twenty-year-old whore. I'm rich because my granddad left me a chunk. But I can't get any money until I'm eighteen except handouts and an allowance, and I'm taking off for parts unknown because I can't stand being used anymore. Nobody gives a damn. My friends, so-called, hang out with me only because I can sneak them enough bread to keep the crack, the ice or whatever hell else they want coming. I was hooked on paint by the time I was eight, still like the stuff; but since it's kid stuff, I've moved up to crack. God, how I need a fix right now!"

So we move along pretty much in silence for the next thirty miles. I sneak a look at his gas gauge, and just as I thought, he filled up back where he picked me up. I start to plan my move.

Should I take off when he goes in to use the phone at the truck stop? He'll likely call ahead to the next town which is Albuquerque and have the cops ready to take me in. But I can see the kind of country we're in, as I see the truck stop the guy keeps talking about in the distance. I'll just wait until we get there to decide either to run from there or wait until we get to Albuquerque to run.

We arrive at the truck stop. It's no use. I can see already that even a jackrabbit couldn't hide around this joint. If I run into the brush, I'll last maybe two hours with no water. It'll be the sheriff that finally takes me in, and he would probably take me the thirty miles back home where the driver picked me up. I have no identification on me, and if I can get away from the driver in Albuquerque before the cops get me, I can disappear and make it on the money I've got until I can get a job and find a hangout place. I am staying with the truck for now. I'll give the driver the rest room bit as soon as we get well into the suburbs of Albuquerque.

The guy comes back and starts the truck going and hasn't been near a gas pump. He probably knows that I know what he's done. He really turns on the talk when we get going. "What shit," I think, "might as well entertain him with some truth and some lies. After all, he's not being a bad guy. It's my problem. He's taken care of his problem."

"Why don't you tell me all about yourself, kiddo," he says before the truck gets up to cruising speed. Well, there it is. It's "kiddo" now — not "honey" and not "lady." This is his way of getting up the nerve to tell me what is going to happen in about another hour. So I decide to kill the time and maybe lighten up my own load by talking. Maybe I can get him loosened up so he'll go for the rest room bit. I'm glad I didn't use the rest room back at the truck stop in the desert.

"You don't buy the eighteen bit?" I say matter of factly.

"No." No need to elaborate.

"Well, I'm splitting a bad scene. Hope you'll help me, Mister," I say like a good little cowed-down girl should, or at least like I think he thinks I should.

"That's better," he says, "don't know how I can help, but I'm a good listener." I'm usually skeptical of so-called good listeners like my school counselor who tried her best to talk sense into me. Only trouble was she didn't understand that there was no sense in my crazy, mixed-up world. How was I going to act sensibly in a senseless world? I couldn't and I didn't.

"Well," I say, "I guess I'm a typical poor, little, rich girl or a 'little girl lost,' maybe a combination. My family has owned a string of jewelry stores for a long time. My granddad was the only person I could ever trust and the only one who loved me. He raised a family including my mother, another older daughter and one boy, my Uncle Joe. Uncle Joe, together with my mother, is now into the family jewelry store business."

"Uh huh," the driver says. Not bad. That was my junior high school counselor's main contribution to the cause, too. It's the sign of the good listener, I guess. I know I am supposed to go on talking, so what the hell! I talk.

"My mother was kind, a black sheep, I guess. She was pretty wild and refused to make country-club-style friends. She ran with the lower-class kids in school instead. I guess she was on a social-equality kick like all the young people were in those days. Anyway, she married my father against the family's wishes. She was pregnant with me at the time, so maybe it was a shotgun wedding." I kind of snickered at that; I don't know why. "Anyway, maybe I should be glad I didn't get aborted and flushed down the toilet. Naturally, I don't remember the first two years much, and as far as my father is concerned, I don't remember him at all. Never have seen him.

"Anyway, the marriage lasted a little over two years, and I think Alma and Big Joe (that's what I called my grandparents) had a big hand in ending that marriage. It was a family embarrassment as I get it. When it was finished, as I understand it, my mother went totally wild. That is why Alma and Big Joe raised me until I was eight years old — the only happy years I had. Mother married a family-approved guy, Charles Pickens, about two years after her divorce and had a little girl when I was four. The little bitch is nine now, so I was with Alma and Big Joe five years.

"I was happy with Alma and Big Joe; Mother and Charles didn't seem to want me anyway. Okay by me. I didn't like either of them. Both of them were in the business with Big Joe; and when Kathy, that's my so-called baby sister, was about two, mother became the buyer for the stores. I think there are six of them in New Mexico and Colorado.

"The business was doing well and Charles had some businesses of his own. The family was getting richer, and I was happy as punch with Alma and Big Joe. Boy, I really loved Big Joe, and he was nuts about his only granddaughter, I think. We did all kinds of good things together. I can't tell you how I adored Big Joe.

"Well, it came apart about two years ago. Big Joe had a heart attack and died — just like that. I was eleven and I just about died. I still miss him terrible."

I was getting plenty of the uh huh's from the driver, and we were getting closer and closer to Albuquerque. I am thinking about making my move, watching as a few service stations start coming up. The signs say we are still about twenty miles from the city.

"What's your name, kiddo?" the driver asks.

"Ginger," I say.

"Holy cow or holy Joe — it's amazing. I'm Joe Hoppenstein, and I've got a granddaughter named Virginia about your age." At first, I think he is making it up. Then, I know better as he gets all soft-eyed toward me, and I realize I've been talking to him all this time just like I used to talk to Big Joe. Gosh, I feel like hugging him. I decide to tell him the whole works.

"I've been afraid to trust anybody since Big Joe died. I thought when he died that I'd just go on living with Alma, thought she'd need me. She always seemed to like me as much as Big Joe did.

"But it took less than a week for me to find out different. I was eleven at the time, and being so lonely, I took up with the lower-class kinds. Alma didn't like that. She'd nearly driven my mother crazy, I understand, when she married my daddy whom I never knew. I did know Alma considered my daddy trash. Alma was a society lady all the way, and I don't think she

137

ever forgave my mother for marrying out of her class. Alma was constantly throwing it up to me about my trashy daddy. I don't know; maybe that's why I always picked the lower-class kids. Maybe as much as I hated my mother, I wanted to stick up for my daddy. After Big Joe was gone, I started hanging out with those kids; actually, I had started doing paint with them years earlier. Paint sniffing is a low-class form of drug, you know.

"But I had money, and crack came along, and I was buying it for the kids. I was a real heroine to them, I guess. Well, like I said, I got hooked on crack myself, and we did a little ice to just to try it out. All that happened within six months after Big Joe died. I was miserable. I was living with Alma, but she had changed. She went wild just like my mother did before her second marriage. The clincher came when I went into her bedroom to say goodnight after carousing and smoking with my low-class friends and found her shacked up with a dude half her age. I found out later he was a male prostitute. Imagine that — Alma was paying to get laid. Oh, she could afford it all right. But she called me a little bitch and literally kicked me out. Well, maybe I was a bitch. I had made it with several guys when we smoked. And we smoked everything — pot, crack, ice and even plain, old cigarettes. One guy even offered me a cigar, but I turned him down.

"Anyway that was when I moved in with mother and Charles — no other place to go. And that was when my little sister Kathy started throwing fits. 'You're not fit to live with us,' she said. 'Your friends stink.' And then we'd have a ruckus, and mother would take up for Kathy. She was drinking heavy by then, and I still wonder how she did the buying when she was roused all the time. I think little Joe is about fed up and is going to raise holy hell with her. But how can he? She has the same percentage of the jewelry stores as he has and refuses to sell out to him or anybody else. That business is like a bomb ready to go off.

"About then is when I started what they called running away. Some running! The first time I hid out in the back yard three days. They had me kidnapped and my picture on TV and everything. The police cars would cruise up the alley within feet of my hiding place, but they never thought to look. When everybody was away from the house, I'd sneak in and get cookies and milk. But mother finally caught me, and I got the feeling she wished I'd been found floating in the river. Anyway, things went from bad to worse after that. Alma would get real upset when I ran away because the family name and business was at stake. My mother and Kathy just about called me every name in the book. But I kept running away, staying in vacant houses with three guys and one other girl, smoking crack and what they were selling as ice. It all felt the same, the highs lasted only a few minutes, not hours like ice was supposed to do, and the guys would do an awful lot of screwing on us. It was pretty good, nothing special.

"Alma and mother knew all that was happening, and all they thought about it was that I'd screw up their reputations. They didn't give a damn about me. I caught Charles. With his eyes on me funny-like as I began to fill out a good bit. I thought it would be a good joke on my mother to screw with Charles and with Alma paying those male prostitutes and my mother drinking herself to death it would have pretty well completed the picture. My mother was out of town on buying trips a lot, and when she was gone, Kathy would really dump on me like she was the one who had all the money. But according to what the trustee told me, Big Joe willed that Kathy would never get more than half of what I got. I think that is why she hates me so.

"But last night was the end. I'd thought of climbing into bed with Charles all right. I admit it. I'd fantasized about what it would be like for Kathy, a nine-year-old kid to find her daddy in bed with me. Charles wasn't my father, of course, so it wouldn't have been incest. I could never even think of that.

"The real surprise was that one night when my mother had flown to Dallas on a buying trip, Charles slipped into my bed. Imagine that! I was his thirteen-year-old step daughter, and he wanted to make out with me. He snuggled up almost before I knew he was there and whispered, 'Come on baby, find out what a real man is like.'

"Well, it was all right for me to fantasize about it, but when it happened this way, I really couldn't take it. I jumped out of bed and Charles was after me. 'If you don't do it, I'll tell your mother you came into my room and who do you think she'll believe?' I knew who she'd believe because she'd always hated me. I spoiled a good thing for her years ago. Alma had been kind enough to tell me all about it. 'She wanted an abortion when she was pregnant with you, but Big Joe wouldn't tolerate it. If it wasn't for Big Joe, you wouldn't be here causing trouble.' And this was my sweet, rich grandmother who had treated me like her own until Big Joe died. I'll bet Alma was cheating on Big Joe all the time I was living with them. No wonder he had a heart attack.

"Well, do you see?" I said turning to Joe Hoppenstein who is acting awfully sad. "Do you see why I had to run away? I couldn't stand it. Nobody wanted me. I've been hurt so much I don't want anybody to be close to me now, either. I don't trust anybody. I don't trust you. You have arranged to turn me into the cops. I know it. Now, for God's sake, Joe, do one kind thing in your life. Let me out at the next corner, and I'll disappear. I swear I won't tell anybody about you picking up a minor. I swear it. I swear it!"

Joe has tears in his eyes. I think he cares. But he won't stop. He doesn't stop at all until the cops pull him over. He watches as the cops take me down from the cab. He watches as they rip my purse apart and find the rocks. I hear a cop ask Joe where he picked me up, and Joe tells them. They put me in the squad car and take me to jail. It wouldn't take them long to find out who I was, I knew that. It was a blur after that. I don't know what kinds of things the cops did about me being a minor and all. I don't know, and I don't care. To hell with it!

****

Ginger is now in a sixty-day substance abuse program at Las Cruces, New Mexico. She has been in the center now for twenty days, and no one has visited her yet. When she is "cured," she will be released back to her mother!

The Facts As We Best Know Them

The nation is experiencing a crisis of drug abuse so great as to make a war necessary — a war on drugs. The question has arisen, and an answer or answers must be given. Whose fault is it? Where do the answers lie? These are the questions. The questions are simple. The answers are so complex as to boggle the mind!

The Fault is in the Supply of Drugs.

As one sees gangs of what most people would call hoodlums on the inner city streets selling drugs, it is easy to say or think, "It is their fault. They are destroying our children. Let's send them all to boot camp."

As one reads about the coast guard seizing a ton of cocaine, the answer comes easily — the Andean nations, especially the drug lords and the get-rich-quick traffickers, are the ones at fault. "Let's put more ships in the gulf and more planes in the air. Let's spray the coca fields in South America with paraquat. We can stop this foolishness."

When amphetamine labs are found in the countryside, we know whom to blame. We heap our scorn on these lawbreakers as we see them led to jail in handcuffs and leg irons. "They are to blame for this mess."

Supply Versus Demand

All the answers for the drug debacle we face suggested above speak to the issue of drug supply. The war on these highly visible causes is well under way. It would be a great comfort if we could know that a solid resolution of these issues will win the war. But it will not!

The demand factor is the basic point of fault and the basic point of the battle. Our society has so ordered itself as to create a demand for drugs on a level that creates seemingly unsolvable problems. The blame factor, as it pertains to demand, points in dozens of directions at once and defies us to enunciate a single one or even several basic causes of the demand for drugs.

141

CRACK, COCAINE, METHAMPHETAMINE AND ICE

Bottom Line — The Wounded Human Spirit

It may be trite and it may be useless to say it, but the basis of the drug epidemic is that a myriad of forces have left the human spirit in a condition of confusion and malaise. The human spirit is wounded and shriveling. People see themselves as having little value and see little hope that a spirit which embraces growth, love and caring will ever be revived.

Somehow, we must restore the pride people once had in themselves. We must restore the desire to live lives of dedication to the high purposes of joyous living. There must be a renewed dedication to lifestyles where kindness, gentleness and caring for self and others comprise the guiding principles of every person's private world. We must return to lifestyles, the cores of which are self-esteem and appreciation of the rights of others — lifestyles dedicated to joy and wholesomeness as opposed to sadness and depression. We must discourage the manipulation of humankind for the purpose of securing the almighty dollar at any price. We must move away from the current state of selfish, diabolical, degrading, enslaving and cruel actions, and toward a restored spirit of cooperation and brotherhood.

Where We Went Wrong

These are profound and some will say foolish sentimentalities. The question arises: How did we arrive at a place where humans are so devalued that we, as individuals, seem to be plotting our own demises?

The religious right would say we have left God out of our lives and out of our worlds; the humanists would say we have forsaken our senses of selfhood and the grandeur of being truly human. We have little time or space for philosophizing in this book. Somehow, a way must be found to reverse directions, and a place must be identified as a logical one for a concerted effort at beginning a reversal of trends. We do have time to look at bottom-line starting points where degradation sets in, causing societal breakdowns. In this chapter we will focus on the American family as a wellspring from which much of what is good might flow. In many cases to say the least, we are forced to view the conditions of the family as a debacle from which all sorts of evil influence flows.

What Every Child Deserves From His Family

With an eye on the story of Ginger given in Happening Five, we can ask the question: What does a child deserve from his family? The word "deserves" is important because, truth to tell, parents bring to families their own backgrounds where they themselves were victims of a debauched society. It would not be logical to caption this section "What Every Child Can Expect From His Family." We must start with things as they are and move toward things that "ought" to be. Still, as an exercise in what may come to be possible, let us list the things a child logically deserves from his family.

The Naive Intruder

Children come into the world with an inherent although unformed (at birth) free will. But they did not will to be born. Arguably, a child has a right to expect a family with dedicated parents. This author is indebted to John Bradshaw (1) who provides insights leading to the following statements concerning parents. Every child deserves parents:

1. Who are willing, able and eager to supply his physical needs

2. Who will be there for him

3. Who will see him as the purpose of having a family in the first place

4. Who will be not only dependable but also predictably dependable

5. Who will allow him to be different and unique, willing for him to fulfill his uniqueness in ways that do not infringe on the reasonable rights of others, including the parents themselves

143

6.   Who will allow him to grow emotionally as well as physically – this means allowing him, within reasonable limits, to experience and express anger, grief, sadness and especially joy

7.   Who will give him encouragement in developing his personal identity

8.   Who will help him develop a sense of belonging by touching him, having affection for him and cherishing him, thus welcoming him into the human race with warmth and caring

9.   Who will affirm his right to be an individual and to grow toward eventual independent status

10. Who will allow him personal space for private moments, will help him become a functioning social creature

11. Who will provide role models for healthy growth potential.

The Case of Ginger

Let us look back to the case of Ginger in Happening Five. She was unwanted in the first place. She was shifted off into a family (her grandparents' home) that offered some need fulfillment, but she became a pawn between Alma and Big Joe, her grandparents. Alma was a pseudo-mother who did not really care, a mother who had already produced a daughter who was unable to function normally. Big Joe, in all his purported kindliness, took on Ginger as a wife substitute using her to gain the companionship he could never get from his wife Alma. Alma, for her part, rejected Ginger immediately upon his death because she secretly hated her.

In her third family group (her mother and her stepfather's home), Ginger was an unwelcome intruder. The only need Ginger had which was met were the needs money can buy. She was not encouraged or even allowed to seek and to find her own identity. She became a world outcast who, in spite of the comforts of the family money, developed no sense of self-worth, no sense of belonging, no concept of loyalty and no reason for living. It was impossible for Ginger to grow into a normal, secure and well-adjusted person under these rigorous circumstances.

A Frustrated Child Seeks Solace in Drugs

A child who has all the things he deserves is still under peer pressure to use drugs, because he is among cohorts who do not have the advantages he has. The American family system has decayed to the point that a majority of any child's peers are sure to urge any other child to join them in their disenchantments.

Drugs are everywhere. Their very presence is a function of decayed societal infrastructure. And since drugs are everywhere, the children who lack the kind of selfhood gained only in a loving family atmosphere will likely succumb to drugs. They must succumb because they desperately need the release from their cruel personal worlds that drugs seem to provide. Peer pressure wins because the child has already become a victim of an insane society.

As far as our fight against drugs is concerned, we can point convincingly at peer pressure and declare that peer pressure must be reversed — that peer pressure must turn around and exert pressure against drugs rather than for them. Indeed, significant strides are being made in effecting this reversal in some sectors. These issues are succinctly reviewed in Chapter Six. We can have and we are having schools without drugs.

But we must ask a deeper question: Why has peer pressure among the young been toward the use of life-destroying drugs in the first place? This is a sobering question and the broadest, most comprehensive answer is to say that society is at fault. While that is unquestionably true, it doesn't

145

give us much of a handle for attack. We must attack the specifics of a society, which in a global sense, ultimately is to blame for any debacle which is either allowed or encouraged. We shall devote this chapter to a look at the American family, hopefully providing information and insights into how the family is contributing to the drug problem and how the problems in American families may be alleviated. We must reveal the facts about the decaying family life in America.

The Dysfunctional Family

There is a sentiment sweeping across the nation that the family is in trouble and that these troubles are spawning dysfunction in which one or more family members become scapegoats upon whom are heaped the garbage of the dysfunction. Many factors enter into the change in family structure: two-income households, moral decay, divorce, infidelity and poor parenting. Many books have been written on the history of the changing and decaying family structure in America, but we shall not give a full analysis of that phenomenon here. We will look more to the results of the dysfunctional family and less to its historical or current origins and dynamics.

Are Family Members Who Become Drug Abusers At Fault?

Several recent books have carried messages to victims of family abuse and dysfunction; and basically, the message to these, including those who have capitulated to drugs, has been, "It is not your fault; you are the victim of a family system gone mad." These insights are probably correct. But those of us who earnestly seek solutions in addition to insights must respond, "Granting that young persons have been victimized by a faulty family system which forced them directly or indirectly into drug use, is it wise to have them believe that they are not at fault?"

This author does not believe it is wise to comfort those with drug problems with the assurance that they are not to blame. Whether it is inevitably true or false is not as important as creating a climate in which the person feels that he must develop and maintain motivation deep within himself to win his personal war. Any message of "no blame" is likely to work at cross purposes to treatment, which must result in autonomy that

146

the abuser earns for himself. Even if the drug abuser is a child of eight, he will not always be a child of eight, and he must move toward maturity and self-determination that will stay with him for a lifetime. Taking away his sense of blame is not likely to help.

While it seems unproductive to play that tape, "You are not to blame," to the abuser; as treatment specialists, we must know that the blame does lie, in large part, in the dysfunctional family, and we must make efforts to support self-direction in the abuser by helping to remove the stresses which resulted in drug abuse and by helping to remove the obstacles to growth. With all this in mind, we can move on in our discussion of the dynamics of the dysfunctional family that could be central in pushing individuals toward drug abuse. Any member of a family may be pressured by the faulty family system, first toward relief from stresses through drug use and then, as stresses continue, to addiction.

Parental Injunctions

Parents have families and are themselves often products of dysfunctional families. There really is no place where it can be said, "The buck stops here." The only place the buck can stop is with the abuser who can and must say, "Regardless of circumstances and no matter what caused the situation, I am going to get under my own load." However, as helpers, we must realize that: 1) Caretakers must act on behalf of children and minors because, regardless of rhetoric, they cannot autonomously get under their loads. (Caretakers and counselors must realize that minors will be unable to get under their own loads until the addiction can be brought under control.) 2) No one who abuses drugs at any age can get under their own load without first receiving help in the form of medicine and counseling to break the shackles of addiction, thereby making autonomy possible.

Parents, who create a family by first entering a relationship and then having children, comprise a subculture which makes the rules and regulations for the family. The cultural backgrounds from which these parents have come will affect these rules and regulations. Through living in a family unit, a person is subjected to verbal, conscious, nonverbal and unconscious beliefs, attitudes and rules to which he falls heir and sometimes falls victim.

In the language of transactional analysis, the child is subjected to parental injunctions. Injunctions are commands, usually nonverbal, which give messages to growing children within a subculture. Examples of such messages are: Don't be a child. Don't be successful. Don't be independent. Don't be as smart as I am.

Parents themselves, even those having the best intentions, command out of their own insecurities that their children live by their rules — rules which often create chaos. These injunctions are, for the most part, issued so that parents may be protected within their own neurotic-need systems. For instance, a parent who is physically unattractive is threatened by a beautiful child. Parents who see themselves as lacking in intelligence are threatened when their child seems more intelligent than they. Parents who are poor social mixers are threatened if their child seems likely to become more personable that they. It may be difficult to imagine these things; and indeed, there are happy exceptions wherein a parent who feels himself to be substandard can still unselfishly wish his child to be gifted. Parents usually can wish the best for their children in some areas of endeavor, but each parent likely has his own vulnerable areas wherein he cannot respond appropriately to the needs of a growing child. Such a parent is not willfully being mean or cruel. We can hope, however, that such parents can come to see their errors and correct them.

Henry was an unwanted child. Of course, his parents never told him that. However, when they wish to go on vacation they confide to each other sadly, "We just can't go. Henry has asthma and he would probably have one attack after another in the mountains." Somehow, they manage to say this where Henry can hear it. Henry gets the message that he is a bother and is unwanted. It seems unavoidable that if a child is unwanted, the parents will get the message to him — often with open anger rather than subtlety.

Competition in the Family

One of the more destructive areas of relating between child and parent is competition. Because of problems of conflict deriving from their own upbringings, many parents feel compelled to be a chief competitor with children who, to say the least, are playing on an uneven field.

It was Chuck Martin's first year as a little league baseball coach. His son Ned was first-string pitcher, and Chuck wanted Ned to be great. They lost their first two games, and it seemed like these twelve-year-olds just couldn't hit the ball. The opposing pitchers had been way ahead of his batters who struck out one after the other. So, Chuck took the bat and proceeded to administer two very resounding lessons to his team, one on how not to pitch and one on how to hit. "Throw your best pitch, Ned," he yelled. Ned did and Chuck hit the ball over the fence. "Throw another," he yelled, "and you guys watch how I get the bat on the ball." Another ball over the fence!

Chuck was really having a good time with the third and fourth over-the-fence hits. Ned felt like crawling in a hole, and the other "hitters" got worse than ever in the following game.

Thus, a parent who is under the goad of succeeding in physical strength will actually compete with a child. The father feels elevated when he can knock the ball further than his twelve-year-old son or when he can lift heavier weights. Rather than allowing the child to win, the father must win in order to be elevated in his own eyes. The child quickly identifies himself as a second-class citizen in such a family, and self-esteem is really bludgeoned.

Success Identity or Failure Identity

A child's emotional tone with his world is developed early. The Freudians speak of oral optimism versus oral pessimism. The child who is held closely and lovingly and who is kept comfortable (dry) and well-fed will see the world as a beautiful, bountiful place. He likely will develop what Glasser refers to as a "success identity."(3)

By contrast, the child who receives little tactile stimulation, hears no loving words and is hungry and wet much of the time sees the world as a harsh, forbidding place. He is likely to develop a "failure identity."

Many children, because of neglect or abuse, develop the feeling that, "I'll never amount to anything; I'm not worth anybody's time or effort." Self-esteem plummets as the child devalues himself. And why would he do that? He does so simply because he hears the demeaning words from caretakers or feels the demeaning neglect.

Yes, success breeds success, and caretakers can make or break the child, can shape a life-long personality component, by praising instead of scolding. Children need to succeed. They ought not to be pawns in an adult's struggle to build his own ego. Obviously, "success identity" spells high self-esteem.

Healthy and Unhealthy Reasons for Wanting a Child

Most opposite-sexed persons who develop a lasting and intimate relationship want children. Why? Having a child who is a part of oneself is the ultimate fulfillment, every person's lease on immortality. To be sure, there are other reasons for desiring a child, some healthy, some unhealthy. It is safe to say that parents typically want their children to be extensions of themselves — there is nothing unhealthy about that on the face of it.

However, when either parent develops the motive in child-rearing to have a child in order to make himself happy and has little or no thought of the child's happiness, there is likely to be dysfunction. A child should make parents happy, but the total existence of the child should not be to fulfill a happiness goal. When this is the case, the child's entire existence is saturated with parental demands that he bring happiness to them. If he doesn't, he is a failure. "Failure identity" happens often to children whose parents divorce — the child feels he should have made them happy, but he failed at his assigned job, to bring about the happiness of one or both parents.

Parents' Happiness Should Not Be a First Priority.

Parents must give the child a right to be an individual. Parents must wish this child to be fulfilled in all the ways which coincide with that child's individuality. In many cases, this makes for at least temporary unhappiness in the parents. Parents have no right to prioritize their own happiness over that of the child.

Children have little or no understanding of why they came into the world. Parents must not allow a child to feel that they are the only ones who have rights and privileges. The child must be made to feel that his feelings count. Few feelings are more demeaning, more self-esteem-robbing than for a child to feel that his total existence is for the benefit of someone else.

The Child Has a Right to His Own Priorities

As a child grows, he develops his own priorities, and he should feel no stress if these do not coincides with his parents' ideals. The message some children receive from parents is: "We had you in order that we could be happy; you are not making us happy, therefore you are a failure."

Such a climate develops dysfunctions which may take many forms. Being at times rebellious, the child may major in making his parents unhappy. The game is then played out by the rebellious youngster: "The more unhappy you are, the happier I am." There is dynamite in a relationship of this type, and using drugs can be an expression of the rancor the child feels when he realizes his parents never intended him to have autonomy.

The Late-Appearing Child, A Special Challenge

When a child comes along late, say he is ten years younger than his next-in-line sibling, parents should recognize that careful handling is in order. There are likely to be child/parent and child/sibling generational differences which can cause dysfunction. If the parents favor the late child because they very much wanted him, then there is likely to be sibling rivalry even with older children some of whom may have left the immediate environs. The natural order of things is for the older children to be jealous of this child although, or course, this is not a necessary dynamic.

The child whose parents are somewhat older than those of his peers is likely to compare his parents with peer parents. The generational gap in terms of speech patterns, of dress and grooming codes, of music preferences and other ad infinitum has the power to create disharmony between parents and child. This disharmony often becomes exacerbated by the condemning attitudes of older siblings. It is easy for chasms to build between late-appearing children and parents, and this animosity may result in warfare that develops into mutual-exchanged, aggravating behavior. Using drugs is often one of these acting-out avenues for such children.

If the child was truly unwanted, the likelihood of a lack of harmony is greatly increased. In a time when peer pressure is great, chasms of any kind between child and parents should be carefully monitored, and parents must take the responsibility for keeping the avenues of true caring open. The clear expression of this caring relationship should be constant and consistent.

Feelings of Abject Dependency Must Be Disallowed

The child is truly dependent on his parents. Must he know and feel that? Absolutely not! It is possible that the child may feel himself to be a treasure and that his parents would remain unfulfilled without him. The child is not likely to feel his parents are dependent upon him, but it can work this way. Some children are allowed to manipulate parents by withholding their love and making their parents miserable. This cannot be allowed either. Parents walk a very fine line, indeed. Children have the power to destroy them, and the drug scene is a graphic example of parents pulled apart by a child who has become aware of his powers. Thus, parents should never allow the child to get a reward for hurting them.

Parents Have Unhealthy Needs

The trouble is that many parents have unhealthy needs to be hurt. Some have been hurt by their parents, and strangely, they both want and expect hurt from their children. Children will try to exploit parents, and once they get reinforcement for that, a lifetime may be lived out with an exchange of hurts taking place. And neither parents nor children really understand the games they are playing. As transactional analysis theory points out, a parent sometimes regresses to the child-ego state, and the child sometimes plays the ego role of parents. Each should play appropriate roles. In healthy families, adults often let the little child within them out to play, and the children understand and appreciate that. Role reversals work both ways and may provide a measure of fun for all when understood. But all must know that these are fun games, and role reversal cannot be allowed as a long-term anomaly, which creates hurtful confusion. Parents are the ones who should know when playing reversed roles are good or bad.

Tom liked to tease Joey, and most of the time, Joey really enjoyed being teased. Tom decided to play a role reversal, and as Joey sat in Susan's lap, Tom said teasingly, "You are stealing my woman, you rascal." A mock tug of war ensued in which Tom tried to pull Joey out of his mother's lap, and Susan pretended to fight Tom off. This is a very tricky game and certainly should not be overplayed. A little such role reversal is fun, but these are treacherous grounds. Joey prizes his mother and could easily be hurt permanently in his relationship to his dad if this game goes too far. The game is fun only so long as Joey clearly wants it to be.

Breaking Family Rules — Guilt Trips

Family loyalties and rules pertaining thereto can be very important to a child. With adolescents, however, these seemingly hide-bound rules can become burdensome. If the family always has formal dinner at seven, one of the teenagers may wish to be elsewhere. Some parents are sticklers for loyalty to rules beyond reason. If they absolutely hold firm to the rules, they will create resentment because, as children grow older, their lives often need to be free from such rules. Parents often allow such rules as these to be broken and then heap guilt upon the one who has broken the golden chord. Many parents are experts at creating guilt trips.

Cindy, who was nineteen and in a university, had a chance to go to her roommate's home in Hawaii for Christmas. What a wonderful trip it would be! But Cindy's family rule was that the family was always together on Christmas. Cindy broke this rule and had a horrible time, because her mother made it very clear that what she was doing was an abominable thing. "It's going to destroy Christmas for the whole family," her mother declared.

Parents who exercise such strict control, when there is no logical reason for it, create resentments that destroy the proper function of the parent when the teenager (or even adult child) really needs to use that relationship to settle a critical issue. Some parents manage to cripple their children in such ways that the effects last well into adulthood. Many of us are still controlled by voices from the grave.

Abusive Parents

Physical abuse of children is terrible; sexual abuse is reprehensible. Yet, many adolescents run away from home because of outright abuse. In order to make their way, they may become drug pushers and prostitutes. Even so, verbal abuse and emotional abuse may be even worse. The American family is coming under close scrutiny *vis à vis* the effects dysfunctional families are having on drug abuse.

Family Therapy

If a person who is a member of a dysfunctional family should read the preceding pages, it is possible that he could find himself within some of these roles whether he be parent, minor child or adult child. On the other hand, it is difficult to see oneself clearly within a family constellation when you are actually in it. One is likely to avoid reality, to deny his culpability and to cast blame visualizing self-fault. We are all inclined to fight for self-esteem rather than for favorable self-impressions.

Dysfunctional families can proceed for decades, even to family dissolution, without family members clearly discussing the dynamics of the family, the games that have gone on for years and years.(4) For these reasons, family therapy has evolved as a treatment modality.

Family therapy is an attempt to bring the members of the family together physically. Members sit down together with one or more therapists in their midst, and the family dynamics are reviewed. The occasion for this usually arises when a family member or members have become so severely affected by the family's inner dynamics that they experience emotional breakdowns, addictions or get in trouble with the law. Family members may develop an inability to function on the job, in marriage relationships or as persons within themselves.

There is usually one central patient within a family therapy effort. However, every family member usually has complicity in the faulty dynamics which have spawned the presenting problem. No family member is likely to be blameless, and no family member is likely to be free from the stresses which, at this juncture, are affecting one family member more so than others.

Hopefully, all family members may be coerced to join the therapeutic group, but often key members refuse to have any involvement. In such cases, ways must be found to bridge the gap caused by the missing member. Often one of the therapists attempts to sit in for and role play the missing member.

Family therapy is an invaluable tool in treating family dysfunction in general and focusing on the presenting problem(s) such as drug abuse in particular. These groups, obviously, can become vituperative, harsh, explosive and badgering. Therapists must be skilled in keeping discussions within limits and in guiding the clamor toward insights on the part of every member. Family members who thus have become drug addicted, lawbreaking, neurotic-psychotic or deeply troubled can often gain restorative insights which must then, for best results, be further dealt with in one-on-one therapy.

Research in Family Therapy

Family therapy has received strong research input. Murphy (6) explores the unconscious and maladaptive roles family members assume in a dysfunctional family. Such roles are that of the enabler, a person who unwittingly encourages the family to be dysfunctional in order to satisfy neurotic needs of blaming others. Another role is that of family hero who surpasses all the others in gaining honors — academic, athletic or otherwise. This role causes other family members pain by calling attention to their own shortcomings and often promotes jealousy. The scapegoat role is one in which a single family member is singled out as the one responsible for all the family's problems. The scapegoat often seeks relief through drug use and abuse. The lost child role is one in which a specific child is virtually disowned by other family members (a lonely role). The family clown gains an identity as tension-reliever and plays this role at considerable loss to himself because he is unable to express his true feelings. He may feel he must keep up the good cheer no matter how he really feels.

Kymissis (5) presents a systems theory of the dysfunctional family. He sees the family as a system of interacting roles and believes the most beneficial aspect of family therapy is for each family member to become aware of his specific contribution to family dysfunction.

Weitzman (8) encourages the family therapist to dispense specific information about drug abuse to the family. He gives careful consideration to the specifics of female drug abuse and the underlying dynamics typical of female substance abusers.

Barbara Wallace (7) enunciates a developmental treatment model utilizing group and family therapy to bring to the surface the specific reasons family members use and abuse crack cocaine. This treatment model suggest specialized crack residences within inpatient detoxification units and further emphasizes the importance of post-detoxification treatment.

Sue Evans (2) shows how chemical abuse arises out of a sense of shame felt by the addict, as such shame is imposed by other family members. She discusses family systems theory as it relates to the fear of intimacy abandonment and boundary ambiguity. A shame recovery model is offered which emphasizes relationship, recognition, stopping inner abuse and affirming the self.

Bibliography

1   Bradshaw, John. Bradshaw On: The Family. Health
     Communications, Inc. Deerfield Beach, Florida. 1988.

2   Evans, Sue. "Shame, Boundaries and Dissociation in Chemically
     Dependent, Abusive and Incestuous Families." Alcoholism Treatment
     Quarterly. Summer Vol. 4 (2). 1987, pp. 157-179.

3   Glasser, William M.D. Reality Therapy: A New Approach to
     Psychiatry. Harper & Row, Publishers. New York, 1965.

4   Kaufman, Edward. "Critical Issues in Family Research in Drug Use."
     Journal of Drug Issues. Fall Vol. 15 (4). 1985, pp. 463-475.

5   Kymissis, Pavlos. "An Integrative Approach to Family Therapy."
     American Journal of Social Psychiatry. Winter Vol. 4 (1). 1984, pp.
     47-52.

6   Murphy, John. "Substance Abuse and the Family." Journal For
     Specialists in Group Work. Vol. 9 (2). May 1984, pp. 106-112.

7   Wallace, Barbara. "Cocaine Dependence Treatment on an Inpatient
     Detoxification Unit." Journal of Substance Abuse Treatment. Vol. 4
     (2) 1987, pp. 85-92.

8   Weitzman, Jack. "Engaging the Severely Dysfunctional Family in
     Treatment." Family Process. Vol. 24(4). December 1985, pp. 473-
     485.

Chapter 6

Drug Free Schools: Possible But Difficult

Happening Six — Mark, the Narc

The Facts As We Best Know Them

Schools Now Have the Tools for Drug Control
Drugs of Choice Among Students
Closed or Semi-closed Campuses
Peer Counseling
The DARE Program

Happening Six — Mark, the Narc

He had noticed her first in English class. She dressed like the "creamos," but she had more to say to the "have-nots." "Real class," he thought; "but why don't the other 'creamos' even notice her?" He'd found out that her name was Wendy. He would have picked that name for her. He found he couldn't keep his eyes off her. Pretty enough, sure; but it was more than that — the way she tossed her hair, her moves. "She's a lot of woman," he thought. Looking around, he noticed the other guys were not seeing what he was seeing, feeling what he was feeling. "Okay, by me," he thought, "to each his own."

Mark came to Will Rogers High only two weeks ago at the beginning of the spring semester. Mark knew what he was and who he was. The DEA had found a pretty nice little house for his mother and his two little sisters. Mom had had it rough, he knew that. His own father had been killed in a construction accident when he was four. Mom had remarried, had the two babies by that son-of-a-bitch, had taken his abuse and beatings while he Mark had listened; and then, she had slipped a kitchen knife into the bastard's gut while he had her bent over the kitchen counter. She'd been no-billed by the grand jury, of course.

But they were a proud family. Mom's father was a prominent dentist, and her mother was a lovely lady who moved with the country club set in Houston. Mark knew that Mom and he had done the right thing to move, to put hundreds of miles between the old life and the new one. The Drug Enforcement Administration had arranged most of it. Mom was now a receptionist-secretary at the agency office here in St. Louis, and Mark knew he had his own work to do. It wasn't a permanent arrangement, he knew that — a year or two at the most.

They had trained him well in Houston. After he'd dropped out of high school following the "incident," Lieutenant Scruggs, the director of the Houson DEA Unit, had spotted him at the juvenile center. How did the assistant special agent know he was different? Maybe it was kind of like how he knew Wendy was different. Anyway, the lieutenant had taken him under his wing. After all, he hadn't committed any crime; he had just been picked up with the crowd he was doing pot with at the skating rink. Sure, there were pushers in the half dozen they had picked up, but he wasn't one — just a school dropout trying to make it, trying to keep from being bored to death while Mom was waiting for the grand jury to get it together.

Mom had really screamed about it. "Absolutely not," she had yelled. "You are not going to be a narc. This family doesn't stoop so low as to get in the gutter. We've got our pride, and we'll make it one way or another; and we'll do it without any hand-outs from Jenny and Pops, either." Mom had always called her own mother by her first name.

But it had been rougher than Mom could have imagined. She had been no-billed by the grand jury. However, the people who hired secretaries and the people with Jenny and Pops at the church and at the country club hadn't no-billed her.

Mark had taken a job at McDonald's, in spite of Mom's demands that he go back to school. He was heading down the dirt road and knew it. The crowds he ran with got rougher and rougher. The ASAC had told him, "Mark, I know a good kid when I see one; but if you keep running with that bunch, in six months, you are going to be pushing pot and rock, maybe meth and ice. Let's make a deal. Work with us at the DEA, and we'll train you to get into a high school where you are not known. You can go undercover for us. Good money, Mark — not like you can make pushing. But think of your little sisters and your mom! You can switch sides right now in this war, but in a few more weeks, you'll be forever on the wrong side. It is not a pretty picture where you're heading, Mark. It's nothing but trouble, and you know it. Let me talk to your mom, Mark. I've followed her case; she's had it rotten up to now. Your family is going to need help. We'll move your family to St. Louis, Mark, and you'll get a check every month. But it's not gratis. You've got to deliver for us."

So, the ASAC talked to Mom. And she screamed "No!" at him, too. But as things became rougher, and it seemed that they'd have no choice but to move in with Jenny and Pops, she came around little by little.

Mark realized he hadn't heard a word the English teacher had said when the bell rang. He kind of hung back while others filed out, hoping to catch Wendy's eyes. And he did — a lot more than that! Wendy marched right up to him, her dark eyes flashing, and he thought he'd lose his breath. "You're kind of new around here, aren't you, Mark?" Gee, she even knew his name.

"Yeah," he finally got it out. "New and green."

"Well, we won't let you stay green long," she said. It was amazing. Here Wendy was making like a spokesperson for the whole school. And he knew that absolutely no one else, kids or teachers, gave a damn about him one way or another.

"Hey, man," he told himself, "you're not the shy guy. The chick is coming on to you. Make your move, man."

And he did. Twenty minutes after school, they had their heads together over burgers and shakes at McDonald's. He'd wanted to look the golden arches over, thinking he'd use his experience at Houston to make a few bucks here in St. Louis.

That all happened on Wednesday. They had their first real date Friday night. It was better than he could have hoped. Wendy was downright intoxicating. After that first date, he carried her around with him in his head day and night. Her perfume never left him, even when he was cutting onions at McDonald's. Willie Nelson was an old coot, but he had it right, "You're always on my mind."

Mark fantasized everything with Wendy. He'd deck the guy that tried to muscle in. He was her champion; he had glorious sex with her every chance he got. She was his and his only. "I've never been in love before," he thought.

The sex? Fantasies were great, but nothing like the real thing! Wendy had played him like a musical instrument. Not too much gusto at first. "Not so fast, fella," she had said. But she knew where she'd wanted to go with it all along. She knew how to make a guy feel like a raunchy tiger. "Boy," he thought, "has she ever got her hooks in deep." Sex and love or love and sex — which came first — it really didn't matter to either of them. Man, this was living! He wished he'd never have to think about the DEA again. But Mark had been contacted by a member of the Drug Enforcement Administration even before he and Wendy had made their heart-felt commitments to each other. He'd met with the special agent in charge last night. They had set up the sting for April. Mark was getting his checks regularly, just as the Houston ASAC had promised.

Already, he had done pot with about six guys — the usual places, rest rooms, behind the band hall, backstage in the auditorium but mostly outside where the smell wouldn't be detected. Will Rogers had it all just like in Houston. In Houston he had learned how to drag on the joint enough to make the tip without inhaling. He'd been briefed real good. "You'll have a drug test going in, Mark, and when you are on the stand after the sting, we'll have to give you another test. You've got to be clean, Mark. The defense attorneys will crucify us if they can prove that you, the informant, are nothing but another freak, junky or boozer." It wasn't that hard to do — to keep it out of his lungs. It was really tough when he and Wendy were sharing a joint because he really wanted to get high. She was having greater sex than he was, and that was tough. But he managed.

Funny. All the sex education classes had said booze and pot, even cocaine was a turn-off for making it with a girl. Baloney! Booze had never turned him on that much! But pot really opened the heavens wide for him; and he knew that it did for Wendy, too. But everybody was different when it came to what any of it, either uppers or downers, would do to a person. There are as many responses to any drug as there are people who take them. They'd impressed that on him at Houston.

But it wasn't pot the cops and the DEA were so uptight about. Cocaine was the target, especially crack or rock. Ever since some wise guy had learned to mix powdered coke with baking soda, cooked it off, and then broke what looked like peanut brittle without the peanuts into chunks or rocks, it had been a new day in the drug rackets.

Mark had been told at Houston that the pot they were now getting was probably ten times as powerful as what the kids had had in the sixties, and he'd been told that creating rock was the absolute worst thing that could have happened. With the little straight copper tubing they called pipes, you could stuff in a little steel wool leaving just enough room at one end to push in a rock or several little ones. When you put the other end in your mouth, applied match or lighter to the rock and sucked that smoke into your lungs, you would get an instant high. It would take a poet to describe the feeling.

This was what they'd told him in Houston. They'd called it "the rush." Stupid guys! They hadn't thought he already knew about rock. Or did they? No matter. Mark knew he'd been lucky. He wasn't one of those whose body chemistry hooks in with the cocaine to create an instant addict or to send a person straight to the hospital with a heart attack or a seizure. He'd known a few kids in Houston who had gone through those kinds of things.

He'd just let his teachers in the DEA at Houston tell him the things he already knew far better than they did — some of them were probably as straight as sticks. But one thing they didn't seem to understand was that you might more or less target rock for a sting, but pot was really the up-front culprit. Mark had never known a kid do rock without getting into it through pot. Oh, he'd told the DEA guys this both in Houston and St. Louis, and they'd at least pretended to understand.

So, after the DEA guys had contacted him and had assigned him to Assistant Special Agent Vicha, Mark turned on all his radar. Up to now, he had only done pot with a bunch of the guys with one or two toughie girls in some of the groups. So far, he hadn't been able to identify the pushers at any level; but he knew they were there, and he was dead ready for the primo. Good thing he had gotten a little into rock, otherwise he wouldn't be able to recognize the primos. These guys at DEA just had to know he was pretty street-wise. He hoped they weren't stupid enough to think he didn't recognize cocaine when it hit his lungs.

He'd never forget the day or the date — the day because of what happened, the date because agent Vicha had insisted that he keep a daily record of what he had seen, complete with names and everything. March 15th! Talk about your day of infamy. Well, even that wasn't a strong enough word. After the last class, he was moving across campus when Fred, one of his pot smoking buddies, stepped out from the corner of the band hall and beckoned. "Not today, Fred, I need to get to McDonald's," he thought; but he knew he'd do well not to create any doubts. He was getting well-known and accepted at Will Rogers, so he went and turned the corner behind the band hall.

As he approached the bunch of four or five, he recognized all the guys; then his mind stood still. He knew he couldn't cover his surprise, but he knew he must. There stood Wendy. "My God," he muttered under his breath. "Not that, please, not that." Why should he be so surprised was a thought that forced its way into his head and probably kept him from coming unglued.

"Hi, Wendy," he said simply as if this were an everyday occasion. But with that, another thought forced itself into his mind. "Every bastard here knows about Wendy and me." It just didn't make sense. Not then, not at once, but soon it became clear.

The joint was in Wendy's hand, and she smiled as she passed it. "You're next, Mark." So he took it and made his drag. His brain exploded. He had been trained in the techniques how to avoid getting pot or anything else into his lungs, but he wasn't prepared for this. As a result, his breath caught in his throat, causing a gag reflex for some reason. He fought mightily for control, and at first, he thought he'd covered okay. Mark knew what was happening because he'd had it before and had been expecting it any time. Still, it was a jolt!

"God! This is the primo. There is rock in this joint," he thought, and Wendy had passed it to him!

"Strong stuff," he muttered aloud as he passed the joint along. He looked all around into eyes that had changed, and he knew what was in their heads. They all knew it was primo. Wendy knew it was primo. Every guy and gal there knew it was primo, and they knew that he knew. That put suspicion into all those eyes. Only a real steady user, maybe only a narc, would recognize the difference.

But while that very sobering thought shot through his brain, Mark's strongest emotion centered on Wendy. He couldn't believe it! Wendy on rock! "No! No!" his inner voice screamed. And then it hit him. "She's sprung," his inner voice told him tauntingly. "Your true love — the love of your life — is sprung, and you are the world's biggest, most gullible fool." Now, he knew why the kids in English class, at least the straight ones, wouldn't even look at her. How stupid could you get?

They had already made a date for the evening. Mark dreaded it but knew he had to keep it. The moment they were alone in the car, she turned to him and made everything that had happened on March 15th so far seem like nothing, "Mark, honey, you're a narc!"

"What a curious contraption the human brain is," Mark's mind flickered. She's making poetry, "Mark is a narc." But then, he knew it was just a defense his brain had used to give him just enough time to grasp the horrible implications of what she'd just said.

He pulled over to the curb and looked deeply into those dark eyes. What was he expecting to see? Anger, hurt, disappointment, confusion? What he saw was a strange combination of sadness and caring. "She really cares about me," he thought. He was surprised at his own thoughts; he was really mixed up for a moment.

"And you, my darling — you're a pusher! You don't care how many kids get ground to death under the rock you're selling."

Wendy caught a gasping breath, tears running down those silky cheeks he had loved to caress. "Oh, Mark, you don't understand," she stammered.

"Try me."

And she did, but he wasn't buying, at least not at first. Not all of it, at best. He knew how the truth got twisted in the minds of users. "My mother is a hopeless alcoholic. She can't work. She's divorced, and I have a little brother and sister to take care of, Mark."

166

"And I suppose that takes a thousand a week, or is it two thousand, Wendy?"

"Oh, Mark, what can I say? I love you, Mark. Consider coming on in and pushing with the rest of us, sweetheart. We'll make it big, then get out, get married and raise a family."

"No can do, kiddo. I'm committed to the DEA. I'll have to break it right now — the sting was coming in about a month. I don't have many names but...."

"You have mine, Mark."

"Yes."

"Would you ...?"

"No choice, Wendy."

"Mark, I'm so afraid for you. I'm not the only one who caught on. I haven't talked to any of them yet, but believe me, several of them knew at the same time I knew. Mark, please get out of this for your family's sake; for your own sake and, believe me, Mark, for my sake. You don't understand. There are two small gangs in St. Louis; some kids are no more than twelve years old. They're all connected to the dope men. And those kids are tough — they carry guns and knives, Mark. There have been four murders in the last two months. The police aren't onto the gangs yet. Mark, you are in great danger!"

"And so are you, Wendy. You can't afford to be seen with me. Get out of the car and walk away. Do it, damn it, before I start blubbering. I love you, Wendy. Go!" And she did.

****

Mark was found dead later that night in the parking lot of an Eastside bar.

The Facts As We Best Know Them

In the public eye, schools are hotbeds of drug use and general decay of moral values, especially inner city schools. Is this assessment correct? Yes and no. Sadly, there are schools where drug use is rampant, where nonstudent as well as student pushers do vigorous business, where the lives of all students are in danger and the profession of teaching has become nightmarish. On the other hand, all kids are not bad, and some schools have firm control of the drug situation. The following is from "Growing Up Drug Free: A Parent's Guide to Prevention":

Despite the grim stories that fill our newspapers and dominate the evening news, most young people do not use illicit drugs, they do not approve of drug use by their friends, and they share their parents' concern about the dangers posed by drugs.

Successful prevention efforts, whether in a family, school, or community setting, have many elements in common: a concern for the welfare and well-being of young people, dedicated adults who are willing to devote their time and energy, and an unwavering commitment to being drug free.

That commitment led a small group of parents in Bowling Green, Kentucky, to form Bowling Green Parents for Drug-Free Youth. The organization has worked closely with the local schools and community to provide training and education for all members of the community, and it has raised more than $35,000 to help finance its efforts. Questionnaires administered to students in grades 7-12 for 6 consecutive years have shown a steady decline in the use of alcohol and other drugs.(2, p. 27)

Schools Now Have the Tools for Drug Control

Certainly, many communities are gaining control over drug abuse in schools. The nation's schools very well may be the battleground of greatest effectiveness in America's war against drugs. Why?

Peer Pressure Must Be Reversed

Peer pressure is undeniably among the chief motivators for youngsters to enter the chemical world. It is not naive to say, "If we can create a reversal making peer pressure our chief ally instead of our chief enemy, we will have won a major battle."

Youngsters do not spend all or even a major portion of their time in school; but when one considers the outreach factors of school relationships, it turns out that schools and school-related activities comprise a major portion of the time factor for adolescents' waking hours, at least while school is in session. Consider the six to seven hour school day, the extracurricular activities and sports. Consider the friendships made at school and the hours of telephone time spent by students talking to each other. Consider private parties that are actually focused around relationship clusters originating in school. Next to the home, school is the most important center of life for the six to seventeen year group.

Cooperation is the Watchword

The major effort the schools make in controlling drugs is to make drug use unpopular. Making drug use unpopular and unproductive for students takes many forms. "Get tough" policies which encompass the campuses themselves, school properties and the "immediate surround" of school properties have had dramatic effects on drug use.

There is a growing liaison among school boards, school personnel and local law enforcement. The trend is that school boards sanction "getting tough" at school so far as drugs are concerned. They get laws passed that make enforcement by school personnel possible. Then, they refuse to crumble under pressures of irate parents who exert negative pressure on "get tough" school policies.

Local law enforcement is cooperating much more fully with schools which have "get tough" policies. Where schools

169

are lax on drugs, law enforcement personnel are likely to feel powerless. Now, they can operate in school environs with new authority — the federal government has passed laws which make search procedures legal on school properties. State laws make it possible for law enforcement personnel to make searches for drugs almost anywhere and certainly on campus. School personnel such as principals, vice principals and security guards are being fully supported in some schools on a "get tough" regimen. Principals are being given authority to suspend and expel students. A very valuable addendum to the school's armament against drugs has become the police officer whose assignment is confined sometimes to a single large school and immediate environs. Sometimes, the police officer serves several smaller schools and environments. These officers, of course, can enforce any law either on or off campuses. School boards cooperate with local police even to the point of paying all or part of the salaries for these arms of the law.

"Get Tough" Policies Are Winning

That the "get tough" policies of schools aided and abetted by the DEA, and local law enforcement officers are working are easily discernible and easily documented. According to a Department of Education handbook "Schools Without Drugs":(5, p. 22)

Eastside High School (Patterson, New Jersey) is located in an inner-city neighborhood and enrolls 3200 students. Before 1982, drug dealing was rampant. Intruders had easy access to the school and sold drugs on the school premises. Drugs were used in school stairwells and bathrooms. Gangs armed with razors and knives roamed the hallways.

A new principal, Joe Clark, was instrumental in ridding the school of drugs and violence. Hired in 1982, Clark established order, enlisted the help of police officers in drug prevention education, and raised academic standards. Among the actions he took were:

1.   Establishing and enforcing strict penalties for breaking the discipline code. In reference to drugs, he stated emphatically, "If you're smoking or dealing, you're out." He acted on his warning, removing 300 students from the roll in his first year for discipline and drug-related violations.

2.   Increasing the involvement of local police officers, known as the "Brothers in Blue," who visited the school regularly to speak to students about the importance of resisting drugs.

3.   Raising academic standards and morale by emphasizing the importance of doing well, requiring a "C" average for participation in athletics, and honoring student achievements.

As a result of actions such as these, Eastside has been transformed. Today there is no evidence of drug use in the school. Intruders no longer have access to the school; hallways and stairwells are safe. Academic performance has improved substantially: in 1981-82, only 56 percent of the 9th graders passed the State's basic skills test in math; in 1984-85, 91 percent passed. In reading, the percentage of 9th graders passing the State's basic skills test rose from 40 percent in 1981-82 to 67 percent in 1984-85.

Fear as a Weapon Against Drug Abuse in Schools

It may be reported with confidence that the "get tough" policies in school systems using them are paying off. Illegal drugs, as well as tobacco and alcohol, are disappearing where sanctions are strictly imposed. This reality goes against research studies which support the contention that "you can't accomplish anything by scaring kids."

The claim that you can't scare kids is undoubtedly true as it pertains to reckless driving by adolescents. Showing them gory wrecks of cars and torn, bleeding bodies seems to have little effect. Perhaps, we have learned something about the effectiveness of varying degrees of fear and varying styles of fear as it pertains to changing behavior patterns. Actually, the failure of fear tactics in the past was derived from the "it can't happen to me" feeling that young as well as old embrace. These messages causing fear always come from outside the individual.

The fear being used successfully on campuses today is one which instead seems to carry the message, "it can and will happen to you." This message always comes from positions of authority. The key to success with recent policies and performances of "get-tough-and-generate-fear" tactics is that no one is immune to the rules. School officials have the capacity to know who is doing what; and regardless of who the transgressing student is, he can and is being made to pay the price of transgressing the rules.

A chief innovation in creating the type of fear which reduces drug usage on school campuses is the development of sting operations. In school after school where a minority of students have seemed to be thoroughly out of control, the local drug enforcement unit has placed undercover "narcs" into schools. The sting operations which follow have been front page news nationwide, and the evidence is that penalties were exacted in spite of the pleadings of parents be they poor, rich or powerful.

It gets the attention of both adolescents and parents when one hundred students, out of a possible 2000, are expelled for a full year because of drug use or drug trafficking, without regard for the social standing of their families. A school may be changed from utter chaos to calm through concerted, determined, sometimes harsh, but even-handed application of greatly strengthened rules — rules which originate in state legislatures, are seconded by school boards and are supported by law enforcement personnel.

Actually, law enforcement personnel are immensely proud of their part in bringing schools from drug domination to drug control. Faced as they are with the frustrations of seeing more hardened criminal types being sent into the revolving prison door, they are greatly mollified to see that school rules are moving out the troublemakers successfully while making a good education for the majority a possible reality. According to "Schools Without Drugs":

> Northside High School (Atlanta, Georgia) enrolls 1400 students from 52 neighborhoods. In 1977, drug use was so prevalent that the school was know as "Fantasy Island." Students smoked marijuana openly at school, and police were called to the school regularly.
>
> The combined efforts of a highly committed group of parents and an effective new principal succeeded in solving Northside's drug problem. Determined to stop drug use both inside and outside the school, parents organized and took the following actions:
>
> 1. Formed parent-peer groups to learn about the drug problem and agreed to set curfews, to chaperone parties, and to monitor their children's whereabouts. They held community meetings to discuss teenage drug use with law enforcement agents, judges, clergy, and physicians.
>
> 2. Established a coalition that lobbied successfully for State anti drug and anti paraphernalia laws.
>
> 3. Offered assistance to the schools. The school acted on the parents' recommendations to provide drug prevention education to teachers, update its prevention curriculum, and establish a new behavior code. Parents also helped design a system for monitoring tardiness and provided volunteer help to teachers.
>
> The new principal, Bill Rudolph, also committed his energy and expertise to fighting the drug problem. Rudolph established a tough policy for students who were caught possessing

173

or dealing drugs. "Illegal drug offenses do not lead to detention hall but to court," he stated. When students were caught, he immediately called the police and then notified their parents. Families were given the names of drug education programs and were urged to participate. One option available to parents was drug education offered by other parents.

Today, Northside is a different school. In 1984-85, only three drug-related incidents were reported.(5, p. 14)

Drugs of Choice Among Students

There is an amazing variation of drugs used by elementary and high school students. It may be stated with impunity that marijuana is still the number one illegal drug of choice while alcohol closely follows. But the marijuana our youngsters are obtaining today is from five to twenty times stronger than it was ten years ago. However, a study made in 1987, which asked sixth graders what drugs peers had pressured them to use, shows crack cocaine is challenging marijuana for second place with about thirty-three percent of the sixth graders reporting peer pressure to use marijuana and about thirty-one percent reporting pressure to use crack.(1)(3)

Marijuana has one quality that on the one hand is helping to control it, and on the other hand, is moving students toward the more dangerous drug, crack cocaine. Marijuana cannot be used indoors and escape notice because of its smell. New, more expansive laws of search have placed marijuana users in jeopardy. Crack use occupies the most threatening role of any other drug. According "Schools Without Drugs":

Crack use is the fastest growing drug problem in America. Most alarming is the recent availability of cocaine in a cheap but potent form called crack or rock. Crack is a purified form of cocaine that is smoked.

1. *Crack is inexpensive to try.* Crack is available for as little as $10. As a result, the drug is affordable to many new users, including high school and even elementary school students.

2. *Crack is easy to use.* It is sold in pieces resembling small white gravel or soap chips and is sometimes pressed into small pellets. Crack can be smoked in a pipe or put into a cigarette. Because the visible effects disappear within minutes after smoking, it can be used at almost any time during the day.

3. *Crack is extremely addictive.* Crack is far more addictive than heroin or barbiturates. Because crack is smoked, it is quickly absorbed into the blood stream. It produces a feeling of extreme euphoria, peaking within seconds. The desire to repeat this sensation can cause addiction within a few days.

4. *Crack leads to crime and severe psychological disorders.* Many youths, once addicted, have turned to stealing, prostitution, and drug dealing in order to support their habit. Continued use can produce violent behavior and psychotic states similar to schizophrenia.

5. *Crack is deadly.* Cocaine in any form can cause cardiac arrest and death by interrupting the brain's control over the heart and respiratory system.(5, p. 8)

Methamphetamine Resurgence

Prior to 1987, the number one drug used in the nation's schools was methamphetamine. This drug was used under the street names speed, crank or crystal among others.

In the summer of 1988, the crack epidemic began, and crack became a drug of choice in the nation's school while methamphetamine slipped in popularity. The NIDA has issued a new report heralding the resurgence of methamphetamine. Whether or not methamphetamine will re-invade school environs in force will be determined by price factors among other things.

The popularity of methamphetamine in school environs has been based upon its access in pill form. It is true that the wider use of methamphetamine across the nation has been via IV administration. Even so, pills were always the popular form on school campuses for obvious reasons. It is mandatory that we keep a close surveillance on the rise of methamphetamine use on school campuses as this dangerous drug makes its comeback.

Closed or Semi-closed Campuses

It goes without saying that students will not use drugs if there is no supply. Most of us have witnessed scenes, via television, of exchanges taking place between pushers and students in full view of everyone. Perhaps, this is partially media glitz, but few would doubt that this happens regularly where there is no source of caring or determination to prevent it on the part of school officials or law enforcement personnel. This situation is changing rapidly, and there are a number of facets to this change.

Closed Campuses

This author recently went to a large inner city school to research the problem under consideration in this chapter. I had visited this school several times before over a five-year period on other missions. I had noticed the looseness of conduct among students, even the exchange of drugs for money and stairwell smoking of tobacco.

On this visit, however, things were vastly different. There were no students hanging out anywhere, including the parking lot I attempted to access. I was startled by a police whistle when I pulled my car into the lot. A kindly uniformed gentleman approached asking courteously what my business was at the school. He showed me the visitor's parking area once I had explained that I had an appointment with the principal.

In my interview with the principal, I commented on the visible change of campus atmosphere and was told, "You can credit that to the closed campus, Dr. Moser."

He went on to explain that students were not allowed to leave campus once they came in the morning except on parental request or an emergency. "No one is ever on this campus who doesn't belong here," he said confidently. I believed him implicitly.

Then, he explained the reasoning behind the closed campus. Theretofore, pushers could walk onto campus, freely displaying their wares. There had been a network of student pushers and non-student pushers. Efforts were made to keep non-students away from campus by threat but the supply network was seemingly unstoppable. At the noon break, the students had been free to race their cars, use drugs or tobacco and to carouse about, causing a heavy rash of tardiness for afternoon classes. Many students just didn't return after the noon break. "Some schools have just shortened the lunch break, but we have completely abandoned ours," the principal confided. He explained the carefully monitored schedule for a "cafeteria" period worked into the schedule over a period from 11:30 A.M. to 1:00 P.M.

New Personnel

"It's different now," the principal told me. Then, he went into a very informative explanation of the new "get tough" policies put in place by the school trustees. These consisted of the following: 1) The campus would be closed from the time of beginning of classes to the time of ending of classes. 2) Cafeterias were improved, and food prices were slashed. 3) Rooms were provided in which brown-baggers could eat their lunches with soft-drink vending machines available. 4) Two security guards were hired to intercept anyone having no business on campus. 5) A police officer who had full credentials and full standing with the local police was hired through a contract between the trustees and the police department. 6) New laws of search were enforced. 7) The rest

177

rooms were monitored between every class for signs of smoking. Tobacco use, alcohol possession or use and any illegal drug use were forbidden. 8) For those who were apprehended for cigarette or alcohol use, there was a two-day suspension. With the second suspension, the student was sent to "alternate school," a school lacking amenities usually cherished by students. 9) For those who were apprehended using or possessing illegal drugs, there was automatic expulsion for the balance of the school year, and legal charges were pressed against them where applicable.

The police officer was assigned a three block circumference patrol with authority to "move along" any loiterers or to arrest any pushers who were soliciting. State law had given more leverage to person and vehicle search on the city's streets, and these laws were being highly effective in getting the word out to would-be dealers and pushers.

The police officer was given "carte blanche" within the campus to arrest anyone, student or otherwise, who might fall within the legal dimensions of arrestable offenses. Apprehended persons were removed from campus and taken to jail with parents being duly notified according to the legal statuses of minors. The principal praised the closed-campus concept as a chief means of drug controls. I left this school convinced that schools with "get tough" policies fully covered legally can and do control drug traffic and drug use where the determination to control is present.

New Laws

The routines the principal described to me all have Federal law behind them and state laws often go beyond Federal law. The Supreme Court recently reaffirmed that the constitutional rights of students in school are not "automatically coextensive with the rights of adults in other settings." This ruling gave broad powers of authority in the effective enforcement of local school rules.

The Comprehensive Crime Control Act of 1984 makes it a Federal crime "to sell drugs in or near a public or private elementary or secondary school." This new "schoolhouse law" specifies a 1000-foot perimeter of protection out from the boundaries of school premises. The sale of drugs to minors has been further attenuated by allowing prosecutors to double the sentence of the pusher who sells to a person under eighteen as opposed to an adult.

At Some Schools Drugs Are Still Tolerated

It may seem from all that has been said that drugs are under control in the nation's schools. That is an overly optimistic view. Clandestine use and sale of drugs still occurs even in schools where every shred of delegated authority is in full use. Astute students usually find ways of doing what they wish, especially if they are addicted and must support drug habits by pushing.

Moreover, in spite of all that has been said, many schools continue to tolerate open defiance of rules and laws. For many schools, things haven't changed very much.

Let's Listen to the Kids

Over the last several years, parents have often been guilty of apathy as was the case for crack cocaine use in schools. As a matter of fact, many of us believed our kids were less than truthful when they told us that crack could be had for the asking on their school grounds. Crack use has become epidemic because we were slow to believe the use of any drug could escalate at such an unbelievable pace. And now comes ice!

Speaking before the House Select Committee on Narcotics Abuse and Control, John C. Lewis, M.D., Director of Health, State of Hawaii, stated:

Faced with the serious problem afflicting our youth, it becomes imperative that we begin to listen to them as we gather information. What they are saying is that crystal meth is available and easy to get. And that they are getting it from other students.

These 'dealers,' well aware of the highly addictive nature of this drug, will initially give

179

away free samples as bait, and once their peers have used it, the hook is set. A former 'ice' addict and dealer who has gone through treatment and is now a peer educator shared that in his experience as a dealer, he never met anyone he gave a free sample to who did not get addicted.(4, p. 13)

In order for the "get tough" policies to succeed, the following must prevail:

1. School boards must be willing to take the "flak" that comes when they put "get tough" policies in place. One would think any school board would be willing to do this. But many school board members are fearful that they will be hounded by parents to get their children excused from the "get tough" rules. Some are even fearful that their own children might bear the brunt of "get tough" policies.

2. Principals and other personnel must be found and hired who have the fortitude to make "get tough" policies work. Some who have long tenure with the school system just don't have the courage and stamina necessary.

3. Law enforcement personnel must cooperate fully. It is amazing to see police watch illegal transactions with drugs and do absolutely nothing. But it is happening everywhere — not just in school environs.

4. Parents must be committed to "get tough" policies. No parent should endeavor to beg off his wayward offspring. But, as we all know, this is a sticking point.

5. The student bodies, summarily, must desire drug free campuses. Just a majority so desiring will not do it. Students must have courage enough to give information concerning violations of rules, even if they must incriminate themselves.

Kids in mainland states are reporting an inexpensive smokable drug called croak, a mixture of crack and methamphetamine HCL. Being cheaper and more available than ice per se, various mixtures of crack and methamphetamine are gaining a large following among mainland student population in the same way crack did in the 80's.

Peer Counseling

The success or failure of a school in remaining drug free will depend upon a change in student attitudes; in other words, peer pressure must become identified with abstinence. One way this is being accomplished is by having students volunteer as peer counselors.

In the State of Hawaii, the Department of Health has established a Peer Education Program, a joint effort of the Department of Health and the Department of Education, to address the needs of our youth through the direction of our youth.

Trained peer educators are working with peer coordination in their schools in a variety of ways to educate their peers not only about the dangers of crystal meth but to get them to think about the reasons not to start....

In addition, the peer coordinators and educators are working on developing support groups for students, inservices for teachers, school wide activities promoting drug free lives and strategies to help friends who are on crystal meth.(4, p. 13, 14)

Students Influencing Students

The peer counselor must be a popular, likeable student known widely among the students. Star athletes and honor students who can gain the respect of fellow students are the types needed. These students can do a great deal in one-on-one relating and in group presentations to demonstrate that the popular thing to do is to avoid drugs.

According to "Schools Without Drugs":

Commodore Stockton Skills School in Stockton, California, is a magnet school serving 1,000 students from diverse cultural and social backgrounds in kindergarten through eighth grade.

Four years ago, a drug-related incident involving seventh and eighth graders prompted the formation of a Substance Abuse Task Force for the School District composed of parents, educators, and other local authorities. This task force formulated a school policy that mandates the following:

1. Teacher training on the substance abuse policy and curricula.
2. An integrated curriculum to prevent drug abuse in all grades.
3. Development and implementation of an education program for parents.
4. A coordinated intervention system for identifying high-risk students.
5. Referrals for counseling or treatment for drug use.
6. Parent and student support groups.
7. Solicitation of outside funds to help implement anti-drug programs in the school.

Students, parents, educators, and community groups have been especially active in planning and carrying out innovative, drug-free activities including a celebrity volleyball game, "Say no" bowling tournaments and dances, and poster and bookmark contests.

Commodore Stockton focuses on honing students' basic academic skills, instilling good study habits, and training students in responsibility and citizenship. The school's organization and discipline are highly structured. Parents are asked to monitor homework, to maintain standards of discipline, to reinforce students' respect for others, and to foster personal responsibility at home. Each month, parents of Commodore Stockton students donate 400 volunteer hours to aid teachers. The school received the California Distinguished Elementary School Award for academic achievement in 1989.

As a result of Commodore Stockton's program, behavioral problems are infrequent, attendance is high, and more than 80 percent of the students test at grade level or above. In addition, area police report juvenile drug arrests from every school in the city *except* Commodore Stockton.(6, p. 16)

The DARE Program

The Drug Abuse Resistance Education program originating in Los Angeles has become a prototype of community involvement through the schools to achieve improved student attitudes about themselves as well as achieve a commitment to stay drug free. This program has been widely copied, and many chapters of DARE are functioning throughout the United States including Hawaii. The description below taken from "Schools Without Drugs" explains this concept: (5, p. 36)

The police department and school district have teamed up to create DARE (Drug Abuse Resistance Education), now operating in 405 schools from kindergarten through grade 8 in Los Angeles. Fifty-two carefully selected and trained frontline officers are teaching students to say no to drugs, build their self-esteem, manage stress, resist prodrug media messages, and develop other skills to keep them drug free. In addition, officers spend time on the playground at recess so that students can get to know them. Meetings are held with teachers, principals, and parents to discuss the curriculum.

Research has shown that DARE has improved students' attitudes about themselves, increased their sense of responsibility for themselves and to police, and strengthened resistance to drugs. For example, before the DARE program began, 51 percent of fifth-grade students equated drug use with having more friends. After training, only 8 percent reported this attitude.

DARE has also changed parent attitudes through an evening program to teach parents about drugs, the symptoms of drug use, and ways to increase family communication. Before DARE, 32 percent of parents thought that it was all right for children to drink alcohol at a party as long as adults were present. After DARE, no parents reported such a view. Before DARE, 61 percent thought that there was nothing parents could do about their children's use of drugs; only 5 percent said so after the program.

Bibliography

1   Brower, Kirk J. and Anglin, M. Douglass. "Adolescent Cocaine
      Use: Epidemiology, Risk Factors, and Prevention." Journal of
      Drug Education. Vol. 17 (2). 1987, pp. 168-180.

2   "Growing Up Drug Free: A Parent's Guide to Prevention." U.S.
      Department of Education. Washington, D.C. 1990, pp. 27-28.

3   Johnson, L.D. et al. "Drug Use Among American High School,
      College Students, and Other Young Adults." National Institution
      on Drug Abuse. Washington, D.C. 1986, pp. 250.

4   Lewin, John C. "Testimony Before the House Select Committee
      on Narcotics Abuse and Control." Honolulu, Hawaii. January
      13, 1990, pp. 1-16.

5   "Schools Without Drugs." U.S. Department of Education.
      Washington, D.C. 1986.

6   "Schools Without Drugs." U.S. Department of Education.
      Washington, D.C. 1989.

Chapter 7

Drug Abuse Control at Colleges and Universities

Happening Seven — Queen Bees Have No Stingers

The Facts As We Best Know Them

A New Day in Drug Abuse Concerns in Colleges
and Universities
Rites of Passage
The Shift of Values on Entering College or
Universities
New Demands on College Administrators
Concern about Illegal Drugs
Substances of Choice on College and University
Campuses
College Athletics and Drug Use
New Directions for Student Freedom
National Collegiate Drug Awareness Kick-off

Happening Seven — Queen Bees Have No Stingers

Joe Petty is a third-year student in pre-medical education in a University in Los Angeles. He says he is lucky to be alive. Here is his story:

My father Jesse Petty was in Vietnam for his tour of duty in 1964-65. Yuwan Bul was the daughter of a surgeon with the South Vietnamese Army Medical Corps. Yuwan's father was killed the year before Dad got to Nam. He and Yuwan, my mother, must have had a torrid love affair because when Dad was shipped back to Diego, Mother was pregnant with me.

Dad was an electrician with the Marine Corps, and somehow, he pulled the strings to get Mother out and to San Diego where I was born. Dad is a good man but a very plain man who is content to stay blue collar all his life. Mother and Dad now live in Oceanside, and although both work, there has never been enough money. The reason, I guess, is that they saved money back to put me through medical school.

I call my mother Yuwan. She is tiny, beautiful, very bright and adorable. She seems all at once to be a fragile flower, a cuddly toy and a delightfully beautiful flame which attracts many moths — everybody, really male and female. Anyone who doesn't have her attention seems to be begging her for it.

She was sad to leave home, but it was the only way. She brought out three things besides the clothes she wore. One of them was me. The other was some family jewels which she hid somehow and sneaked out. The third thing she brought out was a determination that the child within her was going to be just like her dad — I was going to be a doctor.

I am Amerasian but don't look it. I look much more oriental than most Amerasians. I know my mother and dad were afraid that I wouldn't be accepted in school and everything, but I had no trouble at all. After all, this is America, and this is Southern California. And I was determined to make people like me just as they liked Yuwan.

I grew up straight. My dad is Roman Catholic, and my mother is, too. She has some French ancestry, I think. Actually, I look more oriental than she does. She is exotic, effervescent and charming having a touch of aristocracy about her. She learned English in school over there and has quite an accent, of course. But she speaks Vietnamese, French, Chinese and Korean. I don't think anyone ever found out why she learned the Korean language. Dad wouldn't try to learn any language but what he calls American. My mother taught me to speak a little Vietnamese and some Korean. She never seemed to care much for French or Chinese.

Yuwan was the queen of the hive at our house, and Dad was good humored about it. He adores Yuwan, just as everybody seems to adore Yuwan. She knows how to captivate people, and I learned how she did that. I'm sure she taught me that on purpose, thinking I might have a little trouble. But she was wrong. We Americans are all nice, and, of course, I was born in the good old USA.

Two things I didn't like about my childhood: First, we were poor. I think that was hard on Yuwan, too. She was upper-class in Vietnam, but not so in America. She never complained, but neither of us liked being poor. I knew I was smart enough to make it in medical school, and Yuwan pushed me all the way. I didn't mind.

The other thing I didn't like about my childhood was the strictness. I never smoked anything, and although Dad drank beer and smoked tobacco. Yuwan would always tell me where Dad couldn't hear, "You're too smart for that, Joe. One thing you're not is stupid, and booze and drugs are stupid." I felt a little out of it when all the kids used pot, especially at parties. I got by, pretending to take a drag now and then, and Yuwan never smelled anything on my breath. I know she tried every once in a while. She'd throw her arms around me when I came in from a party, and I knew her nose was the most active part of her. I hated not being able to be like the other kids, but I never told Yuwan I hated it.

Finally, I got to the University, and there I used a little marijuana, also a little speed. I had to and I wanted to. Oh, I'd see Yuwan's face every time I used drugs, and I really didn't get hooked, not even on crack. I liked crack so much, it scared me off; I knew I couldn't handle it.

Actually, I think being Oriental-looking helped me a lot getting in and getting all my professors to like me. I'd wow them with a little Vietnamese talk now and then and would throw in a few Korean phrases I knew. Neither the students nor the professors ever knew the difference.

During my third year of pre-med was when it happened. Sure, it was tough academically, but I really wasn't having that much trouble. Three guys, who drove Jaguars and Porches and obviously had a lot of money, started making friends with me, getting me dates and so on. That's where I met Mama Coca. If you don't know it, Mama Coca is cocaine. Sure, I knew crack was cocaine, but these guys snorted it like real big wheels are supposed to do. They let me snort some, and it really was great. I think I liked being with those wealthy guys more than I liked the cocaine. Sure, I knew why all this friendship bit was happening. They figured they'd need to crib off me on important tests, and I studied a lot with them. They always made me feel real smart somehow.

I'd never heard of ice until they mentioned that they'd heard there was some around. I'd used speed and was able to handle that, and I figured that if we could get some ice, then why not. I found out more about why they liked to run around with me. I'd wondered about it a lot. They had sports cars and money, and all I had was an old beat up Chevy. I could barely keep gas in that.

"Why don't you get us some ice?" Chris asked me one night while we were all cramming for a chemistry exam. "We need something special."

"Why me?" I asked.

"Oh, we'll give you the money. Don't worry." I didn't like that superior air. "We hear that the pushers who have ice are all Oriental, and they're real hard to locate — not like crack or speed. They are gun shy and won't sell to just anybody no matter what he drives.

"Here, take my car and these five centuries. Go down by the docks and park. When they get where they can hear you, say something in Jap or whatever. I'll bet you can get them to come to you."

Well, I did it. First, I tried Vietnamese and then a few words in Korean. I knew the Korean words for money and cold but didn't know the word for ice. The cold and money words got the job done. I was proud as a peacock sneaking back into Chris's apartment with the ice.

To make a long story short, I got hooked hard on ice. I couldn't afford it. But I had struck up a good buddy relationship with this one pusher. He spoke English, too, but he was mostly Korean, I think. He'd let me have a few papers of ice on credit because he knew I could sell part of it to my friends and keep paying him. It worked fine until the time came for mid-term exams, and I needed all those papers just to keep myself going. I can't believe I did it, but I got into hock for five thousand dollars before exams were over.

I didn't know what to do, so of course, I asked the pusher for more time and more ice. He said "no" in four languages. I understood all four for the word "no." I was sunk, and I knew it. I had to have the ice; I didn't have any money, and I was in hock for five thousand. I figured it out — I was dead-ended.

Then, the call came. I can't remember what language the guy used, but I got the message. It was simple. "Get the money or you lose your head!" And I thought all those mafia enforcers on TV were just media hype. I had absolutely no question about it. "This was for real!"

Well, that was a little over a year ago. I nearly went wild. I finally narrowed it down to two things I could do, and neither of them was good: Run like hell and don't stop, or go tell Dad and Yuwan. I knew I couldn't run fast enough, or far enough so I crawled back to Dad and Yuwan. I had my speech all ready. "I'll drop out of the university. I'll go to work with Dad. Help me get the money, and I'll do anything." Of course, I knew I'd have to tell them how I'd been doing some drugs ever since high school. I just couldn't think of anything else to do. It was absolutely the hardest thing I've ever done, but I did it. I thought they'd both scream and rant, but they took it like champions.

I don't pretend to know how they managed it but I have a real solid idea. I know Yuwan used to spend a lot of time just gazing into that lacquered jewelry box. She only wore those gems privately, but oh, how she loved them!

What I know is that they put me in a detox center and then sixty days of therapy with a lot of shots. Man what a lot of shots! But I loved them — meaning Dad, Yuwan and the shots. I was the most cooperative patient they ever had at the center.

I had to stay out of pre-med a whole year. But here I am back again, and Yuwan may just have one jewel left — me. Her foolish son, the best urologist in the State of California. Well, give me another five or six years, and you'd better believe — I'm going to make it now. By the way, I've got a Korean fellow-student and friend now. Her name is Mai Sung. I can't believe it. She met my mother, and between the female mutual admiration society that quickly developed, I heard her gasp, "But Yuwan Bul is Korean for queen bee." I saw Yuwan shush Mai quickly, then they whispered and giggled a little. Afterwards, I asked Mai what was going on, but all she would say was "girl talk, Joe San." What a crazy world!

****

Dr. Joe Petty is a urologist in private practice in La Hoya, California. He has a sports car now, the best Japanese car in America. Yuwan is still Yuwan!

The Facts As We Best Know Them

A New Day in Drug Abuse Concerns in Colleges and Universities

Administrators at colleges and universities are becoming aroused concerning their functions *vis à vis* combatting growing drug abuse on campuses. Over the years, campuses have been near the center of activity in terms of drug use and abuse. This is only natural since campuses of higher education are extensions of campus life in public and private secondary schools. Actually, there is an added dimension to drug use and abuse on college and university campus since parental surveillance has most often been removed, and these post-adolescents have become young men and women free from parental domination, coercion and control. They often are unable to make the transition to autonomy without confusion and hurtful behavior.

Rites of Passage

It should be noted that colleges are largely attended by students who were in high school before the passage of legislative actions that have today made possible "schools without drugs." "Get-tough" policies being enforced at many high schools now. Attitudes and behaviors concerning drug use that were inundating secondary schools a few years ago have been passed on to college and university campuses. Actually, only a small number of high schools even pretend to be drug free, even now. Many students who were users on high school campuses become users on college campuses; students who were pushers on high school campuses also often carry this behavior forward.

The Shift of Values on Entering College or University

It would be a happy thought that when freshmen enter a college or university, they suddenly take on adulthood, therewith making them free from pressure or habit insofar as drugs are concerned. Unhappily, however, we know that adulthood is no magic land where old habits are reversed and new pressures are inoperative. Actually, there is a different level or derring-do and anti-establishment feelings any place people

193

come together in groups whether the groups are race riots or Sunday School picnics. In such groups, there will be added pressures to deviate from norms which might be thought of as healthy and free from stress. Mr. Brian Bailey and Ms. Lisa Dieter-Borisky are central figures in the following (4, p. 14):

Substance abuse prevention at the college level begins each year with the incoming class of freshmen. Successful prevention programming necessitates a thorough understanding of the freshmen "mentality" and some knowledge of student behavioral patterns prior to enrollment in college. Coordinating a variety of drug and alcohol prevention programs at the University of Maryland Baltimore County have enabled Mr. Brian Bailey and Ms. Lisa Dieter-Borisky to develop seven "assumptions regarding the attitudes and developmental states of traditionally-aged college freshmen, relative to drug usage":

1.   Most freshmen, particularly in urban areas, are at least somewhat familiar with alcohol and drugs, even if they have not used them;

2.   Many freshmen begin college with the belief that college students lead a wild lifestyle with regard to drugs, alcohol and sex;

3.   Freshmen are not accustomed to making many decisions for themselves;

4.   Freshmen often feel invincible; they do not connect consequences with unwise, unsafe or unhealthy behavior;

5. Freshmen have a tendency to look outside
    themselves for the "right answers" to life's
    questions;

6. Freshmen are eager to feel socially
    competent in the college environment;

7. Peer pressure is ultimately a voice from
    within rather than from without.

Some young people, who have been able to resist peer
pressure in high school or elementary school, have reported to
this author that their introduction to drugs occurred at Sunday
School, church or at church-sponsored outings. These are
environs wherein peer pressure was not expected, thus, they
were unprepared to handle it. In a similar way, many college
freshmen, having resisted peer pressure during earlier
schooling, take their first drink, smoke their first joint or use
their first crack or ice as they come under a totally new peer
pressure indigenous to college dormitories or fraternity-sorority
houses.

There has always been a measure of "hi-jinks" behavior
on campuses where freshmen subservience is a way of life and
where rushees for fraternity-sorority affiliations are constantly
faced with servile demands by so-called superiors
(upperclassmen). In this atmosphere, alcohol use and abuse has
been a modus-operandi of initiation rites; and in late years,
young people in servile roles have been put through drug use
regimens ad infinitum via initiation rites. The above, while
important considerations, are only tips of several icebergs within
campus life. Alcohol and drug abuse on college campuses have
been models of heads-in-the-sand attitudes on the parts of
college administrators.

New Demands on College Administrators

As Robert L. DuPont, a clinical professor of psychiatry
at Georgetown University, has said, "If I wanted to make a
model of alcohol and drug abuse, I couldn't do better than the
modern American college. Parents, faculty members and
administrators have not intervened to help students because of

195

the common notion that drug and alcohol use is part of the 'experimenting' that students must do."(7, p. 9) We can hope this laissez-faire attitude will vanish under the impetus of the war on drugs. We should hope that special efforts at educating college students against the use of dangerous new drug forms, especially crack and ice, will come as a result of new pressures on college administrators.

Havens of Impunity

College and university campuses have always been havens of impunity for drug users, including the use of alcohol by students under the drinking age. This has been true of fraternity houses in particular. Many such houses are assumed to be a part of the physical campus, when as a matter of fact they are sometimes not. Local law enforcement officials are very reluctant to invade these hallowed halls with search warrants and the like although new laws of search would sanction such actions.

The liaisons between local law enforcement and campus security police have typically been hazy. Campus security police have often maintained a laissez-faire attitude toward drug and alcohol use on campus, and local law enforcement groups have, to a large extent, abided by the unspoken but implied wishes of colleges to provide their own security and policing systems. Thus, many college or university campuses have become hotbeds of illegal drug use. Some have unknowingly provided safe havens for students who are pushers both off and on campus and for non-student pushers and dealers. Methamphetamine labs and the manufacture of LSD, PCP and other drugs have often blended into the protective coloration of on-campus and off-campus housing facilities. These facilities are usually in such proximity to the campuses that the responsibility for law enforcement in these environs becomes fuzzy. The jurisdiction of campus police and that of city police is a cloudy issue in most cases, and enforcement becomes a certain duty of no one.

Historically, the principal concern of college administrators *vis à vis* drugs has focused on alcohol use. This has been true because alcohol abuse at colleges and universities has resulted in much DWI, and these cases always bring a measure of ignominy to campuses. College students are in the highest category of drivers' risk factors according to insurance research.

Concern about Illegal Drugs

For years most institutions have distributed handbooks to incoming students stating rules of appropriate behavior including drug use, which while given authoritatively, seem to become downgraded to suggestions except where serious conflicts and behaviors evolve. For instance, alcohol in dormitories may be forbidden by fiat, but the rules are disregarded until and unless there is a violent or boisterous event.

Administrative Double Binds

College administrators have experienced several double binds. Controlling alcohol use has been difficult because alcohol is legal. Although some college-age students cannot legally purchase alcohol, all may use alcohol with impunity. Business interests near campus living quarters frown upon mandated restrictions while parents often demand an "in loco parentis" attitude on the part of disciplinary functionaries at these institutions. Thus, some schools have tried to control alcohol only on campus and at sponsored functions. Others have chosen to do nothing other than deal on a case by case basis with those, who once under the influence of alcohol, perform behaviors which reflect on the institutions.

Another double bind occurs with illegal drugs. The tendency in many state colleges and universities has been to ignore the use of illegal drugs in private quarters even if those private quarters are institutionally owned and under administrative control (dormitories). On the one hand, the institution feels threatened in performing a policing function. On the other hand, the institution feels threatened by objections and even lawsuits from parents whose young people have been subjected to unwanted examples and behaviors of illegal drug users. With all this, one should not be surprised that the typical attitudes of administrators has been one of "live and let live" on the one hand and "get involved only when disaster brews" on the other hand.

Things are Changing

The time has come, however, when few college administrators can maintain a laissez-faire attitude about drug use on campus, especially illegal drugs. The trend is to issue student handbooks spelling out the limits on alcohol use and entirely forbidding the use of illegal drugs.

In order to provide themselves knowledge, backing, motivation, and stamina for the task, most colleges and universities have been eager to become involved in organizations which are currently fostered under various auspices giving direction and sustenance to efforts to curb drug use and alcohol. The U.S. Department of Education released a report showing that fifty-seven percent of colleges and universities had no drug abuse prevention programs and that seventy-five percent had no explicit written policies about illegal drugs.(6) The Chronicle of Higher Education reports that the U.S. Department of Education has led they way in creating a national higher-education network for exchanging information about drugs and alcohol abuse programs. This group has been designated as the Network of Colleges and Universities Committed to the Elimination of Drug and Alcohol Abuse. Money for supporting the network was included in the 1986 Drug Free Schools and Communities Act.

U.S. Agency Workshops

Demonstrating the seriousness with which the Federal Government is viewing the college and university campuses as principal targets in the war on drugs, the U.S. Department of Education, the Department of Transportation and the Department of Health and Human Services are joining forces in promoting regional workshops among 120 selected institutions utilizing ten workshops each designed to be attended by approximately twelve college administration representatives. These workshops, according to Vonnie Veltri, give structure and coordination to administrative efforts. Veltri, senior associate in the research department of the Department of Education, said, "The substance abuse efforts on college campuses have been occurring in very fragmented ways ... We saw a need for colleges to work as a team on a comprehensive plan to deal with drug and alcohol abuse."(12, p. 25)

Alcohol and drug use policies are, in general, being made more strict on campuses across the nation. Campus drug use problems tend to follow regional patterns wherein certain controlled substances are more of a problem at some institutions than at others. This pattern usually conforms to the availability of substances in the area. Whereas Dallas, Texas is known as "speed city," Miami has almost no methamphetamine supply but does have an abundance of cocaine. The one substance in constant and universal supply is alcohol, and most drug users on campuses combine alcohol with whatever else is available. Many college and university students are wary of drug use other than alcohol. Thus, alcohol is the most abused substance on campuses nationwide. Another reason, of course, is that neither possession nor use of alcohol is illegal for students over twenty-one.

Substances of Choice on College and University Campuses

The State of Virginia has developed the first statewide policy in the nation with its Substance Abuse Statement Developed for Higher Education (17). This effort has evolved from the State Council of Higher Education on request of the Governor of the Commonwealth of Virginia. All institutions of higher education in the Commonwealth are being asked to review their policies and to "ensure at a minimum, the issues of enforcement, education and prevention, and counseling and referral."

With due attention to regionalism in campus drug use, it is demonstrated through several studies that alcohol and marijuana take first and second place among substances used on college and university campuses. Recent studies have also revealed a leveling off or even a reduction of marijuana use.

The Growing Prominence of Cocaine

The drug of ascending prominence on campuses today is cocaine. There are many reasons for this, the principal ones being availability and low price of a widely-known drug which has inundated the nation in its smokable form. Also cited as an aspect of crack's appeal for college students is that cocaine has for centuries been the glamor drug, the drug of choice of the wealthy, the symbol of the jet-set, the most prominent drug of mention among prominent actors, rock musicians and athletes. All of these are regarded by college-age youth as subjects of awe and admiration.

A recent survey of college youth found that one in three college students have tried cocaine. The U.S. Secretary of Education has enunciated the role of college and university presidents as being primary in bringing about change.(13)

A study at the University of Michigan, done under the guidance of the National Institute on Drug Abuse (10), found that 30 percent of all students had tried cocaine by the end of their fourth year. The growth of cocaine use at Arizona State University from 1970 to 1984 showed that in 1970 only 2.5 percent of students had tried the drug while in 1984, 44 percent had tried it.

Student dealers in cocaine, especially crack, are a significant part of the campus problem nationwide. "If your habit gets worse, you've got a clientele of people who can help you support your habit right there," says a Department of Education spokesman (13, p. 35).

Cocaine, Drug of Choice for Social Reasons

The campus environment is an ideal breeding ground for cocaine use. "While many students start using the drug simply because it makes them feel good, others may use it as a substitute for relationships. Instead of working out their fears and complex emotions, they opt out to get instantaneous satisfaction from a drug."(13, p. 35) On the other hand, cocaine which is known as an "orgasmic drug," is a logical drug to aid an inexperienced student in entering sexual relationships which are an approved,but threatening element on campuses to many students. "Also, because the drug tends to inflate the user's ego, students who feel they cannot meet their college's academic demands or are afraid they will never succeed in the work world, may take the drug to escape their insecurities and worries."(13, p. 35)

The Most Harmful Drug on College Campuses?

Determining which drug form is most dangerous on college campuses is impossible in an overall assessment because of regional differences in preference, availability and amount of use. The Institute for Social Research at the University of Michigan conducted a survey financed by NIDA and reported that approximately thirty percent of all college students will use cocaine at least once before their graduation.(13) Nicholi (14), working in The Journal of American College Health, speaks of an on-going usage and experimentation with cocaine among college students.

In another article, Nicholi (14) presented a study of amphetamine use on college campuses, citing amphetamines as having a variety of implications for both physical and psychological health.

College Athletics and Drug Use

A number of disasters occurring to prominent college athletes because of drugs have been big media items. Athletic programs in colleges and universities have gotten out of hand. The National Collegiate Athletic Association struggles as it tries to cope with controversial issues such as testing athletes for drug abuse, new academic standards for freshmen athletes, the role of college presidents in governing sports and the integrity of college athletics.(8)

Athletics and Scholastic Integrity

Criticisms are being leveled at college athletics on the claim that athletes use colleges and universities as stepping stones to professional careers. Academics have been seriously compromised in concerted, but unwise efforts some schools are making to enhance their athletic programs with attendant damage to scholastic integrity.

John R. Davis, the president of the N.C.A.A., states, "We believe that in some instances the demands on student athletes' time are a very serious incursion into their academic life. We feel there ought to be some restrictions placed on practice and competition, both at home and away."(8, p. 23)

Athletics and Drug Testing

John B. Slaughter (8, p. 24), chancellor of Maryland's College Park campus, is adamant in his criticism of the lack of coordination between athletics and academics. "I believe that all major universities, particularly the public ones, have an obligation to examine and strengthen the relationship between the athletic and academic components of the institutions," he said. Mr. Slaughter supports the N.C.A.A.'s drug-testing plan which calls for random testing at championships. "Unquestionably, mandatory drug testing is needed," he said.

The N.C.A.A. has issued a compromise statement on random drug testing. Still holding off on a random testing procedure for all recruited athletes, N.C.A.A. ruled in favor of "randomized drug testing at championships." Many are urging the N.C.A.A. to go much further, at least to "scheduled" drug testing of athletes who regularly perform. The N.C.A.A. presses on in its quest for logical realities within a context of confusing pressures.

New Directions for Student Freedom

College has always been a place where the young person, set free from restraints, has been able to exercise open-ended freedom. This is an ideal which is at front center of the reticence college administrators have *vis à vis* intrusion — intrusions even into illegalities well-disguised and acted out in the great and glorious name of freedom.

College students should not expect to live in a world as supportive of tentative experiments in personal freedoms as college campuses have become. In the world of work, for example, many freedoms will be compromised; in marriage many freedoms must be compromised. Many have held that the persuasive atmosphere indigenous to college campuses is a disservice to youth because they become spoiled to levels of personal freedoms. And when they are later placed where such unbridled freedoms must be compromised, they cannot make appropriate adjustments. The divorce statistics are terse examples.

And now, without really wishing to do so, college administrators are having to remonstrate students: "You have long had the privilege of testing the waters, of experimenting in tolerable behavior so far as drugs are concerned. The nation can no longer afford the use of colleges and universities as laboratories in the tolerable extent of personal freedoms. The laboratory must be closed, at least for a time." This is a tough assignment for college administrators, especially those in public institutions. Private and church-related institutions may expect an easier time because such institutions have historically been at least semi-controlled by their governing bodies.

But information is seeping out that the majority of college and university students, who are not really so immersed in drugs as to place a secondary priority on their education, are anxiously waiting for a crackdown on the despoilers of their rights as serious students. The rights of the serious students to gain an education are running pell-mell into the rights of students who wish to experiment with drugs.

Dr. Robert DuPont leads out in promoting this theme as the following report indicates:

To combat substance abuse in the college environment, DuPont believes that it is necessary to foster and develop a student commitment to lifestyles that reject the usage of what he terms 'recreational pharmacology.' He stresses that before this ideology can produce positive behavioral changes, it needs to be 'rooted in the deep and enduring values of colleges to promote the full physical, intellectual, and spiritual development of students.'

DuPont contends that modern scientific research surrounding the processes and effects of drug addiction, and the many tragic drug-related incidents of the past two decades illustrate that the out-dated values of the 1960's can no longer be accepted or applied to the present-day situation. Leaving drug usage decisions to the individual is no longer intellectually justifiable, and 'reflects a reckless abdication of the principle of caring for one's fellow human beings.'

Finally, DuPont criticizes some university faculty and administrators for being reluctant to part with the more liberal values of earlier decades. Ironically, he believes that many college students are more willing to accept a less tolerant and more restrictive attitude to drug and alcohol usage than their educators.(7, p. 9)

The results of these conflicts cannot be held seriously in doubt. The freedom principle is fragile at best, and more important rights cannot be allowed to become captive to the frivolous rights of drug use, abuse and experimentation. Trustee boards and college presidents have a clear mandate, an important one which largely has not been achieved. Dr. Edward Hammond believes that a sea of change has occurred in the permissive society indigenous to American college campuses.

Dr. Edward Hammond believes that over the past thirty years the relationship between student and university has undergone a dramatic change. From 1960 to 1972, the prevailing legal framework, known as *in loco parentis* was transformed and replaced with a more constitutional ideology that granted students additional individual rights and freedoms. In accordance with this new framework, the courts held that students were fully functioning legal adults who, upon enrollment in a college or university, entered into a legal contract which is "enforceable in any court of law, regardless or jurisdiction."

One of the results of this new judicial orientation has been to embroil many of our college campuses in both a legal and a moral crisis. At present, approximately four out of ten institutions of higher education are involved in some form of litigation, resulting either directly or indirectly from drug or alcohol abuse. At the same time, more student freedoms have resulted in increased drug usage which has adversely affected crime rates on college campuses and in the surrounding communities.(9, p. 10)

National Collegiate Drug Awareness Kick-off

The progress and the process of cleaning up campuses from drugs is being taken seriously as evidenced in the National Collegiate Drug Awareness Week Kick-off Conference recently held in Washington, D.C. under the direction and financing of the U.S. Department of Education. The initiation of these conferences came about, however, from the Inter-Association Task Force on Alcohol and Other Substance Issues. The broader goal of the kick-off conference was enunciated as "urging colleges and universities to sponsor education and prevention activities on their own campuses." **There follows a number of contributions made by participants at the kick-off conference:**

Commitment Must Precede Action

Any policy made by a responsible group must proceed from personal convictions and not from a sense of urgency as Dr. Robert F. Ariosto of Connecticut University states:

Because a substance abuse policy involves the regulation of important personal freedoms and individual lifestyles, university administrators must not over-simplify the policy or else they will risk undermining its credibility and effect. Ariosto believes that if policy makers want their guidelines on substance abuse to be effective, first they must carefully examine their own beliefs concerning substance use.(2, p. 15)

A summary statement of direction and purpose was offered by Vonnie L. Veltri, Senior Associate Office of

Educational Research and Improvement United States Department of Education. Ms. Veltri said:

> College and university administrators are well aware of the need to find effective solutions to the problems of drug and alcohol abuse. Current research indicates that substance abuse often results in serious health problems, a decrease in levels of productivity, a breakdown of the family structure and a strain on societal resources. At the collegiate level, substance abuse has been found to inhibit the educational development of students and jeopardize their ability to obtain gainful employment and become a productive member of society.(16, p. vii)

Awareness and Prevention

Mr. Thomas Aceto of the University of Maine offered seven recommendations for enhancing prevention efforts:

> The current substance abuse problem, according to Aceto, can be attributed to a variety of psychological and sociological factors, including the progressive decline in parental influence, the phenomenon of "adolescent invulnerability" and the quest for independence and maturity. These factors, combined with many others, have inhibited a large percentage of young adults from responding to on-going anti-drug and alcohol campaigns. In response, Aceto offers seven recommendations for enhancing prevention efforts at the college level:
>
> 1. Establish as a national priority the creation of comprehensive substance abuse programs at all colleges and universities;

2.   Develop a more sophisticated solution to the drinking and driving problem than establishing the legal drinking age at 21;

3.   Eliminate double standards, and encourage college administrators and alumni to actively participate in substance abuse prevention efforts and activities;

4.   Increase student involvement in the prevention of on-campus substance abuse;

5.   Involve more faculty to serve as role models in substance abuse prevention efforts;

6.   Challenge the federal government to increase its efforts and funding in collegiate drug and alcohol abuse prevention campaigns;

7.   Encourage the alcoholic beverage and media industries to examine and redirect their advertising efforts to reflect a concern for substance abuse prevention. (1, p. 2)

Ms. Elizabeth Broughton, Assistant Dean for Student Services at the University of Florida in Gainesville, offered the following comments along with the program's four main objectives:

The Campus Alcohol and Drug Prevention Project is a cooperative effort involving faculty, administrators, students and community members in an effort to promote "responsible decision-making concerning alcohol use or non-use, and intolerance to illicit drug use." The program's major objectives are:

1.   To mobilize campus resources for the prevention of drug and alcohol abuse;

2.   To provide student involvement and leadership in drug and alcohol educational efforts;

3.   To promote drug and alcohol education as an integral part of institutional services;

4.   To develop a knowledge base and skills training program for drug and alcohol education.(5, p. 4)

Ms. Carolyn Lichtenberg, Grand President of Pi Beta Phi Sorority enunciated a description of that sorority's Aiming Straight Program:

The Aiming Straight program operates under the premise that no illicit drug can be used safely. Thus, all drug usage must be eliminated from society to prevent considerable harm to our next, and subsequent, generations. Aiming Straight members argue that rehabilitation and treatment of drug users is uncertain at best, and that the only effective way to deal with drug use is to prevent it from beginning in the first place.(11, p. 5)

Emphasizing formal course content on drug control in drug abuse education, Mr. William J. Bailey, of the Alcohol-Drug Information Center at Indiana University, Bloomington, describes Indiana's program as follows:

The University of Indiana's efforts to provide students with substance abuse education extends beyond the formalized drug education course, and into a wide range of other course curriculums. Through the university's Alcohol-Drug Information Center, and its Classroom

Support Program, faculty are encouraged to help students find alcohol and drug-related topics for their writing and speaking assignments. To facilitate student efforts in this direction, the Alcohol-Drug Information Center has a ready-reference area with informational files on such issues as drug testing, drinking games and current efforts to curb drunk driving. The program not only promotes increased student awareness, but also enables faculty members to make a significant contribution to the campaign against substance abuse.(3, p. 7)

Drug Testing of Offenders

The issues of drug testing was comprehensively dealt with by the opinions of Mr. Gary Pavela, University of Maryland at College Park:

Pavela raises a second issue concerning drug testing on college campuses. At the University of Maryland, first time drug offenders have the option to participate in a special drug testing program as an alternative to expulsion. The program offers the delinquent student a unique second chance as well as a structured and supervised opportunity to end a potentially harmful drug habit. Although the concept of drug testing implies an inherent distrust of students, Pavela finds this acceptable since the student offender was initially responsible for breaking trust by using a prohibited substance on campus.

Although he supports drug testing for consenting, previous offenders, Pavela does not agree with the policy of random drug testing without reasonable cause. Pavela believes that a policy of this nature undermines the fundamental concept of a relationship built on trust. Without this trust, a university cannot hope to foster the individual and social development of its students, which is an essential part of its overall educational mission.(15, p. 16)

Bibliography

1   Aceto, Thomas D. "The Contemporary Campus: An Administrator's Point of View." Approaches to Drug Abuse Prevention in Colleges and Universities. U.S. Department of Education Booklet. Washington, D.C., October 1988, p. 2.

2   Ariosto, Robert F. "Substance Abuse Policy: Making the Standards Work." Approaches to Drug Abuse Treatment in Colleges and Universities. U.S. Department of Education Booklet. Washington, D.C., October 1988, p. 15.

3   Bailey, William J. "Beyond Awareness: Incorporating Drug Education into the Curriculum: The Indiana University Experience." Approaches to Drug Abuse Treatment in Colleges and Universities. U.S. Department of Education Booklet. Washington, D.C., October 1988, p. 7.

4   Bailey, Brian and Dieter-Borisky, Lisa. "Teaching New Students to Say No." Approaches to Drug Abuse Treatment in Colleges and Universities. U.S. Department of Education Booklet. Washington, D.C., October 1988, p.14.

5   Broughton, Elizabeth. "Assessing Your Campus Environment." Approaches to Drug Abuse Treatment in Colleges and Universities. U.S. Department of Education Booklet. Washington, D.C., October 1988, p. 4.

6   De Loughry, Thomas. "Standards Set For Dealing With Campus Drug Abuse 57 Pct. of College Said to Lack Prevention Program." The Chronicle of Higher Education. Vol. 34 No. 22. February 10, 1988, pp. A31,A36.

7   DuPont, Robert L. "College Life, Breeding Ground For Chemical Dependence or For Immunity Against Substance Abuse." Approaches to Drug Abuse Treatment in Colleges and Universities. U.S. Department of Education Booklet. Washington, D.C., October 1988, p.9.

8   Farrell, Charles S. "Colleges Eye Limit on Time Players Give to Sports, Tougher Tests for Drug Abuse." The Chronicle of Higher Education. Vol. 32 No. 19. July 9, 1986, pp. 23,24.

9   Hammond, Edward. "Network to Promote Drug-Free Colleges and Universities" Approaches to Drug Abuse Treatment in

Colleges and Universities. U.S. Department of Education Booklet. Washington, D.C., October 1988, p.10.

10   Johnson, Lloyd. "Campus Cocaine," The Washington Post Magazine. October 5, 1986, p. 27.

11   Lichtenberg, Carolyn. "Aiming Straight." Approaches to Drug Abuse Treatment in Colleges and Universities. U.S. Department of Education Booklet. Washington, D.C., October 1988, p. 5.

12   Magner, Denise K. "College 'Teams' Trade Information and Experiences in Effort to Curb Campus Drug and Alcohol Abuse." The Chronicle of Higher Education. Vol. 35 No. 43. pp. 25, 26.

13   Meyer, Thomas J. "College Students' Drug Use Down, But 1 in 3 Found Trying Cocaine." The Chronicle of Higher Education. Vol. 32 No. 20. July 16, 1986, pp. 1, 30.

14   Nicholi, A. "Cocaine Use Among the College Age Group: Biological: Psychological Effects: Clinical: Lab Research Findings." Journal of American College Health. Vol. 32 (6) January 1984, pp. 258-261.

15   Pavela, Gary. "Liability and Values in Relation to the Institutional Response to Alcohol Abuse and the Use of Prohibited Drugs." Approaches to Drug Abuse Treatment in Colleges and Universities. U.S. Department of Education Booklet. Washington, D.C., October 1988, p. 16.

16   Veltri, Vonnie L. "Approaches to Drug and Alcohol Abuse Prevention." Approaches to Drug Abuse Treatment in Colleges and Universities. U.S. Department of Education Booklet. Washington, D.C., October 1988, p vii.

17   Virginia State Council of Higher Education. "Substance Abuse Statement Developed for Higher Education." On-Line. Vol. 3 No. 1. April 1987, pp. 5, 6.

PART IV — TREATMENTS

Chapter 8

Treatment in Drug Abuse Centers

Happening Eight — The Story of Sherry Minot

The Facts As We Best Know Them

Happening Eight — The Story of Sherry Minot

There was something unexplainable about it. I felt myself to be a kindred spirit with Sherry Minot when she first came to the clinic. After eight years in this position, I was feeling burn-out setting in. It seemed that nothing was going right. Case after case ended in failure. With the easy availability of crack, it was beginning to seem like a hopeless cause. That is why I was so elevated in spirit when I met Sherry. Here was a good, honest person. She had made mistakes, but she was open and honest with me. I am a licensed psychologist at the Altrusa Substance Abuse Clinic, a private, drug-abuse treatment facility located just off the Interstate in Waxahachie, Texas. The clinic has a catchment area from the vast Dallas-Ft. Worth area.

I asked Sherry to bring Jim along for the next sessions. I usually like to see husband and wife together early in treatment. I knew Sherry and Jim could be rescued from their problems. I usually expect only to get acquainted at the first conjoint meeting, but they both seemed eager to get on with it. They laid all their problems out for me that first session, much more in detail, but essentially the same as Sherry had told me at our first meeting. Usually, I feel I get only part of the truth in early sessions, but Jim and Sherry were so forthright and honest that I knew I was getting the whole picture.

Jim and Sherry were both twenty-eight. Jim was a civil engineer, a graduate of MIT. Sherry had finished her training in nursing at Baylor University. Part of her training was at Baylor Hospital in Dallas. Sherry was a Waxahachie girl and had met Jim when he had come to Dallas to open his engineering business in booming Big D. They had married when Sherry, already expecting a baby, had finished her training.

Jim and Sherry were from conservative, church-going families. Actually, Sherry's father was a Methodist minister, and he kept a tight reign on the family. Sherry always felt sorry for her mother who responded meekly to her father's ironclad rules. Sherry, herself, had had several teenage rebellion incidents — nothing serious. Sherry's parents still live in Waxahachie. Jim was probably even more conservative than

214

Sherry. He had virtually demanded that Sherry forget about a career and be a full-time mother. Sherry had readily agreed. She had been very relieved at the time that she didn't have to leave the baby with sitters.

Jim and Sherry had been very happy together for a while. Jim had bragged constantly about the perfect family they had. Sherry had not been quite sure that they had such a perfect family. She had begun to get bored. By the time baby Joel was a year old, she had wanted to go to work, at least part-time. She could have left Joel with her parents easily enough, she had thought.

But Jim had been adamant. He wanted his little boy to have a full-time mother. The years went on, and Sherry kept hoping Jim would relent about her working. "When he is in school, even pre-school, then you can go to work if you want," Jim had said. "Our family is perfect, and I want it to stay that way."

But Jim's family wasn't perfect. By the time Joel was four years old, a lot of bad things were happening. Sherry started being rough with Joel. She realized she was too hard on him, and she unnecessarily whipped him severely several times. When she slapped him so hard as to bruise his cheek one day, Jim wanted an explanation.

"Oh, he fell against the porch rail," she told Jim looking sternly at Joel, and Joel didn't tell on her. She hugged him hard for that, and loyal little boy that he was, he seemed to understand.

But worse was to come. It started during early summer when a neighbor insisted on taking Joel to Bible School. Without Joel around, Sherry started talking with a nice-looking young man whose back yard joined the Minot's back yard.

Jack Joyner, the neighbor, stayed home as house-husband while his wife worked. He had lost his job a month before. He was bored, too, so the conversations came easily. It came easy, too, for Sherry to go over to the Joyners' patio for iced tea. More conversations followed, and although Sherry had given up cigarettes long ago, she didn't refuse Jack's offer of a cigarette. Jack was a delightfully funny man who, for some reason, appealed to Sherry from the beginning. Actually, she was mesmerized by this man, and the transition was a fast one. From talking, to cigarettes then to marijuana — all of it happened in a matter of two days. Sherry actually entertained the thought that she was getting even with someone for something. It all was so blurred, so impossible. But she did it. It happened.

The house of cards came tumbling when she really got rough with Joel the day the neighbor brought him home from Bible School early. Joel came right through the back gate running toward Jack's patio where the two of them were smoking pot. She hurried to intercept the child before he reached the patio. Joel seemed perfectly at ease with her lie that Mrs. Joyner had called her to come over.

Everything would have been all right, Sherry thought, if she just hadn't become violent with Joel when she got him into his own yard. She hit him really hard over and over with doubled fists. Joel ran screaming with blood streaming from his nostrils. He ran into the street and was nearly been hit by a cruising police car.

****

Sherry couldn't believe that she had been arrested for child abuse. But she knew she <u>had</u> abused Joel. And more than that, the arresting officer had reported that she was intoxicated, intoxicated on pot. He'd reported this because the pot still smelled on her breath. And, of course, there was no keeping Jim out of it. Jim found his wife in jail and his son in the hospital. A big hole had been blown in the bubble of Jim's joyous contentment with his perfect family. Jim was totally devastated and quickly sought the help of Sherry's parents.

Sherry was penitent before the judge, but she lied to him. Her story was that she had gotten the marijuana from and unidentified female neighbor, and the marijuana had caused her to abuse Joel. She had already confessed to Jim that it had been the male neighbor who had given her the marijuana, and Jim had agreed to go along with that story.

The events immediately preceding the coming of Jim and Sherry to the clinic to begin Sherry's drug treatment were plain, simple and swift. The judge, because of the prominence of Sherry's parents, placed the child in the grandparents' custody pending a twenty-eight day treatment for Sherry at the Altrusa Clinic.

Sherry declared the day she was admitted to Altrusa that she didn't have an addiction. She was adamant about that. But Altrusa places all admissions on a forty-eight hour hospitalization rotation complete with detoxification procedures and drug screening tests.

****

The above was the very believable story Jim and Sherry told me with openness and candor. I would have believed them completely except that I knew more than they thought I knew.

I had the print-outs on the drug screen showing both marijuana and cocaine; I had the tech's written report of Sherry's behavior in ICU for those first forty-eight hours. On the second day in ICU, Sherry had become intensely irritable and then very over-reactive. She'd begged incoherently for "some of that stuff you smoke." She had been medicated with desipramine and had become free of withdrawal symptoms after one extra day in ICU.

The time came for my second meeting with Sherry. She didn't seem aware that I knew about the crack use. I tried to develop an atmosphere of trust with her. She was easy to talk with, and she gave me a graphic replay about what had happened — about her boredom and how Jack Joyner had offered her the marijuana, how the drug had made her violent with Joey and how she had been severe with him before, but not really abusive. Sherry was an attractive woman who made me feel secure when it should have been the other way around, I thought.

I listened intently, nodding and making leading remarks to draw her out.

"You aren't buying, are you, Dr. Gaylord?"

"I beg your pardon," I said. I was a little shocked because, up to that time, I had believed her implicitly.

"You aren't buying into my bullshit."

I was surprised because I was simply acting the way I felt. I trusted her. I was also surprised at her language. I knew the language cloaked a lot of anger — anger I had not seen when she and Jim had met with me earlier.

So Sherry told me the whole story. It wasn't easy for her to admit that the smoking with Jack Joyner had progressed from cigarettes, to marijuana and to crack cocaine. "I had never had cocaine before, although I used a little pot in high school just for a lark," she said. "I'm terribly ashamed."

"Cocaine does make some people violent," I said. "However, I can't help but wonder whether or not that was the first time you had abused Joel."

"Oh, yes, absolutely; it was the first and only time," she said. "I'm ashamed of hitting Joel, that is, hitting him with my fists. Oh, I had whipped him before, sometimes maybe too hard like I told you before. But I think I ought to tell you this, too. The cocaine turned me on sexually, and Jack took unfair advantage."

I was really shocked, realizing that I should not show it. "That's a common effect of crack," I admitted, regaining my professional demeanor with effort. I don't know why I was so shocked, but I was.

"I want my baby," she blurted out. "I don't care what happens to me as long as I get my baby back."

"But, Sherry, you know that you wouldn't want your baby unless everything was all right, unless you are over your drug problem," I said.

"I don't have a drug problem," she said. Somehow, the way she said it caused me to believe that her craving was still there in her gut. I had received a note from the medical director

218

saying that Sherry had refused medication to control craving. He said he did not believe Sherry would need medication. It is my experience that so-called drug problems are really masks that cover deeper problems. But she was right. I didn't think that either pot or the cocaine used over a short period would cause the kind of violence she had used with Joel.

"I don't have a drug problem," she repeated sternly. "You can't get a drug problem from using a little marijuana and crack for a week or so, can you?" And even before I could say anything, "Sure, it made me hit Joel, but the marijuana and crack are out of my system by now. Don't you think so, Doctor?"

****

Sherry was assigned to a small group where I was the designated therapist. Annette Lockett was my co-leader in that group. We always try to have male and female leader-therapists in every group at Altrusa.

Besides that, Sherry was to attend a family group where she and her husband would meet with a dozen or so other parents, who most often have older children in Altrusa. We try to make the family groups as cosmopolitan as possible so that a wide array of experiences can be shared. I knew I would get reports from the family group leaders on Sherry because she was assigned specifically to me.

My next contact with Sherry was a second conjoint session I had requested with both Sherry and Jim. I really liked Jim. He was an humble man, faced with problems he'd never dreamed possible. He wasn't a naive person and seemed open and willing to cooperate. However, I felt there might be hidden problems between these two.

The atmosphere between Sherry and Jim was not cordial — not at the beginning. Each seemed to wait for questions from me, and when I did ask some things about early backgrounds, the marriage and so forth, they took turns answering without looking at each other. It was like an agreement — you field this question, and I'll take the next one.

219

But I refused that format, of course. I asked Sherry, "What do you like most about Jim, and what do you like least about Jim?" And as she started to answer, I said, "Don't tell me; look straight at Jim and tell him."

Sherry told Jim without hesitation about her loneliness and boredom. And she began to shake, almost losing control, "Damn you, Jim. What do you think I am, a slavewoman?" She turned loose quite a volley on Jim. He was visibly shaken.

"Now, Jim," I said, "tell Sherry what you like and don't like about her."

But Jim could only sputter. He was so shaken, he couldn't get anything out at first. Finally, he said, "Sherry, I just don't understand why you've done this to our baby. I just don't understand it at all."

And Sherry opened up on Jim again. I didn't interrupt because I felt she needed this catharsis. I believe Jim thought so, too.

From a slouched position and without looking at her, Jim said, "I'm sorry, Sherry. I absolutely promise to do better. I'm to blame, not you, Sherry. Give us another chance. Please!"

And then he raised his head in an almost defiant way and said, "Sherry, I never told you about my problem. I didn't think it was necessary. But now, I want you to know. I got on several drugs my junior year at MIT, LSD for one and then cocaine and speed. I had to spend six weeks in drug treatment, Sherry. And I still crave the damned stuff. But I kicked it, Sherry, and you can sure kick a little marijuana habit. I know you can, and I'll help you."

Sherry gasped, "You used cocaine, Jim? I don't believe it."

"But it's the truth. I've pretended to be all this square because I don't trust myself to be anything but square. I've been afraid to turn loose and let go. I'm scared, Sherry, scared that I might get under pressure and get back on that stuff. But I can do better, darling; we can learn to play. I don't have to work every day. I can take a lot more time off than I do." There was abject pleading in his eyes.

****

My next session was with Sherry alone. Sherry began the conversation.

"No more bullshit!" she said looking me squarely in the eyes. "I've got plenty to tell you, and you'd better be trustworthy. If you're not, I'm really in trouble."

"Okay, Sherry." I didn't confirm or deny my trustworthiness.

Sherry told me in detail about her use of crack with Jack Joyner and about the affair that had gone on for about a week with him. She vowed over and over that she would never do that again. This was on the tenth day of her stay at Altrusa. Although she seemed to think this was an abject confession, there was really nothing new. She'd told me all that before.

"You think I can pick up my baby and go home now?" she asked forthrightly. "I'm okay now."

"Sherry, three things I must say to you," I spoke firmly. "First, the judge did you a real favor by not taking Joel away from you completely.

"And second, and I think more importantly, you were abusing Joel before you say you took the crack." And holding up a palm toward her to keep her from interrupting, I continued, "Third, you probably still have a craving for the drug, and you might just find a way to get it again. No, I think you'll have to stay the full time. But in another week, you will be allowed to go out for dinner with Jim, see Joel, see your parents and have a few hours to make future plans for all of you."

Sherry hung her head and nodded. She understood what I had said, especially about the craving. Still, I was optimistic. She had used crack such a short time if we could believe all of the story she'd told plus what the tests had told us. Actually, drug screens cannot reveal how long a person has used a drug. Still, I knew what a powerfully addictive drug form crack is, and I wasn't conceding to myself that she'd only used it during her affair with the neighbor.

The breakthrough came during group. There were eight people present, six patients, Annette Lockett and me. The group began as usual. Up to this time, Sherry had been very reserved in group.

A young woman named Yvonne was talking and crying at the same time. Annette led Yvonne into an emotional flashback of Yvonne's relationship with her father. Yvonne started talking about how bad her father always made her feel. "He always ignored me. It was his darling sons he really loved. They were a hunting and fishing team. They talked about nothing else but sports of one kind or another. Both my mother and me were like dirt to him. He thought he was king and Mother was dirt. God, how I hated him when he slapped my mother around. He never touched me, but I think I would have preferred a slap to being ignored.

He never really wanted me, a girl. He hated me, and he was terribly angry with my mother for having me. Because of me, he treated my mother awful. She had to go to the hospital twice when he beat her with his belt." Yvonne screamed as if she was being hit with the belt. She was out of control. "I hate you, you fucking bastard. I hate you." Yvonne collapsed in shuddering sobs.

I don't know why, but I caught Sherry's face out of the corner of my eye. Her face was flushed. She was very angry, it seemed, but still saying nothing. I knew a nerve had been touched.

"Can you relate to any of that, Sherry?" I asked her reluctantly, not really wanting to leave Yvonne.

Sherry exploded, "You idiot! You didn't cause the beatings. How can you be so screwed up? It's you mother's problem, not yours. If I had been your mother, it would have been your asshole father's problem. I would have killed the son-of-a-bitch." I had never seen Sherry worked up like this, and I knew we were into pay dirt. I glanced at Annette, and a slight shake of her head convinced me that we'd do well to go with Sherry, almost unprofessionally leaving Yvonne sobbing. Both of these women were wide open, but we couldn't go with both at once, or so I thought.

"Stay with your feelings, Sherry," I urged. "We are all with you." And looking around, I saw that I was right. The other five group members were with Sherry. I didn't understand it, but I've learned to expect in groups that when a very quiet patient like Sherry gets emotional, the group goes with that one. Clearly, the entire group was empathizing with Sherry, not with Yvonne. But more to my amazement, Yvonne had stopped crying, and even she was caught up in Sherry's outburst.

"You tell 'em, baby," Yvonne whispered, but loudly enough to get Sherry's attention.

Sherry started to weep bitterly. It was a new experience for her. Seven other people were suddenly with her in her world of pain. That had never happened before. All these people knew about Sherry, knew she was here because she had beaten her child, and child beaters always have a strike against them in group. But they were all with her now. I think for the first time in her life, Sherry felt accepted, felt it was all right to be a human being full of mistakes, full of hurts, full of anger. The effect on Sherry was magical, whatever caused it. I've seen this often in patients, especially in group therapy. Something changes in a twinkling of an eye, and that person is never the same again. They are opened up, they are vulnerable; but having felt the acceptance of others, they come out of their shells. It seems that most people have to hit bottom before they can really make progress. And Sherry had definitely hit bottom!

Finally, Sherry gained control enough to talk, aware that all eyes were upon her. "I never told anyone in my life I hated my daddy. The damned pious hypocrite! I hated him when he beat my mother, and I hate him now. He was supposed to be a man of God, and he put my poor mother through hell. She never did a thing that pleased him, and just for the pure hell of it or more like for the pure joy of it, the bastard whipped her with his belt like she was a little child. I watched in horror every time. I felt every lash of the belt, and I wanted it to be me, not her. I was the only other person who saw or knew. My mother was pure and sweet. She didn't deserve to be whipped. I deserved it more than she did because I hated him. The fact that she seemed to worship him made me hate him even more," Sherry began to sob uncontrollably again; and Yvonne, far from feeling forsaken after her own painful outburst, walked around the table and took Sherry into her embrace. There were no dry eyes in the room. Grown male psychologists cry, too; and while Yvonne's pitiful outburst hadn't broken through what I thought was my impregnable professionalism, Sherry's outburst did. Sherry made me just another human being, as subject to pain as the next one. Group was over. What to do next?

It was a week from Sherry's outburst to my next individual session with her. I had planned very carefully for this one. I spent a lot of time planning. I knew several things would have to happen. I wrote them down: 1) Sherry must develop her insights concerning why she started hurting Joel. 2) Sherry would have to develop insight into why she had the affair. 3) Sherry would have to tell Jim both about the affair and about using crack. 4) Sherry would have to deal with her hatred for her father.

Talk about the best-laid plans — Sherry came in smiling and before I could muster my professional, carefully-thought-out approach to the agenda, she said, "You know what, Doctor Gaylord, I know now why I was so mean to Joel. I was taking out on Joel my anger at both Jim and my father. Jim was a lot like my father, you know. Oh, Jim wasn't mean, he never struck me, but they both feel women are creatures instead of human beings."

"Oh," I said.

"And what's more, I know why I had the affair, even why I smoked the marijuana and then the crack. And I've got to tell Jim all about that, explain it to him and ask him to forgive me."

From that point, for the balance of the therapeutic hour, Sherry thoroughly mesmerized me. After the session, I wondered why people even need psychologists.

The third weekend of her four-week stay at Altrusa, Sherry was allowed to go out to dinner with Jim. Those were the rules for people who made good progress.

Sherry left Altrusa at the specified time. I was glad to write the judge a letter reporting her good progress. So far as I knew, she and Jim were ready to live happily ever after. I never knew how Sherry made peace with her father or whether she even did or not. People can't be happy because of things; they must be happy in spite of a lot of things. Most of my patients gain a reasonable ability to cope with life, when they decide that they themselves are acceptable and indeed are accepted by others just the way they are. In order to be happy, a person must accept life completely on the terms that life provides. There are no beds of roses.

****

As Sherry sat opposite me after her readmission to Altrusa, I felt the burn-out worse than I ever had before. "I've just got to get away for awhile," I whispered to myself. "I think I'll ask that this woman be referred to another therapist."

Sherry looked me straight in the eye. "Now, Dr. Gaylord," she said. "no more bullshit! I've really got a problem, and I'm ready to face it. I've been using crack now for over a year. I'm the one that first gave it to Jack Joyner. I'm ready for the medication to control my craving because I know I can't control it without help. Jim is hanging in there with me, and Joel is back with my parents. The judge is giving me another chance, and believe me, I'm not going to mess up this time!"

"Sherry, I'm sure you'll understand when I tell you that I feel it best to refer you to another therapist," I said.

"Why, Dr. Gaylord, I hope you won't do that! We have such a trusting relationship already," she pleaded.

I didn't feel I could help Sherry, and I knew that it was necessary for me to take a couple of weeks off. I did.

****

I kept informed of Sherry Minot's treatment during her second stay at Altrusa because, after all, I had a lot of time and energy invested in her. She was an exemplary client all the way, I was told. At present, six months after her second release, Sherry, Jim and Joel seem to be a family living happily ever after.

The Facts As We Best Know Them

Treatment Modalities in Substance Abuse Centers

For those of us who have been practicing counseling-psychotherapy for over twenty years, the formation of hundreds of substance abuse centers, public and private, has forced us into new ways of thinking. Most of us have thought of ourselves as eclecticists. While being trained basically in some time-honored "system" of counseling-therapy such as psychoanalysis, gestalt therapy, behavior therapy or existential-humanistic therapy (to name only a few), we have always reached out from our basic concepts to use bits and pieces of other "systems" in service to our clients.

Existential-humanistic concepts comprise the center from which I have worked. Most of my clients were young, upwardly-mobile persons who had lost their sense of identity and meaning in a confusing, complex society. Many of their values had been lost or compromised. They were in existential crises of one kind or another. They were disenchanted and alienated from their cultures, struggling to find directions for their lives.

Most of my clients, up to ten years ago, were stymied in their growth processes. They were in existential vacuums, needing to establish new and renewed reasons for getting on with their lives. My basic approach with most of them was to establish a trusting relationship with them, trying to show them I cared about them and prized them as immensely valuable human persons, worthy of love and essentially free to break their shackles of confusion and move out of their stalemated private worlds. These concepts are ingrained within the teachings of Rogers (7), Maslow (4) and Patterson (5). The important point is that although their personal freedoms had been temporarily suspended, they really had the abilities to get under their own loads. All they needed was understanding, caring and acceptance. Being basically free to make decisions, reformulate their goals, establish priorities and engage life in more meaningful ways, I had great confidence and, I firmly believe, moderate success in being a good counselor-therapist for these clients.

A New Eclecticism: A Changing World with Changing Emphases

Now that many of us have moved into substance abuse treatment centers with our understandings of human needs and human frailties intact, we are seeing a world in which a broader eclecticism has become necessary. Most of us have forsaken our somewhat narrow "systems" approach and have vastly expanded our reaching-out to embrace and utilize a myriad of old and new concepts. Truth to tell, we have a new generation of clients who occupy front-center of our professional practice of counseling-therapy.

I am faced with a new generation of clients. Not that they are unaffected by the issues they face just as the above described clients were, but they have all those problems superseded by yet another global and all-encompassing one — they are substance abusers. It is my belief that once they have the demon of substance abuse under control, they shall still have the same collage of problems outlined above to deal with because the world becomes more, not less, complex with every passing day. As a matter of fact, it is my contention that most substance abusers are using drugs because they were unable to deal with the types of problems mentioned above. Now that they have taken the "out" of substance abuse, they still have the "old" problems which have always hounded mankind — problems of childhood conflicts, problems of threats to self-esteem growing out of our ultra-competitive society and problems growing out of basic human insecurities.

Substance abusers have become the fastest-growing group needing counseling services, and a myriad of treatment facilities have been created to deal with them. And deal with them we must! The centers will have done their jobs when the abusers have gained control of the chemicals that control them now. Yes, that is true, at least in the sense that the hoped-for breaking of the control the chemicals have is most often the ending place targeted in these clinics. However, I do not think the job of rescuing the perishing will have been done if drug abusers are left only with a "live-one-day-at-a-time" life style. But I confess that this is a logical goal for substance abuse treatment centers.

The Nature of the New Clients

The clients who sit and talk with us in the context of drug treatment centers and who attend our multi-faceted group sessions are distinctly different from clients who simply need to have the shackles to their freedoms removed. These clients (non substance abusers), having achieved this liberation with the help of caring counselor-therapists, move on to embrace their life and their problems with a restored freedom.

Summarily, clients who are in the substance abuse centers are vastly different because of several important factors: First, these clients do not have merely a partial loss of control of their lives and future possibilities as do the others not dealing with substance abuse. These clients have surrendered complete control to chemicals. This is an entirely different kind of loss of control. It is a total loss. This being so, we cannot expect to reestablish self-control solely by means of caring, accepting and otherwise facilitating decision-making thereby making it possible for these clients to get under their own loads. The task is qualitatively and quantitatively different. These victims of substance abuse are incapable of getting under their own loads. It is a sad reality that, although these clients are not all alike, most of them must live out their lives on a level of compromise with the chemicals which they are abusing. Never again, at least in most cases, will these clients be able to be masters of their own fates. True, they may live productive lives but always under subservience to the ever-present threat of having the chemicals once again regain control. The once-an-alcoholic, always-an-alcoholic context of most twelve-step programs will be their albatrosses for the rest of their lives. True, a few persons of prominence are now decrying this truism; but sadly, the evidence supports the "forever-condemned-to-vigilance" proposition.

Let us be more specific about these substance abusing clients. No counselor-therapist of worth ever faced a client without reservations concerning the client's avoidance tactics. All clients resist therapy and have a natural reluctance to be fully known to a counselor-therapist, indeed, to be fully known even to themselves.

The substance abuser, however, is different; if not in kind, he is certainly different in degree. It should be emphasized that the counselor-therapist must be non-judgmental as he deals with a client. On the other hand, it is beneficial to the client for the counselor-therapist to be as fully aware of what is going on as possible. Being non-judgmental in the context of substance abuse is to be paradoxically wary.

We must take the calculated risk of over-generalization in order to describe the substance-abusing client. Certainly, they are not all alike, but there is a common denominator for all of them, and that is that they are in a closed-wall institution. Most often, they are not there of their own choosing. Let us suggest some common mind-sets in these clients. And having a mind-set of our own that all human persons are inherently valuable, we will not be misunderstood — these are not "bad guys." They are struggling with the monsters of their addictions, and that causes them to act in ways they probably otherwise would not act.

Most of the substance abusers are suffering from continuing craving for the drug(s) to which they are addicted. Most of them, especially crack and ice abusers, are depressed and paranoid. The time-honored techniques of gaining a trusting relationship will not work nearly so well with these clients.

Drug Abusers Are Seldom Totally Cooperative

They are most often not committed to the goals of therapy. They are largely not where they are either in one-on-one sessions or in groups without deep rancor and anger within them for having to be there. They are typically under pressure of losing custody of children, of losing jobs, of satisfying parents, of losing inheritances and, above all, they are under the pressure of craving drugs. Thus, they are not as interested in their own self-growth as are self-referring clients. Moreover, they are expert at showing concern they do not really feel.

These clients are deniers by definition. They likely are denying that they have a problem and they are denying that they are denying anything. The thinking of many of them is that they really shouldn't be under treatment at all.

These clients are seldom truly cooperative although they may mimic cooperativeness. They are working within their own hidden agendas. They are trying to figure how they may escape these walls, these intrusions on their rights. Many think the treatments they endure are diabolical schemes concocted by parents, the law, their employers and others ad infinitum to keep them captive while denying them what they think they must have, another fix. However, they deny to themselves and everyone else that they must have another fix. Without wishing to demean them, I must say that these clients are among the most astute con-artists a counselor-therapist will ever face.

Self-esteem, The Beginning and the Ending

Self-esteem is a very important word in our society. Its absence in the person has been heralded as a basic factor in maladjustment, which indeed it is. Everyone knows he must have high self-esteem to feel a sense of self-value. And remarkably, most reasonably educated people know how they have gained a low self-esteem — parents have not given of themselves as they ought, the competitive society is geared to the superior person, failure is disallowed, punishments are dealt to those who do not deserve them, sibling rivalries and hosts upon hosts of other causes.

We are told on good authority that substance abusers are people of low self-esteem. And of course they are! They work constantly and consistently through denial to avoid being conscious of their low self-esteem. But we may be sure that they feel low self-esteem, and when not consciously feeling it, the specter of low self-worth is lurking just beneath the surface.

A naive proposition is that if we can just raise the self-esteem of abusers, then we have scored a direct hit, and the problem will go away. There is some truth here, but more naivete than reality!

We are faced with a circuitous, chicken-and-egg debacle with the drug abuser. Low self-esteem likely was a cause of his drug use. But then, this drug use becomes a chief cause of this low self-esteem. Summarily, then, we cannot from the beginning score a bulls-eye by magically turning up self-esteem with a warm relationship, with inspirational words or with our honest caring and acceptance. It is not true that if the counselor-therapist accepts the abuser with unconditional positive regard, that will cause the abuser to accept himself. These elements of prizing, supporting and accepting are good, even necessary; but they will, at best, only crack the door into the depressive world of low self-worth — low self-worth that came into being by a myriad of life events beginning at birth and culminating in drug abuse which simply makes the crippler, low self-esteem, that much more debilitating.

Why the Segregated Clinic is Necessary

If self-esteem is going to be raised within the treatment context, the effort must come at the beginning, throughout the treatment regimen and must be supported in continuing support-group context, perhaps forever. As a person being controlled by chemicals progresses to a modified self-control, raised self-esteem will naturally follow. But this hoped-for progression can never happen unless concerted, planned efforts are engineered into the treatment process from beginning to end — and even beyond the end of formal treatment.

Clients who are drug abusers must be controlled until a measure of self-control may be engineered via treatment regimen. To start with, the client must be committed to a designated stay in an institution with walls. True, some clients will think this center is nothing short of prison. If being controlled by others for a time does a prison make, then the facility must be just that.

Cognitive Restructuring

The basic problems of drug abusers derive from faulty thinking and learning. Clients must be helped to overcome bad thinking patterns.

In order to accomplish this, most counselor-therapists have adopted confrontational techniques. Counselor-therapists are challenging clients forthrightly, strongly urging them to restructure their ways of seeing their worlds and trying to instill in the clients new ways of thinking and learning.

A large body of literature is being developed along coercive lines with substance abusers. Counselor-therapists must be strong-minded and willing to challenge the faulty thinking of clients who have adopted negative thought patterns. Substance abusers are notorious for blaming others, for dodging responsibility and for engaging in self-destructive modes of thinking. They are irrational in their thinking, and this causes irrational behavior.

For example, consider the woman who left her husband because he was more untidy than she would have liked. "I just simply can't stand to live with a man who doesn't put things where they belong. I deserve better than that."

"Don't you think you have become a victim of irrational thinking to believe that any man you might live with must be perfect?" the counselor-therapist may ask. "What did you expect, a knight on a white horse who would sweep you off your feet and perform absolutely according to every dream you have had about the perfect husband?"

It may be brought out that this woman expects perfection in everything, that she is not perfect herself by any means and that she must change her irrational thinking if she is going to be able to have a successful marriage with any man.

Counselor-therapists who work in substance abuse are fast learning the confrontational methods offered in the writings of Ellis (2), Glasser (3) and Bandura (1) among others.

Acting-Out Therapy

Acting-out therapy is common in substance abuse centers, both in one-to-one situations with client and counselor-therapist and in groups. The counselor-therapist working one-on-one prepares in advance for this type therapy. He has props available in his office for acting out. Usually there are towels to be twisted, pillows to be pounded and a myriad of situational acting-out episodic accoutrements kept on hand.

Anger is the number one emotion which benefits from acting out. A client kneeling in front of a chair, pounding a pillow while being encouraged to verbalize his anger, is a good example. The client is urged to "stay with the feeling" and hopefully will express beneficial cathartic release by physically and verbally acting out his anger against towels and pillows which symbolically represent persons toward whom the anger is directed. The reader may gain more understanding of these methods by studying Self-Actualizing Therapy by Shostrom (8).

The World of Reinforcements and Behavioral Modifications

The substance abuse centers are, summarily, institutions where behavioral control methods comprise a prominent place in treatment. Any institution must be governed by codified rules. The rules for most institutions are given both to the client being treated and to his guardian(s) be they parents, law-enforcement personnel or employers.

Any rule not complied with meets unerringly with aversive conditioning. Institutions do not make mistakes parents often make, being on-again, off-again with rules enforcement. Aversive conditioning is often a prelude to positive behavior.

Thus, clients are denied privileges such as watching television, receiving telephone calls, or they are denied privileges of even conversing with those who may come. Some centers use various "freezes" as aversive conditioners. This may include a freeze on opposite-sexed conversation as an example.

The ASAP center at Van Nuys, California uses the ITP (Intensive Treatment Program) for aversive reinforcement. This program confines the client to his individual quarters for a designated period, not allowing free periods between scheduled activity.

For the client, the regimen consists of little "free" time. Scheduled activities fill most of the hours at substance abuse clinics. Some of these facilities may wish to be known as "toughlove centers," others may decry that term. And of course, there are variations of the toughlove theme in all treatment centers. Treatment centers must run the gamut from mild to severe measures of toughlove because substance abusers run the gamut from totally reprehensible to mildly self-defeating.

Still, behavior control is a chief element in all centers; the methods are custom designed to fit the requirements of a center reputed to be tough as well as the requirements of a center reputed to be not-so-tough. All styles of centers are needed because we are becoming a society saturated by all styles of substance abusers. Choosing a treatment center appropriate for a given individual is usually and necessarily a heart-rendering choice, especially for parents.

Behavior control follows the principles of rewarding desired behaviors (positively reinforcing) and punishing undesirable behavior (aversively reinforcing). Reinforcement of the positive and punishment of the negative are chief elements of the learning process, and learning is the *sine qua non* of any treatment regimen.

In order for reinforcements to be effective, the abuser must be succinctly aware of what behaviors are considered worthy of positive and what behaviors are deserving of negative reinforcement. These are carefully enunciated to the client with frequent reminders.

Contracting in Behavior Control

It is a general rule, that a person under treatment will learn from reinforcement better if he enters into a formal contract. Thus, contracts, both short-term and long-term, are very common in treatment centers. Short-term contracts may be subsumed under a written diary-like declaration of "what I am going to do today to make my program a success." An example of a longer-termed contract is, "If you abide by all rules this week, you may go out to McDonald's with a sponsored group on Friday evening." It could be argued that contracting can become a futile exercise when done too meticulously as touching on minute performances. Each center must contend with this issue.

Contracts are often used between the assigned counselor-therapist and his clients. They are used extensively as agreements between the larger institution and clients. Contracts are written and signed always by the client, in most cases, by the client and a center functionary.

Most institutions work with a levels concept. Everyone begins on the first level and earns status up the hierarchy for appropriate behavior. A client can be "busted" down from a higher level to a lower one. Usually, promotion up the levels-ladder is verbalized in a contractual agreement between the parties. The difference between one level and the next is by calculation a considerable chasm created so as to serve as both enticement and as enforcement.

Contingency Contracting

Many persons are placed in substance abuse centers by employers. Contingency contracting is useful in many contexts, but the contract between employer and employee is the most common as in the following example:

An employer has found that a valued employer is abusing chemicals in manners and degrees as to bring about unproductivity or endangerment within the workplace. The employer who values this worker agrees to pay a significant amount of the treatment costs for services provided that the worker will enter a contingency contract. The written agreement stipulates that the worker may return to his job after treatment, but that he will remain chemically free or surrender his right to work. Usually, the worker's agreement to take periodic drug screening tests is an integral part of the agreement. Such contracting has been deemed highly successful under research studies.

Treatment, A Multi-faceted Project

Detoxification

Clients at closed-wall centers for substance abusers almost always begin in detoxification programs although some centers accept clients who have been through detox centers not in house. This detox program consists of at least forty-eight hours of "drying out." The severely addicted may be helped in this process by drug administration designed to allow the client a less painful withdrawal.

The medical aspect of the center's program is always at the ready. In addition to drugs to ease physical withdrawal, many clients are medicated to ease craving. These medications are invaluable in easing suffering toward the end that clients may be in position to make maximal gains in all aspects of the program.

There are the usual severe cases of depression which must be treated. Attempted suicides are of great concern for substance abuse centers. Various types of self-administered health and life-threatening behaviors are to be reckoned with, and so, medical support personnel are an integral part of any center's armament.

Groups and More Groups

Most substance abuse centers utilize a wide variety of groups. Basically, there are two kinds: therapy group and family group . The dynamics of a group lend themselves well to substance abusers.

Therapy groups usually have two leaders, one male and one female. One of these will be designated as leader, the other as co-leader, but this is by staff duty roster. The clients do not recognize the difference between the leaders, and except for some organizational and reporting matters, little difference exists.

The basic idea in groups is to get the clients to talk. Some clients talk very little early on, but there are always the over-talkers who must be controlled. The clients in a given group are usually the one-on-one clients of the two leaders. In this way, the leaders have a better handle on who in the group needs to be encouraged to talk about or relate to a topic currently under discussion. Sometimes, the agenda is largely unplanned as to content. At other times, it follows pre-arranged topics. Sometimes, the agenda focuses on persons deemed to be ready for maximum gain. Often a topic of current interest is discussed by a number of clients, each of them offering opinions and comments. Then, under the guiding hand of one of the therapists, a topic is maneuvered in a manner so as to bear upon the current quandaries of a particular group member.

If the member reacts to the efforts of the leader, he may very well move into a feeling context, thus relating to the group his private fears and hopes. Thus, opportunities are created for members to discuss their families, relationships of all sorts and, most importantly, their feelings of isolation, of anger, of disappointment or pain. Through this process, the conversation brings buried emotions to the surface.

As a member may express strong feelings of anger, despair or disenchantment toward a significant other person or situation, these expressed feelings may provide catharsis or insight for that member. Other members often voluntarily join in, and in what sometimes seems and sounds like a free-for-all, this or that member may experience something important to him. If a member seems to be moving constructively into understandings and/or catharsis, a leader may encourage that person to "stay with the feeling" hoping that he will move into levels of feeling and understanding he has avoided before.

Then, too, as a leader may sense that an issue under scrutiny within the group discussion may have a bearing on the problem of another member (who is likely a one-on-one client of this leader), the leader may ask, "Can you relate to that, Charlie?" Often this is the best way to get a shy or recalcitrant member into group participation.

Obviously, the group can become highly emotional. The emotion-laden discussions often are a wedge into the deepest problem(s) of some member. The leader, then, has good reason and motivation to bring these revelations into one-on-one counseling at a later time.

A peculiar dynamic of the group is that people will drop their masks more in group than in one-on-one counseling. In a sense, there are as many therapists present in group as there are people present. When a person feels accepted by an individual counselor, he may experience some acceptance of himself and therewith a gain in self-esteem. In a much more dramatic way, acceptance by the full membership of a group, especially as it may deal with a problem the member has never confessed before, does much more to elevate self-esteem than is possible in one-on-one counseling.

Some group leaders favor acting-out techniques. These techniques; such as role playing, role reversal, psychodrama and various techniques in which leaders issue challenges to individual members; are common. These techniques derive from gestalt therapy and self-actualizing therapy (6, 8).

The Language of Groups

Substance abuse clinics do not make an effort to observe strict codes of "proper" speech. In the hope of getting the members to express themselves freely, there is seldom any attempt to dictate speech forms. Thus, the language used in group is usually that typically used by the clients. What some would call vulgarity is standard verbal fare in the group, and although some members may be offended, it is considered a better part of wisdom to allow members to express themselves in their own way.

In essence, group allows members to get down to "gut" level, allows them to say about parents what they could never say to parents. There are recognized pluses and minuses in this lack of decorum, but most centers do not try to control language forms in groups. On the other hand, leaders are expected not to be extreme in language although even they may be "more expressive" in group than they normally would be.

Family Group

Most centers have family group once a week. These groups may include all the clients plus all the parents who will deign to appear. Where center clientele is large, more than one family group is planned, usually on alternate evenings. Center personnel are usually on call to attend any or all family groups with staffing controlled by management.

The family group is seldom a thing of beauty. There is usually a lot of shouting as young people hurl invectives toward parents who often use this setting to relieve themselves of anger, too. A reasonable order out of otherwise probable chaos is managed by several adroit counselor-therapists and techs, as the paraprofessionals are often called.

Family group is usually a setting where parents and adolescents can vent their feelings against another, and that is considered to be the beginning of understanding. Usually, often by pre-arrangement, one family is brought back together in family group. Usually such reunions of families are applauded in family group. Unfortunately, what appears to be a united family riding off into the sunset does not always prevail over time.

Substance Abuse Centers, Success and Failure

Most contractual arrangements in substance abuse centers are for a specified time period, ranging usually from twenty-eight days upward to three months. At the agreed-upon ending time, a number of things may happen

Often one twenty-eight day stay is simply the prelude to another because the client has made no discernible progress. Sometimes, an extra week is agreed to be necessary. Most treatment entities set minimum periods of stay. This period is usually considered to be invaluable. The cooperating client may be allowed privileges as he is seen to be earning them but is rarely released early.

It must be remembered that substance abuse treatment is expensive, and for that reason, some clients are released at the minimum-stay point when, as a matter of fact, they would benefit from further treatment. For many parents and youngsters alike, the ending time is a time for jubilation, and it is hoped that the joy will be permanent. On the other hand, all parties to the contractual stay may feel a sense of dismal failure.

Follow Up is Usually Critical

The relapse rate from substance abuse treatment is unacceptably high. The outcome may be confinement to a tougher love program often in another city, or the outcome may be further degeneration into heavier drug abuse. Much is said about the need of abusers to "hit bottom." Clients "hit bottom" in ways and in time that are largely unpredictable — many never do.

The undesirable probability is that in most treatment programs, one problem (drug abuse) is partially solved while a larger collage of problems still lurk as they did before drug addiction or treatment occurred. Problems stemming from dysfunctional families, faulty genetics, childhood conflicts and other causes ad infinitum should be addressed after the substance abuse is controlled. The better part of wisdom is to believe that the stay in the center is a beginning — a beginning point for deeper long-term therapy, a beginning of dynamic and lasting change within the family context and certainly the beginning of follow-up support. Those who finish their stay at abuse treatment centers are always urged to seek out some type of twelve to eighteen step program, either Alcoholics Anonymous or a similar program more specific to the their addiction.

The substance abuse center resides in a central place in current society. The benefits to many cannot be overstated. That they summarily are in a formative state in terms of techniques, rules and regimens is testimony only to the many varieties of drug abuse and to a society which has created problems too complex for any stylized program to interdict.

Bibliography

1   Bandura, Albert. <u>Principles of Behavior Modification</u>. New York. Holt, Rineholt and Winston. 1969.

2   Ellis, Albert and Grieger, Russell. <u>Rational-Emotive Therapy: A Skills-based Approach</u>. New York. Van Nostrand Reinhold Co. 1980.

3   Glasser, William M.D. <u>Reality Therapy: A New Approach to Psychiatry</u>. Harper & Row, Publishers. New York, 1965.

4   Maslow, Abraham Harold. <u>Toward a Psychology of Being</u>. Princeton, N.J. Van Nostrand. 1968.

5   Patterson, Cecil Holden. <u>Relationship Counseling and Psychotherapy</u>. New York. Harper & Row. 1974.

6   Perls, Frederick S. <u>Gestalt Therapy: Excitement and Growth in the Human Personality</u>. New York. Dell Press. 1965.

7   Rogers, Carl. <u>Client-centered Therapy, Its Current Practice, Implications, and Therapy</u>. Boston. Houghton Mifflin. 1951.

8   Shostrom, Everett L. <u>Actualizing Therapy: Foundations for a Scientific Ethic</u>. San Diego, California. EdITS Publishers. 1976.

Chapter 9

Toughlove — A Sometimes Winner

Happening Nine — Toughlove or No Love

The Facts As We Best Know Them

Toughlove and Behavioral Change
A History of Child-Family Dynamics
The Family Break-down
Adolescent Behavior Under New Values
Enter Toughlove
The Good Sense of Toughlove
Toughlove Outside An Institution
Glasser's Reality Therapy
Institutions for Toughlove
Closed Institutions of Toughlove
In Summary

Happening Nine — Toughlove or No Love

It was a tense moment for every one of them. Janet Sparks, Albert Sparks and their fifteen-year-old son Brad were being ushered into the intake office of Forthright Substance Abuse Center in Birmingham. Having flown into Birmingham the evening before, they should all have been rested occupying a comfortable suite in the Savoy.

None of them was refreshed, however, either in body, mind or spirit. It was down-side all the way. Neither Janet nor Albert had slept. They had agreed that one of them would monitor Brad's door, visible, by pre-arrangement, from their bedroom. They were desperately afraid that Brad would run. Brad definitely had not wanted to come to Forthright. He had been abusive to them about it at home before they left, at the O'Hare airport during a stopover between flights, and at the hotel last evening.

"I am a damned convict," he screamed at them last evening. "You've got me down here where the skinheads can tie me to a tree and strip the hide off my back. Don't you know these people down here are assholes who'll torture your favorite son in their cell blocks?" Looking straight at Janet he screamed, "You bitch!" And Albert floored Brad with the back of his hand full force across the boy's mouth.

"Albert!" Janet screamed. "You know better than that. Don't you see he's not responsible. He's paranoid and he's scared. You know what crack has done to him!" Albert sulked into the bathroom as Janet slumped on the couch fighting the tears.

"A good example." Brad taunted Albert's retreating back as he picked himself up off the floor. "Daddy Albert, the enforcer, has lots of moves he could show these hillbilly pricks down here."

Janet and Albert suspected, in fact, they knew Brad had been using pot over two years ago. They had wrestled with the problems of Brad's bad behavior with the help of his school counselor. They had seen it all: failing grades, sullenness, impudence, sloppiness, hanging out with scum. Brad had made sure that the family was properly tortured. According to him, they were stupid and mean, everyone of them. At first, the older children, both of them married, had tried to help; but Brad had driven them away with insipid, despicable, smart-ass remarks.

Brad had taken over the household in spite of Albert's vicious anger. Janet had fussed with Albert, "We've got to give a little. If we let him have his friends here, maybe we can keep him off the street."

It was totally disgusting! Brad had his dirty friends over constantly. They ate everything in sight! The house was a total wreck. The girls would stay until midnight, but usually one of them (Thank God, it was only one at a time.) came back, slipped through Brad's window and spent the night. How disgusting! Janet and Albert had gone so far as to relieve one another, taking turns at going to a motel just to get a good night's sleep. It was unbelievable; the two of them were being driven from their own home!

Brad's arrest for robbing a convenience store with the help of his cronies had been the shocker and the clincher. Brad had been put in jail that night. The clerk at the store had been put in the hospital from the gang beating.

The media had really opened up on all the parents and families involved. They were all being sued both by the convenience store and by the clerk who had taken such a beating. Thank God, the clerk hadn't been killed!

More than that, thank God, Brad hadn't been killed. He had stolen Albert's German luger pistol which had been used in the robbery. Brad swore that it wasn't he who had pointed the pistol and the clerk, and a gunsmith had testified that the gun couldn't be fired — that there were no shells available anywhere for it. But the sentence had been for armed robbery anyway, and neither Albert nor Janet had thought Brad would get probation. But Dick had come through for them; the judge reluctantly agreed to a ten-year probated sentence conditioned upon Brad's entering a treatment facility approved by the court.

In the hall of the courthouse, Dick had circled arms around Janet and Brad. "You've got to get him out of town and into treatment," he'd said. "The further away the better!" Dick had helped them get Brad into Forthright, but even Dick had seemed surprised when they chose Birmingham. Dick had just raised his eyebrows and said, "That's fine. That's good. Okay. That ought to do it. The court will be satisfied with Forthright."

****

Reviewing the last month in her mind, Janet felt herself torn with pity for her son and with pity, not anger really, for Albert. Albert had always been a great father to all their children. Brad had virtually destroyed the family this last month, himself included, of course.

Janet had been reliving those nightmares all the time they were sitting in the reception room waiting for the director to see them. "Mr. and Mrs. Sparks, you may go in now," the receptionist told them, avoiding Brad's eyes.

Dr. Jaffee, medical director, seated the three of them, shaking hands with Janet and Albert while ignoring the obvious refusal of Brad to shake hands. Janet heaved a small sigh of relief when Brad sat down; she hadn't been sure that he'd even do that.

Dr. Jaffee entered into a somewhat one-sided conversation in which he confirmed that Janet and Albert really had surrendered their own energies and decision-making processes, long ago strained beyond endurance, to Forthright. "You understand, I'm sure, my dear people," he began in an ingratiating manner, "that Forthright accepts only those patients who they feel can be helped. We have done a thorough study of Brad's problems and have freely consulted with the people back in your hometown, Brockaway, including your family physician. We believe we have a center here in Birmingham that can restore your family — give you back you son, Mr. and Mrs. Sparks." he intoned.

"The hell you say," Brad interrupted. "So you are going to give my beautiful bitchy parents back something they never wanted in the first place — me, their son."

Dr. Jaffee did not appear the slightest bit disturbed as he turned his attention to Brad. "Young man," he said with a severe tone, "this center has done the near impossible many times. It would be better if we had your cooperation; as a matter of fact, we shall have your cooperation."

"Bullshit!" Brad sputtered.

"Yes, young man, our center emphasizes control of the patient until he is able to control himself. Our system will only reward desirable behavior. You can fight us, young man, but you will find that our love is tougher than the hate you've brought to us."

Brad smirked. Janet could see the wheels turning in his head. He was so completely unnerving to her. Sometimes, with tremendous guilt, she found herself even wishing Brad were dead. Why couldn't he be normal? Ginger and Albert Jr. had been a first family, and then ten years later when she was thirty-eight, Brad had come along. Why did this have to happen to them? They were too old to endure this, she thought.

"It'll be a second family for all of us," Albert had beamed at Janet, Ginger and Bert in the private hospital room the morning after Brad was born. This little guy is going to make us absolutely inseparable. How wrong he was! It had been hell all the way with Brad; and about fifteen years later, with Ginger and Bert both married and with two grandchildren in their separate incubators, the family was everything but a united one.

Brad had been a problem child from the start. She knew that they had spoiled him early on. Albert's business was flourishing. There was money to spend on their little son. They both vowed openly to give this one everything they couldn't afford for Ginger and Bert.

That had been the beginning of a multiplicity of mistakes. In fact, as they heard it thirteen to fourteen years later first from Brad's school counselor and then from Dr. Knight, a clinical psychologist to whom Brad had been referred, they had done absolutely nothing right. She and Albert had long ago conceded the point.

Ginger and Bert, both normal pre-teens at Brad's birth, had little love for the imposter from the beginning. They had been told that Brad was "high-strung" from birth — first by their pediatrician and then by their family physician. "Some children are born with bad nervous systems," had been Dr. Craft's (family physician) summary statement.

The pediatrician five years earlier had spoken about new advances in medical knowledge. "We know now that many of a child's behavior patterns are inherited," he'd said, and she and Albert had been asked to fill out pages of questions about both family histories.

As Albert had said, "They want to know everything from Uncle Harry's ingrown toenail to what my peak temperature was when I had the measles." It might have been funny if Brad hadn't been so tragic. For Janet's part, she was perfectly willing and ready to concede that it was all her fault; she had been too old to have a normal baby.

But even so, Brad had been very dear to her. Although he was hyperactive and mischievous from the beginning, he had had a special charm for her. He was a cuddler. Once he had tired himself out with his boisterousness, he had always found a ready place in her waiting arms. She had watched him in his crib sleeping, yearning to take him to her. Brad was a beautiful, charming, lovable little one. Janet had recognized the child as her last hope of achieving the kind of closeness she had been too immature to develop with either Ginger or Bert. She had just been too young then and, perhaps, a little resentful of their taking so much of her time. She had wanted so much to get onto a career track when the first ones had come along. And, at great sacrifice, she had done that. As an adjunct to Albert's architectural firm, she had developed her superb decorating skills to a finely honed point. Then, Brad had made his unexpected appearance.

Could it have been possible that Brad hadn't felt her love? The pediatrician had advised that she not give up her career. She had read so much about successful career and successful mothering being possible at the same time. She just couldn't believe Brad had ever felt unloved. She remembered being so jealous of Brenda who had been a godsend as a live-in nanny of sorts.

Janet had reviewed half a lifetime during the thirty seconds or so it took Dr. Jaffee to confirm the financial arrangements for Forthright — arrangements she already knew well from the literature they had been sent. The literature had explained that the costs were the same at all Forthright Centers; the costs were shocking, but if the treatment worked, it would be well worth it.

There was another Forthright in Chicago and one in Milwaukee, but they'd decided Birmingham would be better. "The further, the better," had been Albert's opinion born from despair and, as Janet thought, from his feeling that the family deserved not to suffer further embarrassment. God forgive them! She and Albert had both wanted him as far away as possible. They had had all they could stand.

Janet pulled herself from her reveries as Dr. Jaffee's tone of voice seemed to be moving from trivial to bottom line. "Maybe the literature didn't tell all," she thought. "I'd better pay attention."

"Now, here are some of the most important ground rules," Dr. Jaffee was saying. "Brad will be allowed to call home once a week, but only if he follows the rules. If you, Mr. and Mrs. Sparks don't hear from him, you'll know either that he didn't wish to talk with you or that he did not follow the rules. I say that to save all our energies. Certainly, you can call here anytime you like," he said in severe tones as though he didn't expect it to happen.

"You may visit Brad here as often as you like, provided you call first and secure our approval. Most of the parents live nearby and actually attend the family group meetings every Friday night." Janet couldn't remember that from the literature, but deep in her heart, she knew that they wouldn't be wanting to come every week, meetings or no meetings. For her part at least, she didn't want to sit through any meetings. Besides, she hoped fervently that Brad's treatment would not take over two months. The literature had suggested that as the "norm."

"And I want to make it perfectly clear, Mr. and Mrs. Sparks, that Brad will not take calls from you nor will he visit with you when you come down unless he himself wishes to do so. On the other hand, you may write letters as often as you like, and Brad will be permitted to receive them." The doctor caught Brad's eyes, and Janet was surprised that Brad would condescend to give him even a glance. But Brad seemed interested in what the doctor was saying, and Dr. Jaffee's continuing tone, in emphasizing Brad's rights, seemed to turn Brad on as if Dr. Jaffee had somehow just bestowed knighthood on him.

There wasn't much talk after that. Janet flinched when Dr. Jaffee jabbed one of the buttons on his desk, and a white-jacketed attendant came in as if on cue. "This is it," Janet thought. "I don't think I can stand it. This is what I've dreaded so much for weeks. My darling baby boy! After fifteen years, even though the last two had been totally tumultuous, how could any mother stand by and let a son be led away without screaming?" She desperately wanted to call the whole thing off, but knew she couldn't; the commitment had been made. She knew she couldn't afford to cry now.

It all happened so quickly. The attendant took Brad's arm as if he were escorting him to a waiting limousine. She saw Albert's hand reach out for a farewell handshake with Brad, saw Brad glance at his father with obvious hatred, refuse to take his offered hand and shrink away from Albert as if his father were despicable to him.

"Goodbye Brad," Janet faltered and started toward him for a hoped-for embrace. How her arms ached for him. Her heart was breaking. But Brad didn't even give her a glance, hateful or otherwise. He just stalked away with the man in white.

As the door closed, Janet collapsed into Albert's arms. She could no longer control the shuddering sobs. "I'll never see my little boy again," she thought, again thinking back to Brad as a darling little baby.

Dr. Jaffee's strong voice brought her back. "If you folks want to, you can watch the group intake through the glass in the anteroom to the family group room. They followed him to seats that seemed reserved for them. Several other couples were there and all eyes were glued to the scene occurring in the family room.

The room was filled with young people. They were clapping, gyrating their arms, swaying their bodies and singing songs Janet had never heard. Every male was in dungarees all of the same style and had closely-cropped hair. The girls had on shirts which were all alike. Their hair was all cut in the same way — a straight, bobbed cut just below their ears. They wore no makeup. All of them seemed happy; and, yet, they moved like robots.

Janet saw Brad and several others on an elevated platform. These were the initiates. Brad's hair was long, and he had a seedy look. His countenance was grim and foreboding. Janet's heart went out to him. "It must be tough for him," she thought. And then suddenly, the group broke, and one of the clean-cut, but zombie-like young men took Brad's arm leading him away.

****

They waited anxiously back in Brockaway for Brad's first call. Janet knew that she'd welcome the sound of Brad's voice even if he should demean her, revile her, even curse her. Why didn't he call? They'd assured him over and over that he need not think of the expense. Janet needed to put the blame on someone. "Albert," she said sharply and condemningly, "remember how much you fussed at him when he ran the telephone bill so high that summer when he was at church camp? Remember?" Albert was noncommittal. The two of them had been constantly at each other's throats since leaving Birmingham. She'd tried to work and had gone through the motions well enough. But now, she wanted just to hear the voice of her baby! She'd written Brad three letters telling him how dear he was to them and how much they loved him. They'd received no letter from Brad, and Brad didn't call.

Janet and Albert couldn't agree about it, but Janet secretly made arrangements to fly to Birmingham on Wednesday of the second week, just ten days after taking Brad there. The Center wouldn't dare refuse to let them see him.

"Better call and find out if they'll let us," Albert said when she finally told him about making the reservations. She thought Albert might be angry with her and was surprised at his eagerness.

Janet called Forthright, and after being put on hold as it seemed for endless periods of time, someone came to the phone and said as if it were a very confidential matter, "You'll be permitted to see your son if he wishes to see you. It might be better to clear that with him by letter."

But there was no time for a letter. Janet and Albert boarded the commuter plane, taking a through-plane to Birmingham from O'Hare. Janet was pleased to see that Albert was almost as excited as she.

Albert called the Forthright Center office at 8:30 Thursday morning and asked them to set up a time for them to see Brad. Janet was allowing her thoughts to slip backward as Albert waited out the telephone transfers, holds and what Janet knew seemed like evasive tactics the Center people seemed to have developed so well.

Janet tried to see Brad in her mind's eye, and her memory rejected the most recent Brad, always bringing up the preschool Brad who had seemed to hold his mom in a special category, just as she held him in her heart as a tousle-headed, cuddly, little bundle of joy. "They say we should come at about eleven o'clock," Albert reported. It would be so great to see Brad, and it was just a little over two hours now. It had seemed like eternity.

****

Janet and Albert sat patiently in the waiting room at Forthright from 10:30 to 11:15 before a young man in street clothes approached them. "Oh, Thank God," Janet whispered to herself. "I know he'll really be changed; he just must be making good progress."

"I'm Chuck Snowden," the young man announced himself; and, motioning for them to stay seated, he pulled a chair around to face the couch.

Janet's anticipation was stifling her. Her heart was pounding. "Such a nice courteous young man," she thought, "but he's simply too young to be a physician, psychologist or social worker."

"I'll talk to you about Brad," Chuck Snowden said in a kindly manner. "He's been assigned to me. I'm in remission from crack now. Six months ago, I was right where Brad is now. I understand him better than the professionals do — I've been right where he is."

"But where is Brad?" Janet managed to gasp. "We thought...."

"I'm sorry, Mrs. Sparks. Brad doesn't want to see you now. And maybe it's better that you don't see him. I'm surprised that the Center would let you come way down here right now," Chuck said.

"But why?" Janet asked, feeling tears coming.

"You mean to tell me you people are not letting my boy...." Albert was clearly angry.

"Please, Mr. and Mrs. Sparks, let me tell you. Brad wanted to call you day before yesterday. But he was behaving so badly, they wouldn't let him. It's toughlove here all the way. Every patient must earn every privilege. Frankly, I'd have to agree. Brad shouldn't have been allowed to call you. All he was going to do was to demand that you take him out of here. And your contract with the Center specifies that you cannot take him out short of two weeks."

Janet and Albert were stunned. Janet remembered nothing like that in the contract. But before they could protest, Chuck started talking rapidly.

"The first few weeks is always the worst, folks," he said. "Brad is having a tough time with withdrawal. He is in there right now screaming and cursing everybody. He'd do the same with you. You are lucky he doesn't want to see you. He is very angry with you right now. Surely, you can understand that."

"No, we can't understand that!" Albert said sharply. "We demand to see our son."

"Please, Mr. Sparks. Believe me, you'd just undo what little we've been able to accomplish so far. We have Brad assigned to my group. We are breaking him down little by little."

"But, you're not even a doctor" Albert almost had his hands on the young man's throat.

"Wait, Albert. Wait now." How many times she had stepped into the breach when Albert had lost his temper professionally, socially and even with Ginger and Bert. "Calm down, Albert," she got her arm around his waist, "it'll be all right."

"All right. It'll be all right. Oh, my God," Janet thought. "How am I going to stand this?" This Chuck was telling her that they were breaking Brad. Breaking what? Surely not his body! No! That wasn't it; they were breaking his spirit? Was that what they'd bargained for? On the other hand, they never had any other choice once Brad had become addicted to crack.

****

Walking out of the tunnel back at Chicago, Janet was amazed to see Ginger. "As pregnant as she is," Janet's mind told her, "she is a beauty and a joy forever." Tears came copiously as she embraced her daughter. Albert had his arms around them both.

"The little twirp wouldn't see you, would he?" Ginger treated the question as a fact.

"Ginger you're so sweet but oh, so cruel," Janet thought still holding her as closely as possible, careful not to infringe on her unborn grandchild.

"I came to drive you back to Brockaway and to stay the night," Ginger announced. "I figured you guys could use a little company, because I knew Brad was setting you up for this one."

"But he wanted to call us, Ginger. And they just wouldn't let him," Janet spoke defensively.

"I'll just bet I know what he was going to say if he had called. You wouldn't have wanted to hear it." Ginger wasn't given to subtlety, never had been. Janet had always despised that trait in Ginger.

"Okay, guys, let's get your bags, find the car and go home. I know you're tired."

Tired? "My God," Janet thought, "we're shattered. Every nerve is screaming. Oh, God! What have we done to him?" She'd thought she understood this toughlove thing, but turning him over to a bunch of hoodlums who were still hospitalized, that was too much. How Brad must be suffering, thinking he has been totally abandoned. She knew that Brad in his paranoia had interpreted the Center's refusal to let him call home as a sign that his parents didn't even wanted to speak to him. She just knew that; knowing the way Brad had become in the last few month, she just knew that. This was going to break her spirit. She just couldn't survive this. She knew she couldn't.

****

It was an almost unbelievable, an almost unbearable surprise when Brad called Saturday evening. "Hello, Mom," he said, almost cheerily. Sorry I missed you guys the other day.

They've got me on desipramine now, and I'm feeling a lot better."

Janet could hardly talk, but talk she did. She was glad Albert wasn't around; she wanted Brad all to herself. "Oh, Baby, it's so nice to hear your voice. When do you want us to come down again? Oh, how we miss you, sweetheart."

After they hung up, Janet could not believe it. It was like another world. Brad had called. She couldn't wait to share it with Albert. Brad was going to be all right. They'd go back the next weekend; Brad had agreed that would be the best time. "Oh, thank you God!" she whispered.

****

Nothing was going to go wrong this time. She called the Center at Albert's insistence. "Yes, it would be fine for them to see Brad," they said, "but only if he wants to see you."

On Thursday Albert came down with a terrible cold and announced himself not able to make the trip. It was less than twelve hours from departure time when he gave the trip up.

"Oh, Albert, I can't go, I won't go without you," she announced, knowing full well that she would go if she had to crawl all by herself.

And she did go. And Brad did see her. She remembered Chuck's previous warning, "You should be glad he refused to see you. You wouldn't want to see him the way he is now."

That had been over a week ago; Brad had been at Forthright nearly three weeks. When he came into the visiting room, Janet caught her breath, her heart in her throat nearly choking her. She nearly panicked at seeing Brad. But she fought and regained control. "Brad, sweetheart," her voice said, "it's so good to see you." Her mind could only whisper, "My God, I don't believe it."

Brad was so emaciated that Janet scarcely knew him. "He's lost twenty pounds," her inner voice anguished. "He

256

looks like a ghost." But she went on toward him, realizing that it was she who was closing the distance between them. "Oh, Brad, I've missed you so. Give your mom a hug."

But Brad was very reserved with her. He didn't push her off, but his arms hung loosely while she did the hugging.

"Hi, Mom. Where's Dad?" were his first cautious words.

She carefully explained about Albert's cold. "He didn't want to contaminate you, Brad," she said.

"I'll bet!" had been his only comment as far as Albert was concerned.

For half an hour Janet wrestled for words to get through to Brad. He just didn't respond, didn't seem to feel anything. When he spoke at all, it was only in two-word sentences. "Are you getting enough to eat?" Janet demanded.

"Yeah, Mom." he answered without further comment.

Janet relished that hour she was allowed to visit with Brad. She put every ounce of her strength into that hour. It required all the strength she had. How was she going to keep the conversation going when she was getting so little from him? It was obvious to her that Brad was on heavy medication, and it broke her heart.

They came to get Brad, and it was with relief she saw him go. This feeling surprised and amazed her. As she was repairing her makeup, planning to go back to the hotel, she was surprised to see the young man, Chuck Snowden, open the door and come in.

"It wasn't that good. Right, Mrs. Sparks?" Janet thought that he was a little presumptuous, perhaps a little rude.

"Well,...." she started to speak.

"I know how it is," he said knowingly. "Maybe I can help you some, ma'am. Like I said, I've been through what

Brad is going through and I'm still under treatment, but on a much higher level. Actually, they let me stay in my own apartment now. Oh, I could split, I guess, but I do feel useful around here. And they give me a little pocket money. Not much, but I'm not ready for the big world out there — not quite ready."

"Well, I'm glad ...."

Again Chuck interrupted. "Would you like me to come by your hotel and talk to you, Mrs. Sparks? They don't like for us to talk much to parents here. Actually, there's no mike in this room, but there is one where we talked before. Well,...."

"Oh, yes. Yes, of course, I'd like to talk some more with you, Chuck. I'm at the Savoy, room 1217. When can I expect you?"

And so the new phase began.

****

Chuck came to Janet's room in the Savoy about 7:30 that evening. He seemed at ease, in control from the beginning. His manner was confident, even cavalier. Janet immediately became aware of a flirtatious, effusive, magnanimous air about him. His actions seemed calculated to place him on even ground with her — no age differences, no status differences. He acted somehow like he was the strutting male peacock upon whom female birds of a feather should look adoringly as if proud to be able to survive his effervescent presence. That was it all the way. "We're birds of a feather, you and I. Together, we can take on the world," he seemed to be saying.

It was astounding to Janet the way he took control, seating himself in the most desirable chair, flinging his legs over the arm rest and locking his hands behind his head as he leaned back looking up at her still standing. "We've got a lot to talk about, baby," he said simply. Janet suddenly realized Chuck was high — on what she didn't know.

258

"I know how tough this is on you, Janet," he began while Janet flushed not with the girlish admiration he seemed to expect but with strong anger.

But she controlled herself. "I may really need him," she confided inwardly.

"I can do a lot for old Brad," Chuck said. "He's going to need a good buddy, and I know you want to keep informed about what's going on, sweetheart."

"How can I stand this?" Janet asked herself. "Is this twenty-year-old kid really coming on to me?" But she didn't get those kinds of vibes; it was something else with Chuck. And Chuck didn't take much time letting her know.

"For, oh say, a C-note a week, I can call you every Friday night and let you know what's cooking," Chuck went on matter-of-factly.

"A hundred dollars?" Janet gasped and then quickly recovered. He'd read her right. The hundred would be no problem, and it might well be worth the price.

So the deal was made. He'd call every Friday evening, and she'd mail him cash so he could have it by the time he gave the service. "It's F.O.B. Birmingham," Chuck grinned, making like an entrepreneur.

****

Before getting back to O'Hare, Janet had made peace with herself about Chuck. She'd never tell Albert about this; he'd hit the ceiling. She could visualize Albert cursing and saying, "The son-of-a-bitch is taking you! You are furnishing him his Friday night drug money. How do you know he's not taking crack to Brad?" And she'd made peace with that, too, hard as it was. Also, she'd made peace with the very probable fact that Chuck's price would inch up. "What a peculiar kind of blackmail," she thought as the plane started its descent.

****

Janet stayed glued to the telephone every Friday evening. She mailed Chuck the money each Wednesday, and he didn't fail her. "Honor among thieves," she often thought. She told Albert that Chuck was just doing them a favor in calling collect. Albert accepted it with raised eyebrows. Somehow, Janet knew Albert was neither happy nor enthusiastic about the arrangement; but he never complained, always anxiously waited to hear what Chuck had said.

The first two weeks were reassuring. Brad was doing just fine. "He's not fighting the system nearly as much," Chuck reported. "We'll have him home in no time," Chuck volunteered.

After hanging up the phone, Janet related to Albert what Chuck had said, and she noticed that although it was very early, Albert was already dressed for bed. Oh, how they had slept the last two weeks! They were making up for years of lost sleep. Janet realized that both of them were feeling great relief that Brad was far away and under heavily enforced control. "He can't control himself, so we've done right in getting him under control," Janet thought, her mind returning to the robbery, the trial and the probated sentence. "We were exactly right to get him far away from here."

It was late at night the following Wednesday that the telephone jarred them awake. Albert reached for the phone and listened with bleak sleepy countenance at first, and then Janet saw mounting agitation in his face. "Just a minute, Chuck," he said, covering the phone and turning to Janet. "He's run — he's ran. Oh, what the hell!" he muttered turning back to the phone and to Chuck.

The following twenty-four hours were agonized terror! Brad was somewhere alone in the Alabama countryside — in a ghetto, under a railroad bridge, drowned in a bayou — the thoughts were unbearable. Where was he? Who was he with? Was he in the evil hands of malcontents? Was he being sodomized, gang raped?

The deputy sheriff at Birmingham told them not to come, but to stay by the phone. "We'll get him; we always do," the man sounded like he was enjoying this. "We'll call you the minute we get the cuffs on the bas...er, the kid," he said.

They walked the floor and jumped almost with hysteria every time the phone rang. Albert had a lot of business calls during the day, and he cut them very short, slamming the phone in place as soon as he could and muttering, "Damn!" with every call.

"We've got him!" the exultant sheriff's deputy told them about midnight on Thursday.

Janet and Albert collapsed in total exhaustion. She whispered, "Thank God." She knew Albert did the same, and they slept that night with their clothes on.

Janet and Albert were on the plane to Birmingham by noon Friday. The director at Forthright had told Albert they could speak with Brad over an intercom through a glass window but only if he wished to speak to them.

"Why in the hell are we doing this?" a totally humbled Albert asked her. Janet thought he was feeling just like she was. She knew she felt guilty at having sent Brad so far from them. The month of restful sleep had restored them in a sense, at least their consciences were functioning again. Now, they had to see their son if only through a glass. How she hoped he'd talk to them.

Friday was the family group night at Forthright. Many parents came to these meetings. Janet and Albert had decided when they chose Birmingham that they couldn't handle this, and Brad hadn't seemed to mind. That Friday evening they sat behind the clear glass on one side of the large meeting room. They could see Brad and he could see them. And he looked at them, even smiled a little. He was subdued, a little thinner than last time but seemed different somehow.

Janet was amazed to see Chuck come into the anteroom where they watched. In a way, she was petrified and immediately realized she had forgotten to send Chuck his money. He sat next to her, very closely. She got the message. Seeing Albert's eyes glued on the things going on, she reached in her pursed seizing all the bills she had and pressed these into Chuck's waiting palm.

They watched what seemed an eternity of "sharing" in the group, of shouting matches between parents and offspring and one tearful hugging match among two parents and a seemingly recalcitrant girl. The girl virtually screamed, "I love you Mom and Dad. I'm coming home." Everyone applauded. It all seemed very dramatic, maybe a trifle melodramatic, Janet thought.

Brad sat quietly through all this and finally one of the counselors, calling for quiet, pushed a microphone at Brad saying, "Brad your parents want to talk to you." And so they talked. What she and Albert said was a blur to Janet. But this much she remembered: Brad said through tears Janet knew were not make-believe, "I love you Mom and Dad. I miss you. Please come back next Friday."

And of course, they did. Actually, they became members of the family group the following Friday evening. They were not allowed to touch Brad, they only saw him across the expanse of the room. Brad freely made eye contact with them, and even that seemed light years removed from where they had been.

The usual loud clamor unnerved Janet. They listened as parents bickered with their children, as children hurled obscenities at parents and in one case, as parents and a young man of about seventeen were united. Members of the resident group chimed in. Several young men and women moved around through the jammed bodies, maintaining good crowd control. Some of these were on the higher levels of Forthright's hierarchy, Janet thought. And from time to time, counselors would intervene with, "Stay with that feeling, James. Let your parents know just how angry you are and why."

Janet didn't expect what happened near the end of the two-hour session. She knew Albert didn't expect it either, but it happened. A counselor rose, and, turning to Brad, she said, "Brad, do you have anything to say to your parents?"

And Brad did. He was well-controlled. "I love you Mom and Dad, but I am angry that you sent me so far away. Why did you do that?"

Janet flushed and answered, "We thought it would be best, Brad." Albert said nothing.

Brad looked disdainfully at them, then hung his head and the session moved on as other residents were called on to say something to parents.

****

A month later and after three sometimes stormy family group exchanges with Brad, Brad was allowed to meet with them in a conference room. He had moved into a quiet, almost respectful tone with them. He returned Janet's embrace gingerly and took Albert's hand haltingly. "This is the first time we have actually touched our son in four months," Janet thought, controlling the tears which she thought had gone into permanent drought.

Still another month, and Brad was moved into the Forthright Clinic at Milwaukee in easy driving distance. Albert and Janet became regulars at family group on Friday evenings. In the group atmosphere at Milwaukee, with the encouragement of the top echelon residents, counselors and other parents; the three of them, Brad, Janet and Albert moved slowly into a new relationship.

****

Brad came home after three months at Forthright in Milwaukee. Everyone went through the motions of the new relationship like they were walking on eggs, but little by little, Janet thought that things were improving. Brad was back at Brockaway High. Ginger visited often always bringing the baby. Brad became very fond of little Joe and was beginning to act like one of the family again. Janet felt more relief and happiness than she had thought possible even as late as two weeks ago. Janet couldn't quite understand why she wasn't completely at ease with these new developments.

The Facts As We Best Know Them

Toughlove and Behavioral Change

In traditional family therapy, the family member who becomes addicted to drugs is seen as a victim of environmental stress. No matter how obnoxious his behavior may become, the problem is seen as a family problem, and each family member is involved in causing the addicted one to break under the consummate stresses. It is believed that this person will be able to change only if the family cares enough to rearrange the family dynamics so that undue stress is removed and the addicted one is helped to return to normal living. (Refer to Chapter Five.)

The proponents of toughlove visualize the situation differently. This philosophy poses no less value or concern in the addicted person, but it sees him as a victimizer rather than as a victim. Basically, toughlove propositions do not perceive change in other family members as necessarily a chief focus. It sees the person, who having victimized his family by his behavior, as needing to change his behavior. True, behavior change on the parts of many family members is often seen as helpful, but the central focus is on the one who causes the disharmony. This one is often a drug abuser.

A History of Child-Family Dynamics

The ideal family is usually perceived as a dad and a mom who have married to have a family. Dad is usually the breadwinner; Mom may work, too, but both contribute to the parenting chores. Children are seen as obedient; sometimes feeling rebellious, but always capitulating to reasonable rules of conduct. Every child is different in an ideal family, and Dad and Mom have idiosyncrasies too; but somehow, each family member manages to adapt into his somewhat codified roles so that everyone not only survives but also is reasonably fulfilled.

The European family of the Middle Ages consisted of a mom, a dad and a number of offspring, none of whom had childhoods as childhood is now understood. Around age seven, or as soon as the children did not need constant maternal care, they were thrown pell-mell into an adult world. They went to work in factories, mines or on family farms and were assigned adult tasks. They assumed adult roles. There was no innocent childhood; there were no statutes to protect the young from the hardships of life.

Art Forms from the Middle Ages

A woodcut created in the sixteenth century depicting the story of Jesus and the children shows one person of large size surrounded by eight little men, all with adult faces. Philippe Ariès in his study Centuries of Childhood writes about biblical art: "Isaac is shown sitting between his two wives, surrounded by some fifteen little men who come up to the level of the grown-up's waists: These are their children."(1)

The concept of an innocent and protected childhood began in the seventeenth century. In describing this period, Bettelheim (), in his study of Israeli kibbutzim says, "The children did not infringe on the life of their parents nor the other way around." In this transitional century, children were regarded as needing special attention, but the attention they received, while nurturant and protective, was not intimate.

The Evolution of the Special Stage of Childhood

Childhood as a time of innocence and of intimate relating is believed to have been nurtured by Christianity in the seventeenth century. The descriptions of the family in Jesus' time clearly demonstrated children being cherished, valued and afforded a place of protection, instruction and selfhood. While some cultures may have retained those values during the Middle Ages, it is clear that European cultures did not. Concerning childhood as affected by Christianity, Bettelheim writes: "Henceforth, it was recognized that the child was not ready for life and that he had to be subjected to a special treatment, a sort of quarantine before he was allowed to join the adults."(2) In this era was born the admonitions that a child should conduct himself in ways that would never bring dishonor to his family. It is likely, nonetheless, that many children continued to be treated as chattels and that their lives were not easy ones. However, the idea of education as well as a closely knit family structure were clearly set forth in Western European society in the seventeenth century and these elements of social structure were brought to America. The family scene was one where love was mandated but few other emotions were allowed.

The Birth of Adolescence

It was not until the middle of the nineteenth century that a period between childhood and adulthood was recognized. This period has come to be known as adolescence.

Adolescence found its early identity in the first decade of the twentieth century. It took its place among the recognized stages of life because of evolving institutions. This period in America saw the beginning the modern high school, the college and the armed services. The high school's evolution came about as a condescension to the special needs of youth from ages twelve to sixteen. College, for a privileged few, extended adolescence to about age nineteen. The armed services, ushered in by World War I, helped set the upper limits of the period of adolescence. Adolescence became identified as synonymous with the teenage years.

In twentieth century America, adolescence has been seen as a golden age. Adolescence was also a period of storm and stress, and more emphasis has been placed upon the moratorium it has provided. It has been regarded as a time of preparation for life, and as such, adolescents have been granted a stay from the heavy responsibilities of making a living, of supporting the family and of a pressurized demand to grow up. Certainly, some subcultures, even in America, did not relinquish the teenager to an adolescent moratorium, but the moratorium was more rule than exception.

After the Great Depression and World War II, adolescence became even more golden. The "permissive society" ensued during these years. Babies were born in large numbers, and Freudian psychology reigned supreme. Emphasis was placed upon parents as the ones to be blamed. Children were thought of as either victims of harsh parents and families or as victims of a largess of love. Kindly treatment of the young was the rule and freedom for the young to grow and plan their own futures without domination was applauded.

It was from the "permissive age" that family dynamics now extant in family therapy were derived. Adolescents of this age had no responsibility, often not even for their own behavior. If something went wrong, they could not be blamed; the parents had the blueprints of life, and they were saddled with the building process.

Clearly, children of this age were not taught personal responsibility very well; inherently, they were thought not to deserve the burden of responsibility, so they couldn't very well develop anything other than irresponsibility. If they goofed, then they sowed the wind and reaped the whirlwind. It sounded easy but it wasn't. Many have disapproved of permissiveness, and they have often been proven correct.

The Family Break-down

Things may never have degenerated to the current status if sexual permissiveness and drug use had not become a part of the scene. Some of what has happened in recent years follows: 1) Parents, themselves raised in permissiveness and liberal stances, began to go a little crazy. As a result, marriage vows increasingly became less sacred. Divorces and broken families became the rule. 2) Sexual behavior became explicit, permissive and promiscuous. Children were made aware of sexuality via TV and movies. It became commonplace that Dad and Mother were both openly promiscuous. After divorce, it was just part of the modern world for Mom to have a live-in lover or Dad to sleep around. 3) Both spouses had to or wanted to work, leaving children unattended. 4) Alcohol and drug abuse escalated greatly. Substance use, especially of alcohol and marijuana, was commonly practiced by parents. Children became involved in these substance uses, often with parental consent and sometimes with parental urging. There were new, more potent drugs, and there were entrepreneurs eager to manipulate people into use and abuse.

These are only a few of the changes in family statuses that have ensued during the last decade or two. These new values, often comprising a departure from and contradiction of firmly espoused older ones, have gradually changed the family scene. This dissertation is not a preachment of ultimate rightness or wrongness. It is only the repercussions that count in this discussion!

Adolescent Behavior Under New Values

Under all the changes, how can adolescents and pre-adolescents do other than undergo a profound change? The rate at which these young people are growing up is making them older in many ways than they have any right to be. They are being forced to assume responsibilities for which they are not ready. They usually do not have responsibilities of making their own living so much as they have responsibilities for determining their own values and codes of conduct.

Strangely, in this era, the legal drinking age has been raised to twenty-one while the age for self-responsibility in asserting personal moral values has dropped to twelve. Many factors enter into this anomaly: divorces with broken families, unintended children, working parents seldom at home, multi-families emerging from new marriages, promiscuity of mothers and fathers, early arousal of sexual drives through media and other impacts and, above all, the easy availability of drugs along with the peer pressure to use drugs.

So, the child of twelve becomes responsible for his own behavior! And since such responsibility has been mandated to him, he is expected to assume these responsibilities of moral behavior while inwardly despising the meaninglessness he feels in his gut.

So, we have children and teenagers who spin out of control. They can't seem to understand that the changing world has dictated responsible behavior to them at such an early age. They are confused about growing up in a world gone mad; they become angry because they must struggle with the the responsibility of moral self-guidance, while they are being denied rights which logically should go with moral responsibility. Why can't they drink, use drugs, have sex, stay out all night, race cars, get in jail, become pregnant or whatever else they want?

Enter Toughlove

These child-adults must be restrained from irresponsible behaviors derived from being made responsible for their moral and ethical behavior long before they are emotionally ready. They have no role models who demonstrate a readiness for responsible behavior either.

Neff (4) relates several anecdotes depicting family breakdown. An example might begin with a father berating a twelve-year-old son when he smokes pot in his room. "You can't do that; it's illegal!" the father declares.

"Well, is it legal for you to give me wine at dinner?"

"That's different. Pot is bad for you," the father remonstrates.

"Are booze and wild women, good for you, Dad?" junior inquires.

"You smart-ass kid! I'm going to belt the hell out of you," the father replies.

Then the father and mother on returning from the neighborhood bar, thoroughly drunk, are met at the door by a policeman who tells them, "Your son is in jail for a hit and run." The parents go bananas.

"The only way to deal with that kid," the father says once the smoke clears from the hit and run, "is to put him in one of these toughlove institutions." And so they do, because they must — there is no other course left.

The Good Sense of Toughlove

Toughlove is a way of showing you care by refusing to be bullied by children who, having been reared in horrible ways, cannot and will not control themselves. They cannot yield to common-sense or parental dictums and have taken actions that are stupid getting themselves into deep trouble while also devastating their parents.

The parents, far from blameless, are helpless. The only avenue left for them is to get tough. Even those parents who recognize their own weaknesses and the attendant weaknesses of a society gone crazy, usually wish there were other ways. Indeed, most have tried a myriad of other ways, and everything else has failed; So, they are ready for toughlove.

These parents know what they are about to do is not fair to the child, but they have become so frustrated and directionless that they are ready to say to a child they love very much, "We won't tolerate your behavior any longer." Sometimes they come to say "Shape up or ship out." This is soon seen as no solution, so they reach a compromise which with minor children may be, "We are going to send you to an institution whether you like it or not." With older children who have gotten into serious troubles with the law, "It's either this place or jail, take your pick."

Again, regardless of how parents themselves have behaved — immorally, irresponsibly, or stupidly — there is seldom a referral to a toughlove center that is made without an abundance of tears, guilt and remorse. But sooner or later, parents of children who show them no respect; who bring home their scrubby friends; who booze and use drugs; who steal from their parents or anywhere else they can; who are dirty, unruly, mean-dispositioned, spiteful and incorrigible, take what seems like a step of last resort and commit their child to a toughlove institution.

Toughlove Outside An Institution

Phyllis and David York and Ted Wachtel (6), themselves professional counselors, began a movement which now reaches out to thousands of families who have children who have spun out of control. These authors seem to have been the first to create the one word form of toughlove and have led in the formation of parent support groups across the nation. The program is not a treatment program for problem children so much as it is a support medium for parents. These authors have done much to congeal the thinking of toughlove philosophy.(10)

In describing the growing tendencies for children to run amok they say, "The common denominator is rotten behavior.

There is strong implication that these youngsters might be within the reach of typical counseling and behavior modification procedure except that drugs coming upon the scene change all logical approaches away from normal corrective-coercive procedures and demand a new approach — a toughlove approach."(6, p. 10)(8)(9)

Under the regime of drugs, escalating juvenile crime and sundry elements in the environment, parents and other authorities have lost control.(7) It must be emphasized in the toughlove context that the behavior of problem children is seen at least partially as poor parenting but that parents are not to blame for the crescendo of events that are engulfing them. The thinking is that parents must stop feeling guilty, ashamed, inadequate or hurt. That they are helpless in the face of these rigors is a confession and a concession that must be made in order for parents to get out of the bad habits of giving in to these out-of-control children. The parents must stop padding their children's corners and stop shouldering all the rigors that their children's "rotten" behaviors impose. Parents must quit feeling responsible and guilty because those feelings set them up for further abuse. The blame must be placed squarely on the child. "Looking for family problems and pathology which 'cause' this behavior distracts from the real issue — the responsibility of each young person for his or her own actions."(6, p. 10)(5)

As said earlier, it is a sign of the times that given the condition of a drug-laced society, there may be no alternative to taking away the golden years, the moratorium on responsibility, which adolescents have enjoyed for almost a century. "Most of the young people who are manifesting outrageous behavior are not 'crazy,' they are 'stoned.'" The drug-saturated society is changing the rules for parents. They cannot survive under the drug siege and must seek a way out by declaring their children to be responsible for their own behavior. More than that, they must steel themselves to avoid natural tendencies to rescue their children from the drug dragons, and they must insist that the children suffer the consequences of their action.(6) Children must take responsibility for their own behavior early, because a myriad of factors including drugs and peer pressures have made them antagonists with their parents who must somehow protect themselves from annihilation. Parents are people, too, and have rights to life and the pursuits of their own happiness. And to achieve even a fleeting happiness makes it necessary to practice toughlove.

The premise of the York/Wachtel book is that neither a single parent nor two parents can handle the chore of toughlove alone. Therefore, parents form support groups in which they can share their torments with each other without feeling blame. The support parents obtain in toughlove groups goes beyond emotional support. One set of parents becomes surrogate to the children of another set of parents.

Surrogate Support

For instance, many children because of their "rotten" behavior, usually goaded by drug abuse, wind up in jail. Their immediately plea is for the parents to bail them out, pay their fines and cover the damages they may have done to the properties of others. Such children run up large sums of traffic tickets, steal in order to buy drugs and wreck automobiles. Their antics quickly tax the financial resources of parents, and they are often jailed over and over again. Toughlove indicates that parents should say "no" to pleas for bailing out from jail, at least for a time. This is where support from other parents comes to the rescue. Few parents could survive not knowing about the condition of their children, so other parents go to the jail for them. Ideally, toughlove indicates children should serve jail time sufficient to bring about responsible action. The message should be, "We are not going to rescue you any longer from what you yourself have gotten into. We love you, but we feel you'll just have to tough it out."

Toughlove is difficult for parents who grew up feeling that parents are the natural protectors of their children. To act against their instincts would be impossible unless there were the support from other parents. Even with support, we would be foolish to think any parent can escape unscathed in conscience, in blame and in self-recrimination. The thing to be kept in mind the is survival of parents and the rehabilitation of children. Many are convinced that toughlove is the only way.

The toughlove groups have developed a literature for their members. These are printed suggestions including ten codified beliefs. Among these are beliefs that "parents are people too, that kids are not equal, that parents must take a stand, that efforts must have community support and that blame resides in children as well as parents." The roots of the toughlove movements seem to be based on Glasser's concepts of reality therapy (3). Glasser's contributions to toughlove philosophy is immense.

Glasser's Reality Therapy

Dr. Glasser had an early practice in a reform school for girls in Los Angeles. There, pandemonium reigned until Dr. Glasser instituted the beginnings of reality therapy. Reality number one as meted out to the unruly girls was, "You are here. Accept it. You can't change the rules. You have given up your rights to do that. Do as you are told and don't fight the system. You'll survive better if you face the reality of the situation." A second reality Dr. Glasser emphasized was self-responsibility. "You are the only one who can do anything about your problems. Get under your own load; you are ultimately the responsible one."

With appropriate toughlove administration, many families have managed to survive. When the youngster matures he is often appreciative of his parents' resorting to toughlove principles. True, some never recover from their anger. Again, because of the strangle-hold drugs have on our young people, many cannot change their ways, and institutionalization may become necessary.

Institutions For Toughlove

It can be said that institutions may be catalogued according to the level of dedication to the toughlove principle. The choice of an institution must depend on the level of drug addictions and the level of anger and acting-out the young person indulges. Some toughlove centers are outpatient where the youngsters go daily to participate, continuing to live at home or sometimes with friends. Others, at the other extreme, are virtually prisons where rules are harsh, and by contractual agreement with parents, the functionaries are permitted to deal with each inmate as the maladaptive behavior may indicate. There, obviously, are many colorations of toughlove between the extremes of leniency and harsh authoritarianism.

The Outpatient Program

Neff (4) gives a very adequate presentation of a successful outpatient program in her book Tough Love — How Parents Can Deal with Drug Abuse. The essence of this program is counseling by a corp of young people who themselves have been through the program with a measure of success and who are hopefully able to serve as role models for initiates. The outpatient program usually includes a strong and concerted effort on the parts of family members, who have their own meetings. Through the parents' group meetings, parents offer surrogate services to the children of other parents. Many of these outpatient centers have no medical staff and often no trained psychological staff. They do have liaison arrangements with hospitals for detoxification and medical support for drug withdrawal.

Many outpatient centers derive from religious communities and have a wide range of sectarian emphases. Some have liberal views about the infinite Power of Love, and some are quite specific in coercing the youngsters into specific systems of religious thought and practice. Other outpatient centers are totally free from religious position-taking.

There is wide variation in the requirements for "counselors." Some centers feel that to allow counselors to continue in the hair and dress modes indigenous to the "hip" youth culture is an asset. Others insist on short-haired males without beards or garnishments such as earrings and the like. Female "counselors" run the gamut also in dress, hair and garnishment codes.

The constant reminder issued in these environs is that the parents maintain the toughlove stance, that they do not yield to temptations to "pad the corners" for their children. Where inmates are drug addicts (and most are), there is general consensus that youngsters must live with the one-day-at-a-time principle, that throughout life, they must always consider themselves to be "recovering addicts." It is also generally thought that every addict must "hit bottom" before he can make a recovery but that one day all the turmoil will seem like a bad dream; families will be reunited, even if never close in terms of intimacy. It is unrealistic to believe that all wounds can heal without permanent scarring of all parties concerned.

The general tone of all meetings of youngsters with their counselors and peers is that "love is the theme." Usually, there is insistence on at least demonstrated expressions of love for one another even where there are no religious underpinnings. It is likely true that with youngsters and with their parents as well, group meetings are the core for change and growth. In the groups, caring is a central theme, individuality is honored and growth is allowed at a pace chosen by the individual.

Closed Institutions of Toughlove

An examination of the programs and rules of any toughlove installation will reveal a pattern of constant change. This is as it should be, of course. The changes over the years for specific institutions have gone both ways; that is, some have returned to less coercive, less harsh formats while others have moved toward harshness in toughlove. Youngsters, being as different as they are, need a wide variety of formats.

Toughlove institutions are developing an enormous clientele of distressed parents. Institutions, by and large, gradually develop a reputation and a clientele to fit that reputation. They change their formats to better fit what they see as the fastest growing segment of their clientele. If one could develop a list of such facilities rank ordering them from leniency to harshness, then the list would not stay the same over time.

The Harshest Rules

A list of some of the harsher rules with full acknowledgment that no single institution embraces all of these follows:

Coercion to a Sameness in Appearance

Some institutions strip the incoming youngster of all accoutrements reminiscent of his earlier outrageous behavior and his lifestyle companions. Thus, a youngster coming in with long hair, ornate jewelry, heavy make-up and unusual dress will undergo an overt change to a communal style of male and female sameness.

Young men will have their locks shorn to a crew cuts, will be stripped of garnishments and will be issued plain, standard, but comfortable clothing. Young women will have hairstyle changes to a short bob and will be deprived of all makeup. They will be issued standard garments.

Contact with Parents

Many of the harsher toughlove treatment centers restrict family contact. The youngsters are denied telephone communication of any kind. When parents visit, they are only allowed to talk to them only on intercoms. This is much like a prison environment where visitors and inmates can talk but not touch. These rules are usually relaxed with good conduct over time.

Letters are usually allowed on a limited basis after a period of several weeks of almost total isolation.

At appointed times, parents are urged to come for family group meetings. Again, parents may see but not touch and vice versa. However, verbal exchanges are usually encouraged in the group context.

Work Details

Inmates are usually made responsible for keeping their quarters clean. Failure to meet standards results in demerits which may be removed, in some instances, by performing menial tasks such as grounds tending. Exercising time and facilities are available but must be earned by good behavior. Television in rooms are usually forbidden but allowed in large lounges.

The assignment of manual labor is usually considered unlawful for these institutions. The concept of enforced labor at meaningless tasks (busting rocks) is seldom allowed, depending on state law.

Withdrawal from Drugs

The stated goal is to get the inmate off drugs. The regimen for this varies with the individual and the level of addiction. Medical support is usually mandated by law, but some institutions have in-house or consultant physicians allowing for a harsh approach to withdrawal. Few institutions are inhumane in the strictest sense, but the inmates often do not share this feeling.

Sexual contact is closely monitored and usually forbidden except in group meetings. Sexual acting out is usually punished by withdrawal of privileges or other sanctions.

The Use of Inmates in Treatment

Almost all toughlove institutions operate on a levels concept. As an inmate makes strides toward stated goals, he is moved up in level, usually from level one to level five. Level five inmates are usually approaching release.

As is true in outpatient centers, inmates who have made good progress are pressed into service as role models. In the more rigorous programs, the persons at higher levels are allowed to serve as mentors for those at lower levels. In many cases, this arrangement is harsh in that the upper-level inmates are allowed to become quite rough and demanding of those placed in their limited charge. This is like the upperclassman concept in college. Considerable abuse may arise from these arrangements; considerable growth may likewise be fostered. On the other hand, these arrangements must be closely monitored, or things will get out of hand.

In Summary

The toughlove center should not be a place where youngsters can do as they please. There must be coercion, and there must be experiences for growth. Such institutions, at whatever level of harshness, may be assets in getting a youngster to bottom out. On the other hand, many are hardened by these experiences.

The program of any given institution will bring some youngsters into improved behavior and into control of addictions. All such institutions have failures. There is great need to develop guidelines that could show parent(s) which institutions would have the best possible influence on a youngster. This is almost impossible to do since the harsh centers usually do not wish to go public with specific descriptions of their regimens. Most institutions allow parents to attend an introductory parents group meeting at which time rules are usually explained by upper-level residents.

Bibliography

1   Ariès, Philippe. Centuries of Childhood; A Social History of Family Life. New York. Knopf. 1962.

2   Bettelheim, Bruno. The Children of the Dream. New York. MacMillan. 1969.

3   Glasser, William M.D. Reality Therapy: A New Approach to Psychiatry. Harper & Row, Publishers. New York, 1965.

4   Neff, Pauline. Tough Love: How Parents Can Deal With Drug Abuse. Abingdon Press. Nashville, 1982.

5   York, Phyllis and York, David and Wachtel, Ted. Toughlove Solutions. Bantam Books. Toronto, 1985.

6   York, Phyllis and York, David and Wachtel, Ted. Toughlove. Doubleday & Company, Inc., Garden City, New York, 1982.

7   York, Phyllis and York, David. Toughlove Cocaine: Help For People Who Care About A Cocaine User. Toughlove Press. Doylestown, Pennsylvania, 1985.

8   York, Phyllis and York, David. Toughlove: A Self-Help Manual For Parents Troubled by Teenage Behavior, Revised Edition. Toughlove Press. Doylestown, Pennsylvania, 1988.

9   York, Phyllis and York, David and Olitsky, Gwen. Toughlove For Teachers. Toughlove International. Doylestown, Pennsylvania, 1989.

10 York, Phyllis and York, David. Getting Hurt in All the Hurting Places. Rawson Associates. New York, 1989.

Chapter 10

The Crack in the Emergency Room Door

Happening Ten — The Crack in the Emergency Room Door

The Facts As We Best Know Them

Death from Cocaine Overdose or Toxicity
Effects of Cocaine on the Central Nervous
  System
Conditions Affecting the Circulatory System
Lung Involvement
The Kidneys and the Impact of Cocaine and
  Methamphetamines
Electrolytes and Cocaine-Methamphetamine
  Abuse

Happening Ten — The Crack in the Emergency Room Door

He'd been bone tired when he reported in at seven that Thursday evening. They called Thursday his day off — some day off, when he had to work the 7 to 3 shift after his "relaxing" day. Wednesday, usually a light day in ER, had not been that light yesterday. Still, he'd only assisted in two majors yesterday, one MVA (motor vehicle accident) and one heart attack. But these hadn't been his cases; and neither one had presented any problems for his friend and colleague, Josh Tucker, who'd been pit boss on both operations.

Maybe he'd gotten too much sun on the golf course this afternoon, "Boy! Was I ever terrible," he reminisced, "Why in the hell can't I work that horrible hook out of my irons? Always wind up in some back yard to the left. Damn!"

Helen had virtually pushed him out of the house. "You need exercise, Ted," she'd insisted. He'd rather have just relaxed around the house all afternoon.

Anyway, here it was Thursday night --"The night of the druggies" — the gang had learned to call it. Why Thursday? No one seemed to know.

"Damn crack! Son-of-a-bitch!" And they had finally decided to admit that it was an epidemic. Boy, was it ever an epidemic here in Edwardsville! "We need a special emergency room for the druggies at Saint Albans," he'd reported to the hospital board as chairman of the Committee on Substance Abuse. Fat chance! Sure, they had their special cubbyhole — that was about what it amounted to. Equipment? The best! Breathing machines; stomach pumps; high-tech, read-out stuff all the way. When they wheeled the victim in and the door swung to, they were in their own little world, and by any reasonable standard, it was adequate.

By Ted Tilden's calculations, it was a private hell to the five or more staff who sweated in there. Ventilation? Sure the cool air came in; and the stale, humid, odoriferous air was sucked out — but that wasn't the hellish part. The hellish part was the damn A-bug gear!

"My God!" Ted had reflected seeing himself in the mirror yesterday, "I look like an astronaut." It was body insulation all the way now — not a choice anymore. Gloves, face shields, impervious body covering, every stitch. And even shoe covers, no less. "Somebody is going down and bust his ass in these things," the staff nurse George had said so often it sounded like a broken record.

Two hours in that monkey suit and the sweat had your eyes watery red and was dripping off your tail bone. "Oh, for the good old days when you could turn to the nurse beside you and she would wipe the sweat off your brow like in Dr. Welby," Ted thought.

Ted smiled when he thought about the scrub nurse, Amanda Gentry, who went into that hell hole in the wall pushing a gurney with a druggie on it. Two big guys held the patient down until they could get him or her on the table and secured by leather straps. But, that wouldn't be the case for long. Old Doc Peters, Chief of Staff, had been getting closer and closer to saying outright, "No more restraints!" Wish he'd been here Sunday night when that little 140 -pound guy had gone from the crack rush to the crack rage before they could get the straps on.

"And ice is supposed to be worse than this!" Ted thought. That little guy had lifted George over his head just like a Russian weight lifter handles a dumbbell. And George went 280! George had bounced off the tiled floor and had grabbed the kid in a bear hug before he could really hurt someone. It was really going to be hell when the media zoomed in on some hospital somewhere, headlines screaming, "Patient Murdered By Staff Nurse in the Emergency Room."

But back to Amanda, "God, I really dig that gal!" Ted slipped back into his high-school, hip thought patterns. Amanda always entered the ER with impeccable makeup like she had just come right out of the beauty shop. Eye shadow and mascara, no less. But in five minutes that stuff was streaking down her pretty face. He was glad he could smile about it — he needed a smile. And Manda was one who could make anyone smile. She just didn't fit in this place. She was a pure bred lady; and she had a crush on Dr. Ted Tilden, M.D., surgeon, substance abuse specialist, and all around good doctor.

"Hey," Ted reacted, "my head is getting a little swelled." But he knew he was good. At fifty-five he'd better be good. All those years — university, med school, internship, his ten years at the Cedars in L.A. and now chief of the surgical staff and medical director of substance abuse emergency treatment.

Ted smiled again. He and Helen had a good life — two grown kids both married and doing well. And his oldest son — yes, Helen had been a very understanding number two — Michael had followed in his dad's footsteps and not too far behind him either. Michael would be great. High tech was booming; and no one could even imagine what ER or OR would look like in Michael's time with laser technology and the fast advancing field of total body scanning, tomography and all. He envied Michael and his breed. God, how he'd like to be thirty again!

Not much was going on, but it wouldn't last. Doctor Joe Nash had handled one flesh gunshot wound. The patient had reported it was accidental, and his wife agreed. Amanda had helped Joe with that. The guy wasn't even hospitalized. "Can't make any money for the hospital that way," Doctor Claude Peters, who was the son of the chief of staff, kidded Joe. "Give the lady a chart showing where the heart is," Claude said. This seemed to Ted like a vicious quip; but everybody liked Claude, he could get by with almost anything.

By ten o'clock, the gang was all there. There were five of them on duty including himself, Amanda, Joe, Claude and George — they couldn't get along without George, his brains or his brawn. They had all put on the garb except the headgear and shoe covers.

Ted was sitting in the mini-lounge a few minutes after ten feeling pretty good. "I did get too much sun," he told himself. After all, he was too young to let himself get all that tired.

Ted saw the double doors open as if a giant hand had pushed them. First, he saw the back of a young man; then, as he swung around, he could see the limp girl the young man was carrying. Amanda was already on the way with a gurney. All five came alive like a well-trained drill team.

He recognized the young fellow immediately. Craig Sessions had been the pride of Edwardsville the last two football seasons. Craig saw Ted immediately; and although Amanda and George were trying to disentangle the young woman from Craig's grasp, Craig was obviously trying to thrust her into Ted's arms.

"Doctor, I think she's dying!" Craig gasped.

"Easy, Craig. Let them get her into emergency while you tell me what happened." Ted used a well-modulated tone, seeing panic in Craig's eyes.

"I don't know, Doctor. She just passed out on me. She must have eaten something. Food poisoning — I don't know," he spoke in a jerky, imploring, don't-blame-me tone.

"Where were you, Craig?"

"In the car," Craig said simply.

"Now, Craig, I've known you a long time and believe me this is important," Ted spoke quietly but as convincingly as he knew how. "What kind of drugs were you doing, Craig?" Seeing the panic in Craig's eyes, he continued, "Easy now, Craig, I'm not accusing you; we've simply got to know — what kind of drugs?"

"Honest to God, Doctor," he started. Then head down, almost sobbing, "Crack, Goddam crack! Damn it, I've killed her. Oh, my God, Marcia, I've killed you, baby!" Then Craig broke. He cried great shuddering sobs Ted knew so well. They could come from a 280-pound fullback just as easily as from a distraught mother.

"Okay, Craig, no time for that. Oh, yes, anything else?" When Craig looked at him shaking his head slowly, Ted knew there was more. "Out with it, Craig, we've got to know."

"This," Craig muttered pulling a bottle of booze out of his inside coat pocket. It was about half empty, Ted noted.

"And how old is she?"

"Fourteen, fifteen — pretty young." The way, Craig who was pushing seventeen said it was almost amusing, even under the circumstances.

Taking just enough time to pat Craig on the shoulder, Ted made his way to the trouble he knew waited in ER. It took him just a minute to get into gloves and face shield, put skull cap in place and pull on his shoe covers.

George and Amanda would have things started in ER, and Joe and Claude would be making preliminary assessments. They'd waited on him before going invasive. He was pit boss on this one — would be pit boss the rest of the night.

As he expected, he didn't have to ask any questions. The answers came fast. "Crack toxicity," Joe said quickly. It wasn't a question; it was a statement and Ted nodded back to Joe, knowing Joe would have recognized cocaine symptoms and would have searched for puncture marks on the girl's arms.

"Heart rate 195, blood pressure 190 over 105," Amanda said.

"Okay. How does it sound other than fast, Claude?"

Claude said, "Monitor looks bad. Arrhythmia so bad I can't make out much. She's coming apart inside, Ted. This is a bad one."

"Okay, George, IV's in both arms. Saline for now, but don't depend on gravity flow. Rush it into her fast; and, Amanda, get the catheter in. Don't bother with a bag yet but get a specimen. Have the lab try for a drug screen. We're going to have hell just keeping the kidneys going."

"I think her kidneys are already down," Joe spoke gloomily. That heart is struggling to get blood to the brain. The faster it pumps, the less it puts out and the arrhythmia isn't helping either. I'm afraid we aren't going to make this one, Ted."

"Shut up, damn it, and get those IV's going and intubate her, quickly. Get a stomach pump going now. Get the IV with Valium ready in case she has a seizure, Claude. Be prepared to get it into her jugular vein. For God's sake, don't hit the carotid!"

"God! I know which way the arrow points on a one way street! The profs in med school told us right away the difference between up and down." Claude was actually chuckling. Ted could have choked him except he knew the score. "Joker wild," he thought, "but we need something to keep us loose." Not that it was really helping that much. But Claude was solid, solid as a rock.

"How about her clothes," Amanda was asking, trying to get the catheter in."

"Strip her! Use the scissors, get them all off," Ted almost shouted knowing he shouldn't be rough with Amanda.

"No use, we're going to lose her and we'd better leave her more decent than that," Joe Nash said. "Better send for the priest or whatever."

"Shut up, you fool." Ted was getting angry. He was a fighter, and he knew fighters didn't get angry. Besides, Joe was a good friend, a good doctor. Ted knew that if Joe were pit boss tonight, he wouldn't talk like that. Joe was as scared as the rest of them, and in spite of the gloom, he'd work like crazy.

"George, go out and get her folks' name from Craig. Think he said Marcia." Ted suddenly faced his own panic. "My God!" he thought, "I haven't even looked at the girl." And they say we treat them like slabs of meat on butcher blocks. "Marcia? I know a Marcia." Then quickly, as George was heading out, he said, "Do you know her, George — know her last name?"

"Marcia Sanders," George said simply.

And Ted thought the floor would strike him in the face. Marcia Sanders! He'd played golf this afternoon with Herbert Sanders. Herbert Sanders, his golf and fishing buddy. "Janet Sanders — no, no, I couldn't go into that," he thought. Then, in spite of himself, "Oh, Janet, Janet, what will I say to you if we lose her? God! We can't lose her! She's Janet's lovely daughter. No! No! Never!"

Ted got control quickly, but not in time to stop George. Crisply, he said, "You guys pump on those IV's. You've got to get her kidneys going. Joe, get the needle in her vein; and Amanda, start the injection of Lanoxin into one of the IV's. Work out of a full ampule, and don't go over that amount right now."

Ted was sweating and shaking now. He saw three sets of eyes swing toward him. All three countenances showed the same question on each mind. He knew what they were thinking, "What's new? What's happened? The pit boss is cracking. Not like Ted, not like him at all."

And Ted burst out of there — stopped George just as he was approaching Craig.

"Wait, George, I'll call her parents. I know her. You get back ...." Ted paused, eyes fixed on George, who stood staring at Craig who had his head down, hands cupped over his face. Craig was shaking like a leaf, great globs of sweat pouring off the back of his hands.

"Son-of-a-bitch!" George screamed at Craig in sudden rage. Ted couldn't believe or understand George's anger toward Craig. George slapped Craig's hands apart unnecessarily roughly, Ted thought at the moment. But Craig had the pipe jammed up a nostril. He had been hitting the crack one after the other while they had been in ER; and now he was trying to get just a little more of the freebase alkaloid by making a pocket out of his hands, inhaling deeply trying to get just the very last possible bits of freebase out of the crack residue by sticking the pipe in a nostril.

Worse! The bottle of booze was lying empty on the floor. "Why in God's name didn't I take the booze away when I first saw it?" Ted was cursing his stupidity.

"Can you get him on a gurney by yourself?" Ted asked George and got the expected " are you kidding" look from George.

"Get real, this high school superjock is mine!" George thought, "I can throw guys this size one over each shoulder like toothpicks."

Luckily, Ted remembered Janet and Herb's phone number. In a few seconds Janet's voice was on the line, and Ted was trying to get himself calmed down. Hardly daring to trust his voice, especially with Janet, he made a valiant effort to sound calm. He had had long years of practice speaking with hundreds of anxious parents.

"Janet. Ted here." Her voice instantly took on that seductive, cooing quality that had mesmerized him back so many years before. Even now, he was affected by her voice and cursed himself while the faint glimmer of a long-ago love tugged at his heartstrings. "God, the power of woman on man," was a fleeting thought.

"Ted, darling, what is it? Herb is out somewhere." She was still on the make, adorable nympho that she was.

"Janet," he spoke more firmly and yet with no edge of panic, "we've got Marcia here in emergency at St. Albans. Now, hold it a minute, we don't know yet what — we're doing a little checking ...."

"Ted! Marcia! Well what is it? Has she been in a wreck?" Janet could get hysterical, too, Ted knew; and there was a touch of it in her voice now.

"Janet, get Herb and come on down to emergency. Maybe we can have her fixed up. No! No! She hasn't had an accident — nothing like that. But, she'll need her parents. Come quickly, Janet. Got to go now," he'd managed to end it abruptly with no panic in his voice. Ted gave a mighty sigh of relief as he turned to go back to ER. He guessed he'd called hundreds of parents in his time; but that had been the roughest, he thought.

Entering the room Ted saw the team had split. George and Joe were with Craig — had him stripped, IV's were in place and Joe was drawing blood.

"We've got a rhibo over here. We'll have the lactic count as soon as the lab can get it. He's doubling up on us with chest pain," Joe's voice showed no panic. "We can save this one; but he might have heart damage, assuming he keeps breathing, and assuming his muscles don't dump a butt load of lactic, wiping out his kidneys"

"Good work, Joe. George, get central on the line and tell them to get every staff person here that's on call," Ted said quickly.

"The beepers are going off all over the city right now," George said.

"Good boy! And George, you are going to have to phone Craig's parents. You know his last name. It's in the book I'm sure," Ted said tersely but with a confident tone. In situations like this, George was no different from doctors. Ted required no more, no less from any member of the team than his best. And he always got the best.

And then, his attention swung to the other table. "Marcia!" he muttered. Blood from the IV in the jugular vein was creeping down between her cleavage. The catheter was in place. The girl had never regained consciousness, not at all. "Is it really true like Janet says?" he started asking himself. But his own thoughts were interrupted by two terse statements. Amanda and Claude made their statements simultaneously, but Ted tuned in Amanda's for priority somehow. "We're getting a little trickle," she exclaimed. "Right here on the towel. I'll get another specimen for the lab."

Then Claude who had been bending over with stethoscope held around behind the girl's back spoke in a somber voice, "Her lungs are filling up with fluid, just saline from the IV's, I suspect. It'll go to the lungs before the kidneys a lot of the time, Ted. You know that. Her respiration is very shallow."

Amanda looked stricken. Ted was stricken and didn't show it. "God!" he thought he muttered under his breath as he looked at the girl's features, realizing that his mind ought to be on other things, "she does look like me." Janet had said that she did, when Ted and Helen had visited her room after coming out of the delivery room fourteen years ago. At the time, Helen had been talking excitedly to Herb over in the corner.

"What a beautiful, perfect daughter. We're so very happy for you and Janet," Helen had said sincerely.

Janet had caught Ted's eye and winked. "Look at her, darling." Janet called every man darling, and Helen was used to that. And then, when she was sure Helen couldn't hear her, she said, "She's yours, Ted, look at her; can't you see it? What are we going to do, Ted, darling? You and me and this darling little girl?"

What they had done was nothing. Ted hadn't believed Janet. Their affair had been intense but short lived. But it was a time worth remembering. Janet had gone home for a week, and Herb was out of town the same week. Ted had been lonely; Janet had been and always would be lonely and horny. It just happened, and he hadn't had the nerve to tell Helen. And of course, he'd trusted Janet with that secret, too. How ironic that Janet and Helen had become such close friends.

"I don't like the way she looks at you," Helen had said a million times. And then she always smiled knowingly.

"What does she really know?" Ted's inner voice was whispering.

Ted had not taken his eyes off Marcia during the half minute he'd been in the other world. Now, he looked closely at the movement of her nipples, that being, as every physician knew, the best way to judge the quality of a patient's breathing.

George had always taken on the assignment of peeping through the small glass in the ER door, thus monitoring the waiting room. Suddenly, he sang out, even as he squeezed on the IV in Craig's left arm. "The Sanders people are out there — Marcia's parents."

Ted knew he'd have to go; he also knew Claude and Amanda were doing everything that could be done for Marcia. He stood before Janet and Herb, both in their own way very dear to him. "What's going on Ted? Where is she?" Janet demanded.

And he could have predicted what Herb would say, "We've got the best doctor. Ted, whatever you need, you got — no limit." Herb faced the world with a pocket-book mentality. Always.

"She's come in with cocaine toxicity and O.D., crack I suspect," Ted said calmly not wanting to be too technical. "We're doing ...."

"Crack!" Janet virtually shouted. "She's only fourteen years old. She doesn't smoke anything, much less crack." Ted ignored the non sequitur about the girl's age and using crack. They started now at nine or ten, he knew.

"Look, guys," he said, "it is crack, and crack's very dangerous. You've just got to accept that for now. I've got to get back to her. We're doing absolutely everything we can. I know you believe me on that."

Such consternation he'd seldom seen on faces. "Marcia is very special to them, especially to Janet," he thought.

"Get all the help you need, Ted. I can get a helicopter, if you need it. We'll have her at a bigger hospital in minutes. Just say the word," Herb said.

Ted turned quickly, avoiding Janet's eyes, and went through the ER's swinging doors. Back to disaster, but he wasn't giving up on Marcia yet!

Amanda had a sample of urine now, and Claude was checking the IV bottles and shaking his head. "Want us to keep pumping it into her, Ted? She's your million-dollar baby. We'd do well to get the orderlies in and start washing the body. We don't want any malpractice shit out of this, Ted."

"Damn it, Claude, you're talking like she's dead. She can't die!" Ted saw that Claude had his stethoscope to her heart now, and he knew by the way Claude was moving the scope around that Marcia was going into cardiac arrest.

"Get the paddles, Amanda," Ted ordered.

"Hold it, old buddy. No paddles for me," Claude interjected. "You know damn well paddles are not the thing in this kind of arrest. If she's still alive, you'll kill her for sure. What's happening, buddy? You know your job better than anyone on staff. Something is going on. But I'm not going to get into a lawsuit for using something everyone of us knows is dead wrong."

"Sorry, Claude. Thank you. You're right of course," Ted said with obvious resignation. He went to the girl's wrist, finding her pulse. Ted shivered as he realized he had never held his daughter's soft hand until she lay dying.

"Heart rate down to ninety and falling," Amanda whispered hoarsely. The pulse was weak, and the breathing was barely moving her chest. And then not at all.

"The respirator?" Ted looked straight into Claude's eyes seeking a last desperate hope.

"No, she's going, going gone. Once, twice, three times and sold," Claude mimicked the auctioneer's chant.

"Damn him," Ted thought. "Call the orderlies, Amanda."

From the other table, Joe said, "God's good. Now we can get with the one we can save."

The squawk box boomed from the speaker, "This is the lab. Lactic acid in blood sample marked 'Craig' measures at slightly over 28,000 units. Urine sample shows cocaine and alcohol." Amanda was absentmindedly pasting a label on the urine sample from the girl.

Ted knew his job. Stethoscope to the heart, he could get no beat. There was no pulse. "She's gone," he said sadly. Amanda pulled a sheet over her. Ted was glad there was a back way to the morgue; Janet and Herb wouldn't have to see the body being removed. The orderlies always came in the back way, too.

"Craig's parents are here," George announced. Ted knew his job; but he had another more grueling one, telling Janet and Herb.

Turning to Claude, he said, "Would you talk to them, to Craig's parents?"

"Talking is my best act," Claude said. "Ask any of the women. Getting past the talking is the hard part for me." And Claude went out, patting Ted on the shoulder as he passed. Amanda was crying. This one had been special for her because she had sensed, along with all the others, how special the girl had been for Ted. And then pert, prim, pretty little Amanda, who had revealed little of her inner feelings to anyone, came around the table and without hesitation held Ted tightly to her. Just for a moment — no word — none needed.

Ted turned to go as the squawk box came to life again, "This is Jimmy in mobile unit three. We're coming in with a guy with chest pains, heart rate up, hyperventilation. Over."

"We've about got this one under control," Joe said. "He'll make it."

George turned toward the speaker crouched over like he was about to take on two, 200-pound linemen. "Say it, Jimmy. Damn it, say it. Over."

294

"BCA, my boy. Get ready, George; he's about your size," Jimmy said. BCA. Big crack attack! BCA! They could say it only with the acronym on the air. The television crews scattered over the city really liked this stuff, and they always had a monitor on every unit. After all, the air was a free vehicle for communication, and the units didn't have a protected frequency.

The squawk box sounded off once again, "Code blue, code blue, room 1406."

And prim, straight, but tough little Amanda, from whom no one had ever heard anything but an encouraging word spat it out like a veteran trooper. "Shit!" Ted, on his way out to see Janet and Herb hoped it hadn't been heard out there. Strange, how that one word from that one person gave him the courage he needed to face Janet and Herb.

****

Ted examined Craig in ICU the next day and turned him over to his own physician. "He'll be here in the hospital at least a month. Rhibos with heart damage take a lot of hospital time." Ted thought. He didn't like the odds. Two-to-five — heart attack by twenty-five.

The Facts As We Best Know Them

Crack is made by mixing cocaine hydrochloride with baking soda, cooking the mixture and allowing it to cool, forming a brittle mass which is easily broken into rocks. Chemically, the rocks are obviously a mixture of cocaine hydrochloride and sodium carbonate. The powdered cocaine hydrochloride does not lend itself well to smoking, but the rocks will smolder under heat, releasing a freed-from-its-base vapor, which is high-percentage pure cocaine. The acid salts of the hydrochloride and the baking soda are left behind as residue.

The freebase cocaine is drawn into the lungs; and there, because of the nearness of the pumping heart and the carotid artery leading upward to the brain, the freebase cocaine is diffused through the brain using the intricate system of arteries and veins which interlace the brain tissues.

The Brain, Center of Drug Impact

The brain contains billions of short interneurons resembling links in a chain which assembled, comprise circuitry for hundreds of pathways for impulses originating outside the brain and delivered to the brain via the spinal column (pricked fingers, etc). It also has pathways which activate from sensory inputs, such as seeing a ferocious-appearing dog, the person having already experienced what ferocious-looking dogs can do to him. There are other impulse pathways that are in place to respond to thought patterns which come as one sits with all receptors (eyes, ears, etc.) turned off. A person can think his brain impulses into operations.

The Role of Synapses

These interneurons, being like links in a chain, also are similar to thousands of short electric cords which are joined together at a myriad of synapses greatly resembling a joining of the male and female parts of an electric plug and an electric receptacle (as in the plugging in of a vacuum cleaner). These synapses are necessary to the passing of electric impulses, which bear messages to various parts of the brain. Messages are passed to discrete parts of the brain (a pleasure center, for example) or to the cerebral cortex, where incoming information is processed by thinking and reasoning (3+4 = 7).

The synapses are among our central points of concern when the impact of any drug upon the brain and thus, upon human behavior is being studied. Unlike the electric plug in your home, the synapses are incased in a fluid-filled sac which contains what neurologists call neurotransmitters. Scientists have identified four of these transmitter elements. They have been differentiated from each other chemically and have been named dopamine, norepinephrine, serotonin and acetylcholine. Summarily, the function of these neurotransmitters is to create a means by which an impulse can jump across the chasm between axon and dendrite fingers of the interlacing synapses. It is similar to putting salt into water, thus making the salt water a good electrical conductor. These neurotransmitters are in a constant state of build-up, discharge and building up again (reuptake) in preparation for the ensuing need to furnish electric transmission. The condition of these neurotransmitters at any given moment will determine whether or not the impulse will be passed through to the next neuron in the chain.

Cocaine and Methamphetamine — Impacts on Dopamine

As the cocaine in crack or the methamphetamine in ice enters the synapse by osmosis from the blood stream, the drugs have profound capabilities of changing the operating capacities of these transmitters (2). Cocaine and amphetamines affect all transmitters in various ways, but dopamine has been singled out by neurobiologists as the one most affected.

Recent research has shown that the effects of cocaine on the dopaminergic neuron is at first to sensitize it.(3) This same effect was established for methamphetamines in the early 1970's along with the ability of methamphetamines to bring about dopamine depletion as does cocaine.(9) However, the early effect of methamphetamine, especially the smokable form is to usher in a transient but violent psychotic-like state which probably has biochemical explanations outside the dopamine depletion context. Thus, for a while, dopamine (and other transmitters as well) become supertransmitters, and some neural pathways are more affected than others. One pathway is called mesolimbic since it leads to the limbic area of the brain, where specialized pleasure centers reside as well as mood-modulating centers. The quick pick-up from first use of cocaine and from recreational use over time within limits causes heightened sex drive and fickle mood swings. Another pathway leads to the cerebral cortex and causes an experiencing of heightened energy, elevated euphoria and elevated powers of reasoning and thinking. Still other pathways are affected, one being related to the supply of prolactins in the muscles of the body.

Scientists do not agree fully on what happens under any. circumstance relating to the enormously complex brain; they also do not agree on just what mechanics are involved within the brain from various drug effects. However, there is enough agreement to draw reasonable generalizations about what happens under the impact of cocaine and methamphetamine on the brain.

So far as neurotransmitters are concerned, the central focus is upon dopamine.(4) Consensus among scientists seems to be that the first impact of these drugs during first use and on long-term recreational use within limits is that dopaminergic neurons are, with each new drug hit, overly activated and sensitized, thus helping create the rush.(5) Then the consensus is that with overuse, the cocaine molecules block the reuptake process causing a decrease in or atrophy of these neurons toward the end that dopamine depletion occurs. The term overuse is an almost meaningless one because, individually, every person is a law unto himself. Indeed a single use often becomes overuse because addiction or death can come about with a single use.

Death from Cocaine Overdose or Toxicity

Overdosing on drugs is a common occurrence. An overdose of drugs causes disturbing feelings and odd behavior in some people, sends others to the hospital emergency room and kills some. Most emergency room personnel, having heard that a single use of cocaine or ice can addict, are concerned about this, but are much more concerned that they will receive either a dead-on-arrival cadaver or a living person they cannot save.

Just how much danger is there that these drugs may kill on first dosage or on overdose? The literature and the attending physicians would answer, "Considerable." The unpredictable level of cocaine tolerance may contribute to the nearly impossible task of defining toxic doses.

Verebey et al state, "Cocaine induced sudden deaths are underreported and are attributed instead to heart attacks, strokes and seizures...."(10, p. 518)

As emergency room attendants get the news from incoming ambulance units, they usually entertain the question, "Is it O.D. or is it toxicity?" The concept of O.D. is self-explanatory, the concept of toxicity, not so much so. Suffice it to say that many people have blood chemistries and/or metabolism nuances which cause the first dosage of a given drug to be a life-threatening one. The drug may be cocaine, alcohol, methamphetamine or any other drug or food. Some human systems respond to the introduction of a given chemical with totally unpredictable reactions. Verebey et al (15, p. 518) make this point specifically about cocaine as follows: "An important factor is the individual predisposition or sensitivity to cocaine. Logic suggests that the higher the dose or blood level the greater the chance for toxicity, or that a dose administered orally or intranasally is safer than the same dose administered intravenously or by smoking. But these are generalities. Cocaine induced sudden death can happen to naive subjects and experienced individuals regardless of the dose or the route of administration.... Thus, cocaine abuse is similar to Russian roulette, no one really knows the outcome until the trigger is pulled. We can predict that the rapid delivery of cocaine to the brain through smoking and the current increase in this route of administration will likely increase the toll of cocaine related sudden deaths."

Effects of Cocaine on the Central Nervous System

The impacts of cocaine on the CNS are many, but in terms of life-threatening trauma, there are two basic ones, seizures and strokes.(7) Either can result in death, in permanent disability or in slow, almost always less than perfect recovery.

There are multiple factors in the situations under which a person is rushed to the emergency room after using cocaine or methamphetamine. The person is suffering from the impact of the drug on his body, and he is frightened sometimes to the extent of panic attacks. He is in strange environs, embarrassed and disoriented. All of these factors plus his overall physical condition and debilities of a specific nature (diabetic, epileptic, heart disease, etc.) work together with the drug and immediate environmental impact to bring tremendous stress to the CNS. It should be remembered that elevated blood pressure, heart rate and body temperature are almost always factors in the patient's total condition.

Seizures

If the person is experiencing seizure on entry to the emergency room, that seizure may have dire consequences which include death. In seizure, the brain impulses which normally operate under certain rhythms or combinations thereof (alpha, beta, theta) are thrown into disarray. The victim is seized with brain impulses gone wild bringing about gross body movement, convulsions, severe headaches, nausea and other disagreeable symptoms. As the seizure quiets under medication over time, there is dysphoria. If seizure is the entire clinical picture, vessels in the brain do not rupture.

Strokes (Infarctions)

Seizures are often accompanied by stroke.(6) Stroke entails the rupture of blood carriers which possibly is attenuated by elevated blood pressure (arterial or venous) and can be verified by CAT scanning or by other symptoms such as loss of speech, paralysis, etc. If seizure and stroke happen together, attending physicians must control seizure first even before stroke assessment can begin. Either symptom is serious, together they may be critical.

Seizures are thought to occur because brain wave patterns are scrambled by drug impact; a part of this may relate to malfunctioning neurotransmitters. Seizures per se are less life-threatening than are infarctions (broken blood vessels). On the other hand, an infarction, which floods neural pathways with blood, may be a factor in seizures.

Strokes (infarctions) can occur from aneuristic damage caused by nothing more than intolerable high blood pressure.

On the other hand, cocaine (according to some researchers) causes spasms to occur in the main artery leading to higher brain structures, and this spasming may contribute to extra pressure on the one hand and unpredictable blood flow on the other. Excruciating headaches, obviously, are highly probable under conditions of infarctions.

Conditions Affecting the Circulatory System

A specific symptom of cocaine or methamphetamine impact is the development of arrhythmia of the heart muscle. Undoubtedly this is a function of either the peripheral nerve system conduction or of the autonomic nerve system. Again, arrhythmias may derive partially from drug impact on the brain, from drug impact on the heart muscle or even from fear and panic.

The person suffering from O.D. or toxicity of cocaine or methamphetamine often goes into hyperventilation which is another cause of panic. Severe chest pains often accompany all these developments; and of course, such pain further exacerbates the stresses of heart trauma brought on by the drugs.

Endocarditis (inflammation of the heart muscle) often accompanies drug impact and this condition affects the heart valve, which along with the uneven blood flow caused by arrhythmia brings extreme stress to the heart. Also, there is widespread belief that drug impact brings spasming of the arteries and veins around the heart and that these spasms may function as blockages resembling thromboses. As a matter of fact, some deaths thought to have been thrombotic have on autopsy shown no blockages at all.

Summarily, the heart and its pumping regimen, as well as the optimal maintenance of pressure within the circulatory system, are thrown into violent disarray by drug impact. The heart rate is almost always increased, so the heart is pumping wildly while the incoming blood from the venous system may not be steady because of spasms. The arterial outflow through the left ventricle may not be a steady process, resulting in wildly gyrating changes in blood flow, blood pressure and body temperature.

Under conditions as described above, only a very healthy body in the best condition would sustain itself from infarction, thrombosis or heart failure. Many deaths are avoided by good, astute physicians and their armamentaria of equipment, drugs and laboratories. Death is avoided; but heart damage, which may later result in thrombosis, infarction or protracted heart disease, may be the long-term result of overdose or toxicity.

It should be noted that there are two forms of toxicity. One is, as described above, a violent reaction to a specific element introduced into the body. The other is a gradual build-up toward ultimate toxicity as the drug abuser enters a neuroadaptive practice of increasing dosages to compensate for tolerance effects which gradually bring his body into system collapse. Toxicity may occur on first drug administration or in an ever-increasing progression after the thousandth episode. In other words, toxicity is unpredictable.

Lung Involvement

The lungs and the heart are in very close proximity both from locational and functional standpoints. Without the lungs, the heart would be useless and vice versa. It is unlikely that any visceral organ could escape some impact of drug use. The lungs are in a critical position *vis à vis* the heart.

What often happens is that the lungs collect unwanted fluids as the heart carries on the battle with uneven blood flow and gyrating pressures in the immediate system. Added to that, under rescue strategies, extra fluids are pushed into the body in efforts to reestablish renal function.

Under the rigors of emergency room treatment with so many disparate systems to deal with, the doctors may give the patient too much fluid, causing the lungs to receive an unbearable burden of excess fluids, which may refuse to go where they would be most helpful. The results are often full or partial cardiac arrests, the lungs being incapable of providing the heart muscle with sufficient oxygen. Damage may be done to several systems because of stressors which cannot be optimally balanced by efforts of emergency room attendants who are attempting to monitor all systems. The emergency room personnel must switch treatment emphases from the less critical system failure to the more threatening one. The lungs may comprise the point of most critical focus since fluids once routed into the lungs cannot easily be interdicted or eliminated.

The Kidneys and the Impact of Cocaine and Methamphetamines

Renal function comes strongly into play in any emergency treatment. Renal failure is especially common under cocaine and methamphetamine O.D. or toxicity. Although the renal system has its own arterial blood supply from the heart, the kidneys are adversely affected by any severe stress situation such as extremely high body temperature. Body temperatures derived from smoking ice are reported to soar as high as 108 degrees, Fahrenheit. Under cocaine and amphetamine impact, muscle tissue often dumps large quantities of lactic acid into the kidneys through the bloodstream, thereby causing renal failure. This condition is referred to as rhabdomyolysis.

Parks et al (8) report on the treatment of four patients diagnosed as experiencing acute rhabdomyolysis, two using crack and two using IV cocaine. Three of these patients developed nonoliguric renal failure. The fourth died of hyperkalemia and ischemic bowel.

The functioning of the renal system in monitored early in any emergency room involvement by the insertion of a catheter. Unless the kidneys function to remove impurities from the blood supply, that system will fail within a matter of hours especially if uremic poisoning is added to the load other system components must sustain. Urine must be obtained for laboratory assessment of various body factors including levels of lactic acid and the presence of whatever drug entities may be in the blood. Sugar content must be monitored as well as conditions of acidity and trace minerals of electrolytic importance.

Where rhabdomyolysis is severe, as seems more likely in those who are heavily muscled, who do very hard physical labor, who play strenuous sports or who are on various muscle building regimens, the renal failure brought about by high lactic acid is sometimes irreversible and therefore fatal. The uremic poison brought back to the heart muscle can cause more severe endocarditis and death. Heart damage may occur in a roundabout fashion by renal failure.

Electrolytes and Cocaine-Methamphetamine Abuse

The human body is immensely dependent upon electrolyte balance. These influences, coming as they do in great part from trace minerals in the bloodstream, can wreak havoc in the human body in undersupply or in oversupply. Potassium is one of these trace minerals which in undersupply can cause hallucinations and various psychiatric symptoms.

The kidneys play a pivotal role in providing a balanced supply of trace minerals since active kidneys screen out the excess. When kidneys are not functioning, there is more likely to be an oversupply of trace minerals, especially potassium. Trace minerals and thus electrolyte imbalance is seldom life-threatening but can lead to bizarre behavior which cannot go unattended.

Forms of bizarre behavior, ensuing from electrolyte imbalance caused by relatively long-term use of crack cocaine or methamphetamine, are often identified as paranoid schizophrenia and obsessive-compulsive behavior. According to Acee and Smith (1) reporting exclusively on crack, there are three notable behavioral outgrowths from these psychological states: hallucinations, paranoid delusions and hypomanic behavior. At this stage in methamphetamine abuse, there will likely be more violence than with cocaine abuse although other effects are quite similar. The paranoid content of behaviors at this advanced state are considerably different from the paranoia of early use; with these first users there is little paranoid decompensation, only furtive feelings that they are being closely watched. With long-term use of cocaine or methamphetamine, the behaviors will be considerably more psychotic-like, including open accusations against people and continual, overt searching behaviors.

Bibliography

1   Acee, Anna M. and Smith, Dorothy. "Crack." American Journal of Nursing. Vol. 87(5). May 1987, pp. 614-17.

2   Dackis, Charles A. and Gold, Mark S. "The Physiology of Cocaine Craving and Crashing." Archives of General Psychiatry. Vol. 44. March 1987, pp. 298, 299.

3   Dackis, C.A. and Gold, M.S. "New Concepts in Cocaine Addiction — The Dopamine Depletion Hypothesis." Neuroscience Biobehavioral Review. Vol. 9. 1985, pp. 469-477.

4   Dackis, Charles A. and Gold, Mark S. "Psychopharmacology of Cocaine." Psychiatric Annals. Vol. 189. September 1988, pp.

5   DeWitt, H. and Wise, R.A. "Blockade of Cocaine Reinforcement in Rats With the Dopamine Receptor Pimoxide, but not with the Noradrenergic Blockers Phentolamine and Phenoxybenzamine." Canada Journal of Psychology. Vol. 31. 1977, pp. 195-203.

6   Levine, S.R. et al. "Crack Cocaine Associated Stroke." Neurology. Vol. 37 No. 12. 1987, pp. 1849-1853.

7   Meyers, John A. and Earnest, Michael P. "Generalized Seizure and Cocaine Abuse." Neurology. Vol. 34 No. 5. 1984, pp. 675, 676.

8   Parks, J.M. et al. "Cocaine Associated Rhabdomyolysis." American Journal of Medical Science. Vol. 297 (5), May 1989, pp. 334-336.

9   Pickens, R. and Harris, W.C. "Self-Administration of d-amphetamine by Rats." Psychopharmacologia. Vol. 12. 1968, pp. 158-163.

10   Verebey, Karl Ph.D and Gold, Mark S. M.D. "From Coca Leaves to Crack: The Effects of Dose and Routes of Administration in Abuse Liability." Psychiatric Annals. Vol. 18(9). September 1988. pp. 513-518.

Chapter 11

Relapse Prevention and Long-term Treatment

Happening Eleven — Mama Coca and Senior Batu, You Can't Have My Husband

The Facts As We Best Know Them

Relapse Prevention Demands a Concerted Effort
Dopamine Specificity
Pyrolysis in Crack and in Ice
The Need for a Team Approach
Patient Categories
Recovery Phases in Inpatient Treatment
The Need for Outpatient Treatment
The Depot Drugs
The Role of Conditioned Cues in Relapse
Is Hitting Bottom Necessary?

Happening Eleven — Mama Coca and Senior Batu, You Can't Have My Husband

As I tearfully look down at my tiny precious baby girl nudging my breast, my heart is about to burst. I am so fulfilled with love; my heart is bursting with joy and with gratitude. Thank you, Father, for giving me a perfect baby girl. My feelings are indescribable. She is a perfect baby. Oh, how I was crazy with worry!

I was petrified just hours ago. I'd lived with this paralyzing fear for nine months. I had considered abortion; now I ask forgiveness, Father. Oh, what a choice I had to make! People will say the Church made the choice. No! I made the choice. God had a lot to do with it, but I made the choice. I wanted to have my baby and wanted her to have Bobby's dark hair. I prayed for her to be like Bobby and be like me, too. I hardly believe she's here with me and so perfect.

I confess that my overpowering fear was not rational, but I was afraid for my baby. Bobby was just barely off drugs when she was conceived. He said that Maria Elena would be a token of my belief in him, would prove how much I love and trust him. To give him a baby would make him strong. It had made him strong. He has been free from drugs for the nine months. Since I showed my trust in him, I know he'll never use drugs again, and he will take really good care of Maria and me. Oh, I'm so happy! I don't have to pray anymore for him to stay off drugs; I just thank God for touching Bobby and making the three of us as one. My baby girl is well and fine in every way, no more fear for me to bear.

Oh, how I shook watching those crack babies on TV. Poor little things, jerking and screaming with withdrawal symptoms because their mothers wouldn't stay off crack while they were carrying them. It haunted me all the time. I hated those mothers! How could they hurt unborn babies? Mothers should be of God; these, I saw and knew, we're of the devil. My doctor assured me over and over that Bobby's long drug habit couldn't cause my baby any harm at all because harm comes only when the mother does bad things; it only came through the mother. But oh, how I worried. Could doctors be sure crack babies couldn't come through the father? They seemed very sure, but I wasn't. I thought they were trying to calm me down. It was a long nightmare; now it is a wonderful dream.

But that wasn't all my tortured mind had to endure during those nine months. Every night I awakened in a cold sweat. I had gone with Bobby so many times to see Robby, his twin brother who was shrinking right before our eyes. Yes, Robby had AIDS and was being devoured by demons right before our very eyes. It was so pitiful, so horrible. He smelled of death for weeks before he shuddered and died holding my Bobby's hands. All the while, Bobby was going into the bathroom every thirty minutes for a crack fix while his brother was dying that night. I don't think Bobby could have survived without the crack. He'd been snorting cocaine for years, and there was no way he could have gotten off cocaine with all the loving and close feelings he'd always had for his twin, Robby. He stayed high on rocks while we were in the hospital, and then, he would go home to snort the lines of powder because he crashed so fast and hard from several hours of crack. My heart was sick because he was suffering so much. He was pitiful. He was my husband. We had vowed for better or for worse, and this was the worse part.

But only the Father knows how I really suffered. Yes, crack babies would cause me to cry when I saw them on TV. But the AIDS babies suffered so much, they literally broke my heart and, at the same time, made me so angry at the mothers who had them. How could they? Media hype, Bobby had said. He's just a man. I knew better. Those poor, sweet, little things jerked and screamed and died. Life is so hard! And they hadn't done a thing to deserve that hell. Hell is for the damned who have sinned against God and haven't confessed their sins. I just couldn't stand to see God put those poor, little things through weeks and months of hell only to die in unspeakable agony. I just couldn't stand it at all.

The worst of my experiences was the grinding fear of AIDS. Bobby told me over and over, "I haven't got AIDS. Robby has AIDS. I haven't been homosexual with Robby, I haven't used Robby's dirty needles! How in God's name could I get AIDS from Robby? No way!" Bobby swore, his face red and eyes filled with hate. But I couldn't help being afraid. I was true to Bobby, but I was so pitifully afraid of AIDS I nearly lost my mind. But I held on to my vows — for better or for worse. Oh God, how I had wanted at times to give it all up. But if Bobby had AIDS, I was already infected anyway. I knew that.

"Please, Bobby, take the test," I pleaded. "We've got to know."

"No way," he had shouted over and over, and then, with my begging and with the company's help, he had taken the treatment, had beat crack, was released from the clinic and wanted to have a baby to bring us closer together. Oh God, how I have always wanted babies, but I was so scared. The crack part I believed although it haunted me. A father couldn't pass on crack to his baby. The mind part of me believes that, but the heart part was so afraid.

And the AIDS part was a brutal cross I bore; Bobby wanted a baby as a token of my belief in him. I loved that, because I wanted a baby so much, and I loved Bobby so.

I screamed going into the delivery room. They all thought it was the pain but it was the stark fear that I was about to deliver an AIDS baby, which would mean a few months of torment for my baby and perhaps a few years of slow death for me. "I should not have this baby because Bobby wouldn't take the test," I moaned under my breath during labor. I dreaded to see the baby — really, I couldn't look at the baby. At first, I was so terrified, but the nurse came, saying what a beautiful and healthy baby girl she was.

So, do you see why I am thanking God and looking down at my little Maria Elena, heavenly flower, with a heart filled with joy? Oh, thank you, Father!

****

Bobby and Robby moved to Wailuku from San Francisco. Actually, they came to Lanai City with their father who had a job picking pineapples on Lanai. The boys could not stand that small island with no big city life, so they moved to Maui, to Wailuku — some big city. But it was better than Lanai

City. Wailuku is only a small city, but it has a cannery where both boys got work. I knew very little about Bobby until after I had married him. He was so good looking, very talkative and very affectionate. My mom had a fit about it. "You are a judge's daughter. You are going to disgrace us, Lani. You want to marry this stateside Latino, and you know nothing at all about his family," my mother said. But Bobby was so sweet, so beautiful, and I didn't think it mattered about his family. How wrong I was! And besides, our family has Spanish bloodlines, too. That's why I named my baby after my grandmother, Maria Elena.

It wasn't until after the Company had paid to have Bobby put into the Substance Abuse Center that Bobby really told me about his family. Bobby's family had lived in San Francisco for many years. I was real surprised that Bobby had the drug problem. When I was allowed to visit Bobby, we sat in the shade of the jacaranda trees on the grounds at the Center, and he told me about his longtime drug use. Bobby's family was a big one, and Mom was right — I should have found out about it before I married him. I think I would have married him anyway because Bobby is so nice in spite of his family.

They were natives, descendants of the Spaniards who had settled in California a long time ago. I had read about the hippies at Haight Ashbury, about the gay people and about the drug culture of this mainland city.

His family was big. He had three sisters older than he and his twin brother Robby. But that was just the beginning. He had about twenty cousins, I guess, and most of them were older than Bobby. And, of course, uncles and aunts — they were a real extended family such as I learned about in sociology in high school.

Mom called Bobby and Robby hoodlums right from the start. I don't know why they were so exciting to me. I guess it was because my family seemed so dull with me being an only child of a wealthy family. My father was a judge in the appellate court, and he was sweet and kind, but not much of a family man. My mom was the queen bee at our house.

Bobby's whole family was into the drug scene. His mother was an alcoholic, and it seems that every cousin was a pusher. Bobby smoked his first marijuana when he was eight, and he had shot up speed and cocaine a lot. His favorite was angel dust which I'd never heard of.

Bobby wasn't able to get any angel dust in Wailuku, and he nearly went crazy. He finally found someone who would sell him crack, and that was what saved him from going crazy, I guess. But it was also what nearly cost him his job. Just before he got busted, we were fighting all the time, never made love.. And my mom was on me every minute. I was about ready to call it quits myself.

We had been married six months when Bobby got busted off his job at the cannery for being late and generally messing up. But, thank God, the Company came through for Bobby. I guess he was someone they needed. There was this arrangement Bobby had to sign with the Company and the Union which got money out of insurance to pay for Bobby's treatment. If he hadn't gotten into treatment, I know I would have left Bobby soon. He was getting unbearable.

They kept Bobby at the center for twenty-eight days, and I wasn't allowed even to see him for two weeks. But he was a model patient, they said, and was released after four weeks. They gave Bobby pills to take every other day which they said would help him stay clean. At first he wouldn't take them; said he could go cold turkey. It nearly broke my heart to see him suffer so. He would be all right during the day, but after dinner, he would sit with his hands clenched and sweat breaking out all over. He craved the crack that much. I begged him to take the pills, and finally he had to — it was just too much. He took the pills for about two weeks, then started skipping, trying to get through the craving on his own. I didn't understand how he would fight the good drug when the craving for the bad drug was driving him wild. All he would say was, "You just don't understand, Lani." I surely didn't.

Bobby had to give urine samples at the center once a week during this time of breaking the addiction. That was part of his agreement with the Company and the Union. He had to stay clean, and he tried hard. If only he had taken the medicine like he was supposed to do! He got more and more irritable and said he was going to quit his job. That was plain crazy and I told him so.

And that was when Robby got the infection. I had noticed how much weight he was losing, but it was a real bad scene to find that he was dying with AIDS. It was terribly hard on Bobby, and somehow, I knew that he was making it only because he was using something again. I didn't know what. During the last few days before Robby died, Bobby would go into the bathroom at the hospital every thirty minutes and would come out feeling better. I guess I knew he'd gone back on crack, but I guess I didn't really blame him. I don't think he could have stood Robby's death without something. How he faked out the urine test that week I never knew but he did it someway.

For a few days after Robby's death, Bobby took his medicine again. He'd fooled them once on the urine test and figured he could do it again and again until the crack got out of his system. But Bobby was so depressed it nearly broke my heart.

Then one day he came home all smiles. I knew something was wrong but couldn't figure it out. He was on a high and I knew it. He wanted to make love all the time, but I couldn't please him. He got to cursing me — it just wasn't Bobby. I tried to make him tell me what was happening. He told me it was just that he had kicked both crack and the medicine, and everything would be fine. It wasn't fine; it was pure hell. I was beginning to be very afraid of him.

It was coming up to the day he had to go to the center to leave urine again. Bobby was very abusive that morning, but he never struck me. I didn't dare tell my mom any of this but I was about ready to call it quits. I just didn't want to admit that she was right, but I could see Bobby was getting out of control. He was going to hurt somebody.

And then, the worst happened. Bobby missed a day of work, and we couldn't find him. But we finally did. He was in jail. He had gotten into a fight at a bar and had nearly killed someone. This was the worst time of all. I went to stay with my mom and she begged me to get a divorce. When I got up the nerve to call, the Company man, Mr. Daniels, he told me that Bobby had been using ice. "The fool thought the ice would make him better at the job, and it did for a few days." Mr. Daniels was very angry, and I got angry at him for calling Bobby a fool.

"What's going to happen, Mr. Daniels?" I asked.

"I guess it is all over," he said. "I don't think the Company or the Union will go any further." That was when I went to see Mr. Daniels. I was mad at him, but he really seemed to want to help.

I don't know how I swallowed my pride but I begged Mr. Daniels to help. My mom would scream at me every time I would go down to the cannery to talk with him, but I was determined. Mr. Daniels was very understanding. "It's this damn ice," he fumed. "It is going to be one hell of a bad drug for us. The pushers all have it now, and it is even worse than crack."

Then, Mr. Daniels flew to Honolulu for a conference, and when he got back, he called me. "I think I've got it fixed so Bobby can have another chance. The Company and the Union are really upset about this ice. I put in my best word for Bobby; we'll just have to wait a few days and see."

My mom wouldn't let up, but I was determined that neither crack nor ice was going to break up my marriage. I called Mr. Daniels every day. Bobby got out of jail, and the guy that got beat up didn't press charges.

Finally, the word came. Bobby and I were so excited. They would give him another chance, another twenty-eight days at the center. Bobby would have to be tough, they said, because ice withdrawal is worse than crack.

But there was the big hitch, of course. The insurance company would pay only eighty percent. We'd have to come up with about three thousand dollars. No way! No way! We were broke!

But now that I've got my sweet baby everything looks so good. Bobby went through his second stay at the center with no problems at all. They put him on a new drug, and now he is taking a shot every two weeks as well as pills. I absolutely won't let him quit taking his medicine. I call the doctor at the Center every few days to be sure I know what he's supposed to be taking. And now that we've got the baby, he'll stay clean — I know he will. If he doesn't, I'll not only break his head, I'll take away his baby. Bobby is doing better than ever on the job and I just know we are going to be a great family.

Oh, yes. How did we get the three thousand dollars? I doubt I really need to tell you. My mom came through with it; bless her dear heart. I never even asked her where she got the money or whether daddy knew about it or not.

****

Maria Elena is a year old now. Bobby and Lani are doing well. Bobby has been promoted to a better position in the company.

The Facts As We Best Know Them

<u>Relapse Prevention Demands a Concerted Effort</u>

A dramatic illustration of the power of cocaine craving comes from laboratory studies of rats which became addicted to cocaine through self-administration. Rats described by Dackis et al (2), self-administered cocaine constantly, totally ignoring food and water needs. The rats continued to press the levers to obtain cocaine-laced fluid and starved to death. Thus, cocaine reward may be viewed as among the most powerful "acquired drives" that is known. Pickens et al (11) have demonstrated the same phenomenon with self-administration of d amphetamine by rats.

The focus in this section of the book is upon craving and relapse. Cocaine and methamphetamine in their smokable forms lead all others in their reward and craving power, according to current research. (3) But, it has been declared by those who have been addicted to both crack and ice that the craving for ice is even more powerful than that of crack cocaine.

There is a constant debate as to which is more addicting, crack or methamphetamine. Each drug form has its own advocates. Crack cocaine as delivered to the brain through smoking is no different from cocaine HCL delivered by IV. However, the crack is the more addictive and seductive. Duncan declares that crack, while not a new drug, is, because of its route of administration and other factors, highly addictive.

The effects of cocaine are felt sooner after smoking than by any other route of administration. The onset of effects takes place within five to 10 seconds, the peak effects lasting five to 10 minutes. Smoking also allows users to titrate the dose precisely – that is, to take very small amounts, feel their effects almost immediately, and then take more until exactly the desired level of effects is obtained. On the one hand, this makes an overdose extremely unlikely. On the other hand, the instant gratification thus possible can be highly seductive. It is for this reason, and not due to any difference in the drug effects, that smoking freebase may actually be more likely to result in dependence than snorting, or even injecting, cocaine hydrochloride.(5, p. 26)

The summer of 1988 was a time of hysteria *vis à vis* the crack epidemic. Arguments that crack was not a "new drug" are abundant in the literature of this period. Certainly, cocaine had been smoked since the days of the Incas, but the point is moot as to whether or not crack is a new drug. In the smokable form originating in 1983, crack passes the duck (looks, walks, quacks and flies like) test for "new drug." Ice like crack passes the duck test. The impact and implications are so unique that it may as well be labeled a "new drug."

Dopamine Specificity

In the mainland states, ice is following on the heels of the crack epidemic. Indeed, many crack abusers in the Haight Ashbury District of San Francisco are turning to ice almost gleefully because, at least subjectively, the rush is more sublime and the high is longer-lasting with ice than with crack. Ice, unlike crack, has a distinctive chemical difference from typical methamphetamines that users can obtain on the street, at least as far as potency of the d isomer is concerned..

Most methamphetamines have a d isomer and an l isomer in their chemical make-up. The d isomer is the part of ice which causes both the initial highly euphoric rush and the prolonged high which lasts up to eighteen hours as opposed to about twenty minutes for the crack high. Ice prepared by the ephedrine hydrogenation method is ninety to one hundred percent d methamphetamine. No other methamphetamine on the street even approaches that level of d isomer methamphetamine. Although methamphetamine HCL can be made in the laboratory with very high levels of d isomer, it is shocking that an illicit manufacturer can create a substance in the bathtub with a very high d isomer content. It is true that street distribution of powdered methamphetamine is cut by mixing it with other inert substances thus reducing the purity. However, the cutting of the ice form of methamphetamine is difficult compared to powdered methamphetamine HCL, and the chances that almost pure d isomer methamphetamine will get to the user of ice is very great.

It is easy to see both sides of the argument as to which is more addictive, crack or ice. It may be that the d isomer in ice, made more prominent by the ephedrine hydrogenation method, causes a more intense rush. It is obvious that the prolonged high of ice logically does not serve as an instant reinforcement demand and thus is not as addictive as crack — that is to say, a quick reinforcement via a new hit is not necessary with ice. Yet, the crash is likely more severe with ice when it does come. Individual differences in reaction make this an almost sterile discussion.

Pyrolysis in Crack and in Ice

Bioavailability is a critical issue in the effectiveness of smokable drugs. When cocaine freebase is smoked, there is a great loss in bioavailability through pyrolysis. Crack cocaine is a form which requires heating to a smoldering state, which once begun generally continues until only an ash residue remains. Siegel (12) performed an intensive study of the pyrolysis of cocaine but did not involve crack. Siegel found the loss through pyrolysis of cocaine at 200°C to be about thirty percent, at 400°C the loss is about seventy percent and at 800°C the loss is about ninety-five percent. Thus, only a small amount of active chemical is delivered to the lungs when crack is lighted, if we take the liberty of extrapolating from Siegel's study. The smoldering edge of a burning cigarette, according to Siegel, is likely to have a temperature of about 1000°C. Thus, there logically is little bioavailability from the burning edge of either a cigarette or of crack. That part of the rock which is a centimeter or so from the smoldering edge is volatilized at a lesser temperature. The effective bioavailability comes not from the burning edge, but from parts of the rock that is heated enough to be volatilized but not enough to lose a great deal of bioavailability from excessive heat. Two factors must be considered: 1) If there were not a heavy loss of bioavailability from heat, crack would be lethal. 2) We may be faced in the future with more sophisticated volatilizing pipes or paraphernalia that will deliver immense and dangerous levels of the chemical.

NIDA studies as quoted by Dr. Jerome Jaffe show that ice is volatilized at a much lower temperature.(9) Then, too, the pipe for ice smoking is made so that the flame never comes into contact with the crystal. Vaporization of methamphetamine can deliver over ninety percent pure d methamphetamine.(9) Thus, most of the chemical is bioavailable with the ice whereas a much lesser percent is available with crack. This is one reason the methamphetamine high via ice use lasts so long. Toxic psychoses deriving from ice use can be not only acute but also long-lasting. (9) So, there are many reasons to believe that the bottom-line effects of ice can be more dangerous than those of crack.

Because we have been hard at work trying in treatment facilities to alleviate the craving that accompanies cocaine and methamphetamine addiction, we may hope to find ourselves in a better position to deal with the methamphetamine craving from ice because similar pharmacological interventions will likely work with cravings for both crack and ice. Both drugs seem to derive craving behavior from the same basic neurologic disaster, dopamine depletion.(13) Although it is obvious to many that the dopamine depletion bandwagon is overloaded, evidence is replete that more mechanisms (through thyroid axis activation, for example) and depletion of other neurotransmitters are involved.(2) Depletion of dopamine causes craving for both cocaine and methamphetamine in whatever form they are used. The exact psychopharmacology may differ slightly from one drug to the other, but laboratory studies using animals have found methamphetamines to be more powerful in first activating and then in depleting the dopaminergic neurons. As a matter of fact, it has been strongly suspected that large doses of d isomer methamphetamine cause irreversible destruction of dopaminergic neurons, a total loss of nerve cells.

The Need for a Team Approach

It is generally conceded that psychological approaches to the handling of craving, therewith preventing relapse, cannot succeed without pharmacological intervention. As a matter of fact, psychological therapists and various medical specialities (psychiatrists, neurologists, etc.) have conceded that a team approach is mandatory in order to be able to deal effectively with cocaine and methamphetamines among others of the drug family such as PCP, LSD and designer drugs.

Further, there is a consensus that detoxification centers, which define their end-point of involvement (usually reached in from two to eight days) as "patients physically clean from chemical substances," are largely ineffective in and of themselves in preventing relapse. Without follow-up for at least a year, drying-out processes used alone result in high recidivism rates. Summarily, then, sustained treatment must follow detoxification and the work of the substance abuse center; in order to be effective, it must engage both psychological and pharmacological elements. Even so, relapse after twenty-eight to sixty days in a treatment center is common. With long-term pharmacological follow-up coupled with psychological counseling, success rates can be expected to improve.

Patient Categories

Kosten (10) has contributed mightily by providing several highly logical descriptions concerning such topics as whom to treat, how to treat, when to treat, where to treat and how to match patients with professionals. To begin with, Kosten identifies, specifically for cocaine abusers, three general categories of patients appropriate for pharmacological intervention. These are: 1) those who have developed neuroadaptations to heavy cocaine use. Neuroadaptation means that the patients have entered long-term strategies of increasing dosages forced by tolerance factors, including the use of other counteractive drugs in their abuse repertoires and have otherwise adapted to changing patterns of needs over time, 2) those who have psychiatric vulnerability, meaning that many patients have psychiatric problems as well as cocaine addiction. There are strong implications that their cocaine problems derived from self-medication of cocaine in seeking relief for psychiatric problems and 3) those who have substantial medical risks, meaning that some patients must be treated by taking into account that they have cancer, heart disease or diabetes among other possibilities.

Recovery Phases In Inpatient Treatment

Dackis et al (3) have suggested a three-stage progression for craving based on the assumption of dopamine depletion as the causation factor. These are: 1) intense craving minutes after the last cocaine use, 2) intermediate craving after crashing symptoms abate (This stage may last several weeks.) and 3) powerful craving which is triggered by conditioned cues, which may occur for years after cocaine use has ceased.

Gawin and Kleber (7) categorize the period of abstinence into three phases: 1) crash, 2) withdrawal and 3) extinction. Although there is some disparity among researchers as to whether or not crash and withdrawal should be separated as stages (1). Kosten (10) agrees with the phasing suggested by Gawin and Kleber and gives the following as time factors: crash (2 - 48 hrs.), withdrawal (2 - 10 wks.) and extinction (3 - 12 mos.). Kosten further gives behavioral descriptions for the phases as follows: 1) Crash brings paranoid and suicidal behavior. 2) Withdrawal brings anxiety and depression usually bipolar in nature. 3) Extinction is a time of fighting against conditioned craving cues.

The crash stage is dominated by sleep for many abusers; and if this is the case, no medications need be used. On the other hand, some patients sleep little and demonstrate agitation, even paranoid tendencies. With ice abusers, there is a greater tendency toward psychotic-like paranoid schizophrenic states accompanied by extreme violence. Ice abusers create thorny problems in cases of overdose or toxicity. Emergency room personnel must be wary of incipient violence and be ready to restrain the patient. Neuroleptics such as chlorpromazine for calming may be required. Unless the patient shows signs of neuroleptic-malignant syndrome, extremely high body temperature may contraindicate neuroleptics, and other calming drugs such as Valium or Librium must be used. Suicidal patients must be restrained, of course. Sometimes, suicidal patients will need to be hospitalized.

The withdrawal stage, which begins after the hyper-agitation or sleepiness of the crash stage, brings acute craving for cocaine and/or methamphetamine. At this stage several drugs are helpful in keeping craving controlled. Amantadine and bromoscriptine are two new drugs that have been most often used against cocaine craving. These are fast-acting drugs. The older drug L'dopa, developed many years ago specifically for Parkinson's disease, is a useful drug serving as an agonist for dopamine; in other words, it mimics the function of dopamine. Many treatment centers rely exclusively on the tricyclic antidepressant drug group, and these serve equally well in combatting either methamphetamine or cocaine cravings. These tricyclic anti-depressants seem to reduce dopaminergic receptor sensitivity. Desipramine and imipramine are also effective in preventing relapse by controlling cravings.(8) However, these drugs have a delayed efficacy (up to two weeks) in affecting craving. Best results are obtained from a combination of fast-acting and slow-acting drugs.

The task of matching drugs to patients is a formidable one. Referring back to Kosten's three types of patients: 1) the neuroadaptors 2) the abusers with psychiatric problems and 3) the patients with serious medical problems, it must be said that the drugs named above are often accompanied in administration by serious side effects. The side effects preclude the use of some drugs even with the patient who has no serious psychiatric or medical problems. With the latter groups, however, extra precautions must be taken to avoid exacerbating synergistic incompatibilities between prescription drugs being taken and abstinence-maintenance drugs. The fact is that each patient presents a new experience to the physician-psychiatrist and comprises a study (N = 1) in experimental psychopharmacology.

The Need for Outpatient Treatment

Inpatient treatment with drugs mentioned above is easily monitored. It is a fact, however, that most abusers of crack and/or ice cannot afford inpatient treatment. In the United States, an average twenty-eight day inpatient program costs between $15,000 and $20,000.

Outpatient treatment is preferable for a large number (perhaps most) of crack and ice abusers. But, there are serious drawbacks to outpatient treatment, chief of which is that patients will not faithfully take their medications. On the other hand, most medicines which control craving cause anhedonic effects allowing the same symptoms to occur as set the addiction in motion in the first place. In uncontrolled situations, most neuroleptics, benzodiazepines and heterocyclic antidepressants are effective under controlled situations but may actually be cause-agents of relapse when the patient is self-monitoring because patients do not take medicines as prescribed.

The chronic or slow-acting drugs like bromoscriptine do not take effect in slowing craving until after about two weeks following administration.(4) Many outpatients relapse before these drugs take effect. Some fast-acting drugs cause anhedonia and depression, the conditions facilitating drug addiction in the first place. These two extremes (slow-acting and fast-acting) being unacceptable, every medical practitioner is left grasping for a treatment modality that will or at least might work with outpatients. If there is an answer, it lies in a depot-type drug which will stay in the system for a long period after administration (beginning with the first hour and extending for at least a four week period). Such a drug may have been found in flupenthixol decanoate. This drug has not become legal in the United States to date.

The Depot Drugs

Gawin et al (6) conducted the first credible research with flupenthixol decanoate, and the research on this drug was conducted using an exclusive group of crack addicts. This study illustrates perhaps a somewhat mandated situation. In the first place, the drug is not approved for experimentation on humans in the United States. Therefore, a site where such prohibitions were not in effect was obtained, the island of New Providence in the Bahamas. All the subjects selected were using crack, a drug form of high incidence in this region. So, whether by design or happenstance, this controlled, scientific inquiry was the first to use crack cocaine as a specific in testing flupenthixol decanoate as an antidote to craving.

There are reasons why this experiment was chosen for reporting in this book on crack and ice. They are that: 1) There is good reason to research drugs to be used to combat specific and sub-specific addictive agents such as crack cocaine and ice. 2) There are good reasons to research new drugs for use with a broad spectrum of addictive substances. For instance, drugs should be researched in the hope of gaining tools for dealing with the interlacing methamphetamine-cocaine problem as well as other polydrug problems. 3) There is a need for basic research which may cast new light on treatment methods for the wide spectrum of psychologic-physical problems faced by the human race, whether drug-related or not.

Flupenthixol decanoate is a xanthene thought to function as a craving reducer by blocking dopamine binding at a number of receptor subtypes, especially autoreceptors. The depot duration of flupenthixol decanoate is from two to four weeks. The results were impressive in the research mentioned above. There was a seventy-two percent decrease in craving, and nine out of ten patients reported amelioration of cocaine craving within three days of drug administration. Obviously, more studies on human subjects need to be done. Rat studies are certainly valuable, but extrapolations from rat behavior to human behavior are less than optimal.

Obviously, new drugs with depot capabilities need to be carefully tested. This is of great importance since the vast number of persons needing treatment cannot afford inpatient care.

Research on drugs specific to withdrawal from ice is needed. The desperate needs are dual: 1) Specific drugs are needed to relieve specific problems such as the extreme violence of toxic reaction to ice. 2) Drugs are needed which can be effective in delaying the psychotic states which ice brings about in long-term users.

The Role of Conditioned Cues in Relapse

Relapse into cocaine or methamphetamine use is devastating to a victim who has maintained sobriety for a considerable time. One stumble causes such victims to feel that they are back to square one, and such a feeling often brings about a protracted binge. This binge will likely end only when a true life-threatening set of circumstances ensue.

There are at least two broad-based circumstances which can bring about relapse in a person who has struggled mightily to save himself from a fate worse than death and has been successful for a significant period of time. First, many victims experience highly devastating crises. The death of a loved one where the relationship has been strong and supportive is a good example. Under stress sustained by weeks of watching a loved one die, the victim may be incapable of handling the situation without drugs. The craving for a hit comes on strongly as the stress becomes almost unbearable. The victim tells himself, "I need this; I deserve this one break from this unbearable situation." At this point, this victim needs his support group more than at any other time. One hit leads to another, and as depot-type or slow-acting, anti-craving drugs are depleted, relapse occurs. The victim usually rationalizes that "this won't happen again." However, it is usually the beginning of another bad episode which will end either with a life-threatening situation or with death.

Secondly, the victim who has been "clean" for a considerable period often makes the mistake of returning to old haunts, to old friendships and situations. These old scenes are often identical to those which were present during earlier binges. These old familiar faces and places provide conditioned cues which bring on the old feelings which were responsible for the earlier drug abuse. It has been demonstrated that among the most powerful cues for the return of craving is the sight and smell of drug paraphernalia such as ice and crack pipes. This is why counselors urge victims to change their lifestyles and life spaces during and after treatment. As an example, the dysfunctional family, which spawned the stresses originally causing addiction will do the same again.

Is Hitting Bottom Necessary?

In summary, treatment of substance abuse often fails through relapse if there is not an effective follow-up fashioned with pharmacological and environmental components capable of preventing relapse. Relapses are tremendously painful and destructive of self-esteem. Some say a certain number of relapses are necessary before an abuser can hit bottom and rebound with renewed spirit and ultimate resolve

The success stories that achieve media attention usually do have the "hit bottom" phenomenon, implying that the patient has ascended to a point where he has no place to go but up. It is true that every patient who turns a corner toward improvement (even those who later relapse) can point to a time, an event, something someone said or a special insight. The patient refers to this as, "The point where I began the long journey back."

Two things are clear: First, relapses are unnecessary to a learning process which includes a long-term engagement in one-on-one psychological counseling and growth experiences in heightened self-esteem, developed within group contexts. Second, relapses are not necessary for growth and self-esteem to flourish. For the war on drugs to succeed, relapses must be ultimately avoided. Our energies must be channeled strongly and consistently toward relapse prevention.

Bibliography

1   Bower, Kirk J. and Paredes, Alfonso. "Cocaine Withdrawal." Archives of General Psychiatry. Vol 44. March 1987, p. 297.

2   Dackis, Charles A. and Gold, Mark S. "Psychopharmacology of Cocaine." Psychiatric Annals. Vol. 189. September 1988.

3   Dackis, Charles A. "The Physiology of Cocaine Craving and 'Crashing'." Archives of General Psychiatry. Vol 44. March 1987, pp. 298, 299.

4   Dackis, C.A. and Gold, M.S. "Bromoscriptine as a Treatment of Cocaine Abuse." Lancet. (1) 1985, pp. 1151-1152.

5   Duncan, David F. "Cocaine Smoking and Its Implications For Health and Heath Education." Health Education. August/September 1987, pp. 24-27.

6   Gawin, Frank H. et al. "Outpatient Treatment of 'Crack' Cocaine Smoking With Flupenthixol Decanoate." Archives of General Psychiatry. Vol. 46. April 1989, pp. 322-325.

7   Gawin, F.H. and Kleber, H.D. "Abstinence Symptomatology and Psychiatric Diagnosis in Cocaine Abusers: Clinical Observations." Archives of General Psychiatry. Vol. 48. 1986, pp. 107-113.

8   Gawin, et al. "Desipramine Facilitation of Initial Cocaine Abstinence." Archives of General Psychiatry. Vol. 26 (2). February 1989, pp. 117-121.

9   Jaffe, Jerome. Testimony at Meeting of the Select Committee on Narcotics Abuse and Control. Washington, D.C. October 24, 1989.

10 Kosten, Thomas R. "Pharmacotherapeutic Interventions for Cocaine Abuse." The Journal of Nervous and Mental Disease. Vol. 177 No. 7. pp. 379-389.

11 Pickens, R. and Harris W.C. "Self-administration of d amphetamine by Rats." Psychopharmacologia. Vol. 12. 1968, pp. 158-163.

12 Siegel, R.R. "Cocaine Smoking." Journal of Psychoactive Drugs. Vol. 14. 1982, pp. 272-341.

13   Wyatt, et al. "The Role of Dopamine in Cocaine Use and Abuse." Psychiatric Annals. Vol. 18(9). September 1988, pp. 531-534.

INDEX

A

1960's 34, 35
abruption 70
abusive parents 154
Acee 304
Aceto 206
acetylcholine 297
acting-out therapy 233
adolescence 266, 268
adoption 71
AIDS babies 65, 66, 72
alcohol 33, 36, 66, 67, 68, 171, 195, 196, 197, 198,
199, 205, 207
amantadine 322
Ariès 265
Ariosto 205
arrhythmias 301
Asia 98
Attention Deficit Disorder 72

B

Bailey 194, 208
Bandura 233
Bayview Hunter's Point 76
Bent 16, 18, 20, 69, 97, 103
Bettelheim 265
Blalock 17
Bowser 75
Bradshaw 143
Brazelton Neonatal Behavioral Assessment Scale 69
bromoscriptine 321, 323
Broughton 207

C

Caesarian section 70

K

Kaye 68
kidneys (cocaine and methamphetamine effects) 303-304
Kleber 16, 321
Kleiman 13
Korea 96
Kosten 320, 321, 322
Kymissis 156

L

l isomer methamphetamine 11
L'dopa 70
L'dopa 321
levels concept 236
Lewis 179
Lichtenberg 208
limbic system 70
Los Angeles 92, 93, 117, 123
lost child role 156

M

manufacturers 120
marijuana 32, 33, 34, 36, 40, 174
Martin 69
Maslow 227
Mayo Clinic 66
methamphetamine HCL 99, 317
Miami 92, 117, 199
Middle Ages 264
Minneapolis 92
Murray 33

N

National Collegiate Athletic Association 201

National Collegiate Drug Awareness Week Kick-off Conference 205-210
Neff 269, 274
neurotransmitters 37, 39, 297
New York City 97
Nicholi 201
nicotine 68
NIDA 11, 13, 16, 38, 39, 45, 91, 92, 93, 96, 102, 176, 200, 201
norepinephrine 297

O

Oahu 14
OBGYN 71

P

paranoid schizophrenia 17, 100, 304, 321
Parks 303
Patterson 227
Pavela 209
peer counseling 181
peer pressure 169
permissive age 267
Philadelphia 92
Philippines 96
Phoenix 92
physical symptoms complex 41
Pickens 316
placental barrier 67, 68
plea bargaining 128
polydrug 10, 44, 45, 66, 68, 323
poor man's cocaine 91, 95
poverty 124
probable cause 123
prostitution and crack 77
psychoanalysis 227
pyrolysis 318

R

S

synapses **296**

T

therapy group **237**
tobacco **33, 171**
tolerance **39, 101, 302**
toughlove **32, 71, 234, 264-278**

U

undercover agents **121, 126**
universities **193-210**

V

Van Nuys **234**
Veltri **198, 206**
Verebey **45, 46, 299**
Viet Nam **32**
Virginia **199**

W

Wachtel **270, 272**
Wallace **45, 156**
Weitzman **156**
wholesalers **120**

Y

York **270, 272**